ELEMENTS OF FINANCIAL RISK MANAGEMENT

ELEMENTS OF FINANCIAL RISK MANAGEMENT

Peter F. Christoffersen

ACADEMIC PRESS

An Imprint of Elsevier

Amsterdam   Boston   Heidelberg   London   New York   Oxford
Paris   San Diego   San Francisco   Singapore   Sydney   Tokyo

Academic Press
An Imprint of Elsevier
525 B Street, Suite 1900, San Diego, California 92101-4495, USA
http://www.academicpress.com

Academic Press
84 Theobald's Road, London WC1X 8RR, UK
http://www.academicpress.com

Library of Congress Catalog Card Number: 2003107899
ISBN-13: 978-0-12-174232-4
ISBN-10: 0-12-174232-6
PRINTED IN THE UNITED STATES OF AMERICA
08 09 10 11 12   7 6 5 4 3

To Susan

CONTENTS

2 Volatility Modeling

3 Correlation Modeling

4 Modeling the Conditional Distribution

5 Simulation-Based Methods

6 Option Pricing

7 Modeling Option Risk

8 Backtesting and Stress Testing

PREFACE

INTENDED READERS

This book is intended for three types of readers with an interest in financial risk management: first, master's and Ph.D. students specializing in finance and economics; second, market practitioners with a quantitative undergraduate or graduate degree; third, advanced undergraduates majoring in economics, engineering, finance, or another quantitative field.

I have taught the less technical parts of the book in a fourth-year undergraduate finance elective course and an MBA elective on financial risk management. The more technical material I have covered in a Ph.D. course on options and risk management and in technical training courses on market risk designed for market practitioners.

In terms of prerequisites, the reader should have taken as a minimum a course on investments, a course on options, and one or two courses on econometrics or mathematical statistics. In addition, certain chapters require some previous exposure to matrix algebra.

SOFTWARE

A number of empirical exercises are listed at the end of each chapter. Excel spreadsheets with the data underlying the exercises can be found on the CD-ROM that is shipped with the book. The CD-ROM also contains Excel files with answers to all the exercises. This way, virtually every technique discussed in the main text of the book is implemented on the CD using actual asset return data. The material on the CD is an essential part of the book. Previews of the spreadsheets are therefore shown following the exercise questions at the end of each chapter.

Updates to the material in the book including the data and the answers to the exercises as well as links to further risk management resources can be found at www.christoffersen.ca. Any suggestions regarding improvements to the book are most welcome. Please e-mail these suggestions to peter.christoffersen@mcgill.ca.

ACKNOWLEDGMENTS

Many people have played an important part—knowingly or unknowingly—in the writing of this book. Without implication, I would like to acknowledge the following people for stimulating discussions on topics covered in this book: Torben Andersen, Gurdip Bakshi, Jeremy Berkowitz, Tim Bollerslev, Bryan Campbell, Francesca Carrieri, Susan Christoffersen, Frank Diebold, Jin Duan, Rob Engle, Vihang Errunza, John Galbraith, Rene Garcia, Eric Ghysels, Silvia Goncalves, Jinyong Hahn, Steve Heston, Derek Hulley, Atsushi Inoue, Kris Jacobs, Eric Jacquier, Chris Jones, Michael Jouravlev, Philippe Jorion, Ohad Kondor, Jose Lopez, Simone Manganelli, Tom McCurdy, James MacKinnon, Nour Meddahi, Saikat Nandi, Andrew Patton, Andrey Pavlov, Matthew Pritsker, Eric Renault, Garry Schinasi, Jean-Guy Simonato, Norm Swanson, Til Schuermann, Torsten Sloek, and Jonathan Wright.

I have had a team of outstanding students working with me on the manuscript and on the CD-ROM in particular. They are Roustam Botachev, Thierry Koupaki, Stefano Mazzotta, Daniel Neata, and Denis Pelletier.

For financial support of my research in general and of this book in particular, I would like to thank CIRANO, CIREQ, FCAR, IFM2, and SSHRC.

I would also like to thank my editor at Academic Press, Scott Bentley, for his encouragement during the process of writing this book.

Finally, I would like to thank Susan for constant moral support, and Nicholas and Phillip for helping me keep perspective.

1

RISK MANAGEMENT AND FINANCIAL RETURNS

1.1. CHAPTER OUTLINE

This chapter begins by listing the learning objectives of the book. We then ask why firms should be occupied with risk management in the first place. In answering this question, we discuss the apparent contradiction between standard investment theory and the emergence of risk management as a field, and we list theoretical reasons for why managers should give attention to risk management. We also discuss the empirical evidence of the effectiveness and impact of current risk management practices in the corporate as well as financial sectors. Next, we list a taxonomy of the potential risks faced by a corporation, and we briefly discuss the desirability of exposure to each type of risk. After the risk taxonomy discussion, we list the stylized facts of asset returns, which are illustrated by the S&P 500 equity index. Finally, we present an overview of the remainder of the book.

1.2. LEARNING OBJECTIVES

The book is intended as a practical handbook for risk managers as well as a textbook for students. It suggests a relatively sophisticated approach to risk measurement and risk modeling. The idea behind the book is to document key features of risky asset returns and then construct tractable statistical models that capture these features. More specifically, the book is structured to help the reader to do the following:

- Become familiar with the range of risks facing corporations and learn how to measure and manage these risks. The discussion will focus on various aspects of market risk.
- Become familiar with the salient features of speculative asset returns.
- Apply state-of-the-art risk measurement and risk management techniques, which are nevertheless tractable in realistic situations.
- Critically appraise commercially available risk management systems and contribute to the construction of tailor-made systems.
- Use derivatives in risk management.
- Understand the current academic and practitioner literature on risk management techniques.

1.3. RISK MANAGEMENT AND THE FIRM

Before diving into the discussion of the range of risks facing a corporation and before analyzing the state-of-the art techniques available for measuring and managing these risks, it is appropriate to start by asking the basic question about financial risk management.

1.3.1. Why Should Firms Manage Risk?

From a purely academic perspective, corporate interest in risk management seems curious. Classic portfolio theory tells us that investors can eliminate asset-specific risk by diversifying their holdings to include many different assets. As asset-specific risk can be avoided in this fashion, having exposure to it will not be rewarded in the market. Instead, investors should hold a combination of the risk-free asset and the market portfolio, where the exact combination will depend on the investor's appetite for risk. In this basic setup, firms should not waste resources on risk management, as investors do not care about the firm-specific risk.

From the celebrated Modigliani-Miller theorem, we similarly know that the value of a firm is independent of its risk structure; firms should simply maximize expected profits, regardless of the risk entailed; holders of securities can achieve risk transfers via appropriate portfolio allocations. It is clear, however, that the strict conditions required for the Modigliani-Miller theorem are routinely violated in practice. In particular, capital market imperfections, such as taxes and costs of financial distress, cause the theorem to fail and create a role for risk management. Thus, more realistic descriptions of the corporate setting give some justifications for why firms should devote careful attention to the risks facing them:

- *Bankruptcy costs.* The direct and indirect costs of bankruptcy are large and well known. If investors see future bankruptcy as a nontrivial possibility, then the real costs of a company reorganization or shutdown will reduce the current valuation of the firm. Thus, risk management can increase the value of a firm by reducing the probability of default.

- *Taxes.* Risk management can help reduce taxes by reducing the volatility of earnings. Many tax systems have built-in progressions and limits on the ability to carry forward in time the tax benefit of past losses. Thus, everything else being equal, lowering the volatility of future pretax income will lower the net present value of future tax payments and thus increase the value of the firm.

- *Capital structure and the cost of capital.* A major source of corporate default is the inability to service debt. Other things equal, the higher the debt-to-equity ratio, the riskier the firm. Risk management can therefore be seen as allowing the firm to have a higher debt-to-equity ratio, which is beneficial if debt financing is inexpensive. Similarly, proper risk management may allow the firm to expand more aggressively through debt financing.

- *Compensation packages.* Due to their implicit investment in firm-specific human capital, managerial level and other key employees in a firm often have a large and unhedged exposure to the risk of the firm they work for. Thus, the riskier the firm, the more compensation current and potential employees will require to stay with or join the firm. Proper risk management can therefore help reducing the costs of retaining and recruiting key personnel.

1.3.2. Evidence on Risk Management Practices

In 1998, researchers at the Wharton School surveyed 2000 companies on their risk management practices, including derivatives uses. Of the 2000 firms surveyed, 400 responded. Not surprisingly, the survey found that companies use a range of methods and have a variety of reasons for using derivatives. It was also clear that not all risks that were managed were necessarily completely removed. About half of the respondents reported that they use derivatives as a risk-management tool. One-third of derivative users actively take positions reflecting their market views, thus they may be using derivatives to increase risk rather than reduce it.

Of course, not only derivatives are used to manage risky cash flows. Companies can also rely on good old-fashioned techniques such as the physical storage of goods (i.e., inventory holdings), cash buffers, and business diversification.

Not everyone chooses to manage risk, and risk management approaches differ from one firm to the next. This partly reflects the fact that the risk management goals differ across firms. In particular, some firms use cash-flow volatility, while others use the variation in the value of the firm as the risk management object of interest. It is also generally found that large firms tend to manage risk more actively than do small firms, which is perhaps surprising as small firms are generally viewed to be more risky. However, smaller firms may have limited access to derivatives markets and furthermore lack staff with risk management skills.

1.3.3. Does Risk Management Improve Firm Performance?

The overall answer to this question appears to be yes. Analysis of the risk management practices in the gold mining industry found that share prices were less sensitive to gold price movements after risk management. Similarly, in the natural gas industry, better risk management has been found to result in less variable stock prices. A study also found that risk management in a wide group of firms led to a reduced exposure to interest rate and exchange rate movements.

While it is not surprising that risk management leads to lower variability—indeed the opposite finding would be shocking—a more important question is, does risk management improve corporate performance? Again, the answer appears to be yes.

Researchers have found that less volatile cash flows result in lower costs of capital and more investment. It has also been found that a portfolio of firms using risk management would outperform a portfolio of firms that did not, when other aspects of the portfolio were controlled for. Similarly, a study found that firms using foreign exchange derivatives had higher market value than those who did not.

The evidence so far paints a fairly rosy picture of the benefits of current risk management practices in the corporate sector. However, evidence on the risk management systems in some of the largest U.S. commercial banks is less cheerful. A recent study found that while the risk forecasts on average tended to be overly conservative—perhaps a virtue—at certain times the realized losses far exceeded the risk forecasts. Importantly, the excessive losses tended to occur on consecutive days. Thus, looking back at the data on the a priory risk forecasts and the ex ante loss realizations, one would have been able to forecast an excessive loss tomorrow based on the observation of an excessive loss today. This serial dependence unveils a potential flaw in current financial sector risk management practices, and it motivates the development and implementation of new tools such as those presented in this book.

1.4. A BRIEF TAXONOMY OF RISKS

We have already mentioned a number of risks facing a corporation, but so far we have not been precise regarding their definitions. Now is the time to make up for that.

Market risk is defined as the risk to a financial portfolio from movements in market prices such as equity prices, foreign exchange rates, interest rates, and commodity prices.

While financial firms take on a lot of market risk and thus reap the profits (and losses), they typically try to choose the type of risk they want to be exposed to. An option trading desk, for example, has a lot of exposure to volatility changing, but not to the direction of the stock market. Option traders try to be delta neutral, as it is called. Their expertise is volatility and not market direction, and they only take on the risk about which they are the most knowledgeable, namely volatility risk. Thus financial firms tend to manage market risk actively. Nonfinancial firms, on the other hand, might decide that their core business risks (say chip manufacturing) is all they want exposure to and they therefore want to mitigate market risk or ideally eliminate it altogether.

Liquidity risk is defined as the particular risk from conducting transactions in markets with low liquidity as evidenced in low trading volume and large bid-ask spreads. Under such conditions, the attempt to sell assets may push prices lower, and assets may have to be sold at prices below their fundamental values or within a time frame longer than expected.

Traditionally, liquidity risk was given scant attention in risk management, but the events in the fall of 1998 sharply increased the attention devoted to liquidity risk. The Russian default, the Long Term Capital Management (LTCM) crisis, and the subsequent flight to high-quality assets dried up liquidity in the markets for many more risky securities. Funding risk is often thought of as a second type of liquidity risk, and indeed the LTCM collapse was ultimately triggered by a withdrawal of funding by bank lenders.

Operational risk is defined as the risk of loss due to physical catastrophe, technical failure, and human error in the operation of a firm, including fraud, failure of management, and process errors.

Operational risk—or op risk—should be mitigated and ideally eliminated in any firm as the exposure to it offers very little return (the short-term cost savings of being careless, for example). Op risk is typically very difficult to hedge in asset markets, although certain specialized products such as weather derivatives and catastrophe bonds might offer somewhat of a hedge in certain situations. Op risk is instead typically managed using self-insurance or third-party insurance.

Credit risk is defined as the risk that a counterparty may become less likely to fulfill its obligation in part or in full on the agreed upon date. Thus, credit risk consists not only of the risk that a counterparty completely defaults on its obligation, but also that it only pays in part or after the agreed upon date.

The nature of commercial banks has traditionally been to take on large amounts of credit risk through their loan portfolios. Today, banks spend much effort to carefully manage their credit risk exposure. Nonbank financials as well as nonfinancial corporations might instead want to completely eliminate credit risk as it is not a part of their core business. However, many kinds of credit risks are not readily hedged in financial markets, and corporations are often forced to take on credit risk exposure that they would rather be without.

Business risk is defined as the risk that changes in variables of a business plan will destroy that plan's viability, including quantifiable risks, such as business cycle and demand equation risk, and nonquantifiable risks, such as changes in competitive behavior or technology. Business risk is sometimes simply defined as the types of risks that are an integral part of the core business of the firm and that should therefore simply be taken on.

1.5. STYLIZED FACTS OF ASSET RETURNS

While any of the preceding risks can be important to a corporation, this book focuses on various aspects of market risk. As market risk is caused by movements in asset prices or equivalently asset returns, we begin by defining returns and then give an overview of the characteristics of typical asset returns.

We start by defining the daily geometric or "log" return on an asset as the change in the logarithm of the daily closing price of the asset. We write

$$R_{t+1} = \ln(S_{t+1}) - \ln(S_t)$$

The arithmetic return is instead defined as

$$r_{t+1} = (S_{t+1} - S_t)/S_t = S_{t+1}/S_t - 1$$

The two returns are typically fairly similar, as can be seen from

$$R_{t+1} = \ln(S_{t+1}) - \ln(S_t) = \ln(S_{t+1}/S_t) = \ln(1 + r_{t+1}) \approx r_{t+1}$$

The approximation holds because $\ln(x) \approx x - 1$ when x is close to 1.

One advantage of the log return is that we can easily calculate the compounded return at the $K-$day horizon simply as the sum of the daily returns

$$R_{t+1:t+K} = \ln(S_{t+K}) - \ln(S_t) = \sum_{k=1}^{K} \ln(S_{t+k}) - \ln(S_{t+k-1}) = \sum_{k=1}^{K} R_{t+k}$$

We can consider the following list of so-called stylized facts, which apply to most stochastic returns. Each of these facts will be discussed in detail in the first part of the book. We will use daily returns on the S&P 500 from January 1, 1997, through December 31, 2001, to illustrate each of the features.

- Daily returns have very little autocorrelation. We can write

$$Corr(R_{t+1}, R_{t+1-\tau}) \approx 0, \quad \text{for } \tau = 1, 2, 3, \ldots, 100$$

  In other words, returns are almost impossible to predict from their own past. Figure 1.1 shows the correlation of daily S&P 500 returns with returns lagged from 1 to 100 days. We will take this as evidence that the conditional mean is roughly constant.
- The unconditional distribution of daily returns has fatter tails than the normal distribution. Figure 1.2 shows a histogram of the daily S&P 500 return data with the normal distribution imposed. Notice how the histogram has longer and fatter tails, in particular on the left side, and how it is more peaked around zero than the normal distribution. Fatter tails mean a higher probability of large losses than the normal distribution would suggest.
- The stock market exhibits occasional, very large drops but not equally large up-moves. Consequently, the return distribution is asymmetric or negatively skewed. This is clear from Figure 1.2 as well. Other markets such as that for foreign exchange tend to show less evidence of skewness.

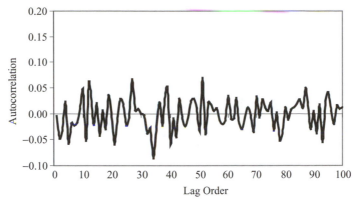

FIGURE 1.1 Autocorrelations of Daily S&P Returns for Lags 1 Through 100. January 1, 1997—December 31, 2001.

- The standard deviation of returns completely dominates the mean of returns at short horizons such as daily. It is not possible to statistically reject a zero mean return. Our S&P data have a daily mean of 0.0353% and a daily standard deviation of 1.2689%.
- Variance, measured, for example, by squared returns, displays positive correlation with its own past. This is most evident at short horizons such as daily or weekly. Figure 1.3 shows the autocorrelation in squared returns for the S&P 500 data, that is

$$Corr\left(R_{t+1}^2, R_{t+1-\tau}^2\right) > 0, \quad \text{for small } \tau$$

Models that can capture this variance dependence will be presented in Chapter 2.

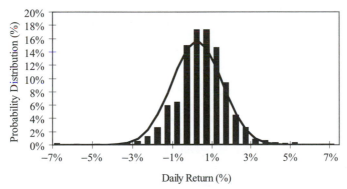

FIGURE 1.2 Histogram of Daily S&P Returns Superimposed on the Normal Distribution. January 1, 1997—December 31, 2001.

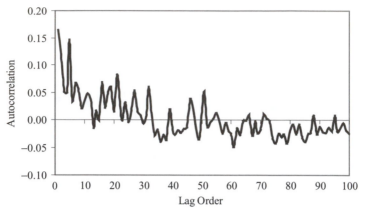

FIGURE 1.3   Autocorrelation of Squared Daily S&P 500 Returns for Lags 1 Through 100. January 1, 1997—December 31, 2001.

- Equity and equity indices display negative correlation between variance and returns. This is often termed the leverage effect, arising from the fact that a drop in a stock price will increase the leverage of the firm as long as debt stays constant. This increase in leverage might explain the increase variance associated with the price drop. We will model the leverage effect in Chapter 2.
- Correlation between assets appears to be time varying. Importantly, the correlation between assets appears to increase in highly volatile down markets and extremely so during market crashes. We will model this important phenomenon in Chapter 3.
- Even after standardizing returns by a time-varying volatility measure, they still have fatter than normal tails. We will refer to this as evidence of conditional non-normality, which will be modeled in Chapter 4 and 5.
- As the return-horizon increases, the unconditional return distribution changes and looks increasingly like the normal distribution. Issues related to risk management across horizons will be discussed in Chapter 5.

Based on the previous list of stylized facts, our model of individual asset returns will take the generic form

$$R_{t+1} = \mu_{t+1} + \sigma_{t+1}z_{t+1}, \quad \text{with } z_{t+1} \sim i.i.d. \ D(0, 1)$$

The conditional mean return, $E_t[R_{t+1}]$, is thus μ_{t+1}, and the conditional variance, $E_t[R_{t+1} - \mu_{t+1}]^2$, is σ_{t+1}^2. The random variable z_{t+1} is an innovation term, which we assume is identically and independently distributed ($i.i.d.$) according to the distribution $D(0, 1)$, which has a mean equal to zero and variance equal to one.

In most of the book, we will assume that the conditional mean of the return, μ_{t+1} is simply zero. For daily data this is a quite reasonable assumption as we mentioned in the preceding list of stylized facts. For longer horizons, the risk manager may want to estimate a model for the conditional mean as well as well as for the conditional variance. However, robust conditional mean relationships are not easy to find, and assuming a zero mean return may indeed be the most prudent choice the risk manager can make.

1.6. OVERVIEW OF THE BOOK

The book contains eight chapters including the present. Chapters 2 through 4 discuss the construction of conditional densities for simple assets such as equities, indices, bonds, and foreign exchange. These assets typically form the basis of any risk management system, and knowing their statistical properties is crucial. Chapter 2 discusses methods for estimating and forecasting variance on an asset-by-asset basis, Chapter 3 presents methods for modeling the correlation between two or more assets, and Chapter 4 introduces methods to model the tail behavior in asset returns that is not captured by volatility and correlation models and that is not captured by the normal distribution.

Chapter 5 introduces simulation-based methods in risk management. We survey data-based methods such as historical simulation and weighted historical simulation and contrast them with the Monte Carlo simulation of GARCH models. Finally, we introduce filtered historical simulation, which combines the attractiveness of conditional GARCH models with data-based methods for obtaining the conditional distribution.

Chapters 6 and 7 discuss option pricing and hedging. In Chapter 6, we discuss how the seminal Black-Scholes model, which relies on constant volatility and a normal distribution, has problems capturing the pricing properties of particularly close-to-maturity and deep in and out-of-the-money options. We then consider alternatives to Black-Scholes that are able to better capture key features of observed market option prices. In Chapter 7, we discuss different ways of measuring and hedging the risk from holding options in a portfolio. Options have nonlinear payoffs and therefore present a set of challenges that are different from those discussed in Chapters 2 through 4, which consider assets with linear payoffs only.

Chapter 8 gives a thorough treatment of risk model evaluation and comparison. We first discuss different methods for back testing (or evaluating the model) on historical data. We finally consider a coherent method for stress testing, which entails feeding extreme scenarios into the model and assessing the performance of the model under these scenarios.

1.7. FURTHER RESOURCES

A very nice review of the theoretical and empirical evidence on corporate risk management can be found in Stulz (1996). Allayannis and Weston (2003), Minton and Schrand (1999), Smithson (1999), and Tufano (1998) present further empirical evidence. Berkowitz and O'Brien (2002) document the performance of risk management systems in large commercial banks, and Dunbar (1999) contains a discussion of the increased focus on the corporate risk manager after the turbulence in the fall of 1998. The definitions of the main types of risk used here can be found at www.erisk.com and in *JPMorgan/Risk Magazine* (2001). Cont (2001) contains a nice overview of the stylized facts of speculative asset returns. Useful surveys of risk management models include Duffie and Pan (1997) and Marshall and Siegel (1997). Useful web sites include www.gloriamundi.org, www.riskwaters.com, www.defaultrisk.com, www.bis.org, and www.riskmetrics.com. Links to these and other useful sites can be found at www.christoffersen.ca.

1.8. EMPIRICAL EXERCISES ON CD-ROM

Open the Chapter1Data.xls file on the CD-ROM. (*Excel Hint*: Enable the Data Analysis Tool under Tools, Add-Ins.)

1. From the S&P 500 prices, calculate daily returns as $R_{t+1} = \ln(S_{t+1}) - \ln(S_t)$ where S_{t+1} is the closing price on day $t + 1$, S_t is the closing price on day t, and ln is the natural logarithm. Plot the closing prices and returns over time.

2. Calculate the mean, standard deviation, skewness, and kurtosis of returns. Plot a histogram of the returns with the normal distribution imposed as well. (*Excel Hints*: You can either use the Histogram tool under Data Analysis, or you can use the functions AVERAGE, STDEV, SKEW, KURT, and the array function FREQUENCY, as well as the NORMDIST function. Note that KURT computes excess kurtosis. Note also that array functions are entered using CONTROL-SHIFT-ENTER instead of just ENTER.)

3. Calculate the 1st through 100th lag autocorrelation. Plot the autocorrelations against the lag order. (*Excel Hint*: Use the function CORREL.) Compare your result with Figure 1.1.

4. Calculate the 1st through 100th lag autocorrelation of squared returns. Again, plot the autocorrelations against the lag order. Compare your result with Figure 1.3.

5. Set σ_0^2 (i.e., the variance of the first observation) equal to the variance of the entire sequence of returns (you can square the standard deviation found in 2). Then calculate $\sigma_{t+1}^2 = 0.94\sigma_t^2 + 0.06R_t^2$ for $t = 2, 3, \ldots, T$ (the last observation). Plot the sequence of standard deviations, (i.e., plot σ_t).

6. Compute standardized returns as $z_t = R_t/\sigma_t$ and calculate the mean, standard deviation, skewness, and kurtosis of the standardized returns. Compare them with those found in 2.

7. Calculate daily, 5-day, 10-day, and 15-day nonoverlapping log returns. Calculate the mean, standard deviation, skewness, and kurtosis for all four return horizons. Do the returns look more normal as the horizon increases?

The answers to these exercises can be found in the Chapter1Results.xls file. Previews of the answers follow.

QUESTION 1

Plots of Returns and Closing Prices

	Raw Data	
Date	**Close**	**Return**
02-Jan-97	737.01	
03-Jan-97	748.03	1.48%
06-Jan-97	747.65	-0.05%
07-Jan-97	753.23	0.74%
08-Jan-97	748.41	-0.64%
09-Jan-97	754.85	0.86%
10-Jan-97	759.50	0.61%
13-Jan-97	759.51	0.00%
14-Jan-97	768.86	1.22%
15-Jan-97	767.20	-0.22%
16-Jan-97	769.75	0.33%
17-Jan-97	776.17	0.83%
20-Jan-97	776.70	0.07%
21-Jan-97	782.72	0.77%
22-Jan-97	786.23	0.45%
23-Jan-97	777.56	-1.11%
24-Jan-97	770.52	-0.91%
27-Jan-97	765.02	-0.72%
28-Jan-97	765.02	0.00%
29-Jan-97	772.50	0.97%
30-Jan-97	784.17	1.50%
31-Jan-97	786.16	0.25%
03-Feb-97	786.73	0.07%
04-Feb-97	789.26	0.32%
05-Feb-97	778.28	-1.40%
06-Feb-97	780.15	0.24%
07-Feb-97	789.56	1.20%
10-Feb-97	785.43	-0.52%
11-Feb-97	789.59	0.53%
12-Feb-97	802.77	1.66%
13-Feb-97	811.82	1.12%

QUESTION 2

Raw Data

Date	Close	Return
02-Jan-97	737.01	
03-Jan-97	748.03	1.48%
06-Jan-97	747.65	-0.05%
07-Jan-97	753.23	0.74%
08-Jan-97	748.41	-0.64%
09-Jan-97	754.85	0.86%
10-Jan-97	759.50	0.61%
13-Jan-97	759.51	0.00%
14-Jan-97	768.86	1.22%
15-Jan-97	767.20	-0.22%
16-Jan-97	769.75	0.33%
17-Jan-97	776.17	0.83%
20-Jan-97	776.70	0.07%
21-Jan-97	782.72	0.77%
22-Jan-97	786.23	0.45%
23-Jan-97	777.56	-1.11%
24-Jan-97	770.52	-0.91%
27-Jan-97	765.02	-0.72%
28-Jan-97	765.02	0.00%

Mean	0.0353%
Standard Deviation	0.0127
Skewness	-0.2377
Kurtosis	2.6624

This is Excess Kurtosis (Raw Kurtosis minus 3).

This formula calculates the starting point of the first bin

The formula increases previous return value by 0.5% if the result is still within data range and gives zero if it is out of the range. Finally, we have bin with steps of 0.5%.

The array formula calculates the frequency distribution of the return data set

The formula returns the normal distribution for the mean and standard deviation given by F3 and F4 correspondently. The Denominator 200 (100% over 0.5% - step in bin) normalizes the function

Frequency Distribution

Return	Frequency	Normal
-7.11%	0.08%	0.00%
-6.61%	0.08%	0.00%
-6.11%	0.00%	0.00%
-5.61%	0.08%	0.00%
-5.11%	0.00%	0.00%
-4.61%	0.08%	0.02%
-4.11%	0.08%	0.08%
-3.61%	0.24%	0.25%
-3.11%	0.24%	0.73%
-2.61%	1.11%	1.79%
-2.11%	2.39%	3.76%
-1.61%	4.62%	6.78%
-1.11%	6.13%	10.46%
-0.61%	11.94%	13.81%
-0.11%	17.99%	15.62%
0.39%	16.80%	15.12%
0.89%	16.08%	12.53%
1.39%	10.51%	8.89%
1.89%	5.65%	5.40%

QUESTION 3

Calculating Autocorrelations of Raw Returns

Date	Close	Return	Lag	Correlation
02-Jan-97	737.01			
03-Jan-97	748.03	1.48%	1	-0.0046
06-Jan-97	747.65	-0.05%	2	-0.0480
07-Jan-97	753.23	0.74%	3	-0.0330
08-Jan-97	748.41	-0.64%	4	0.0234
09-Jan-97	754.85	0.86%	5	-0.0581
10-Jan-97	759.50	0.61%	6	-0.0192
13-Jan-97	759.51	0.00%	7	-0.0234
14-Jan-97	768.86	1.22%	8	-0.0168
15-Jan-97	767.20	-0.22%	9	0.0098
16-Jan-97	769.75	0.33%	10	0.0472
17-Jan-97	776.17	0.83%	11	-0.0524
20-Jan-97	776.70	0.07%	12	0.0601
21-Jan-97	782.72	0.77%	13	0.0396
22-Jan-97	786.23	0.45%	14	-0.0215
23-Jan-97	777.56	-1.11%	15	0.0210
24-Jan-97	770.52	-0.91%	16	-0.0427
27-Jan-97	765.02	-0.72%	17	0.0058
28-Jan-97	765.02	0.00%	18	-0.0296
29-Jan-97	772.50	0.97%	19	0.0365
30-Jan-97	784.17	1.50%	20	0.0003
31-Jan-97	786.16	0.25%	21	-0.0596
03-Feb-97	786.73	0.07%	22	-0.0088
04-Feb-97	789.26	0.32%	23	0.0294
05-Feb-97	778.28	-1.40%	24	0.0189
06-Feb-97	780.15	0.24%	25	-0.0223
07-Feb-97	789.56	1.20%	26	-0.0073
10-Feb-97	785.43	-0.52%	27	0.0665
11-Feb-97	789.59	0.53%	28	0.0060
			29	0.0095

Autocorrelations are small and do not show a systematic pattern.

Calculating Autocorrelations of Squared Returns

Date	Close	Return	Squared Return	Lag	Correlation
02-Jan-97	737.01				
03-Jan-97	748.03	1.48%	0.000220	1	0.1647
06-Jan-97	747.65	-0.05%	0.000000	2	0.1187
07-Jan-97	753.23	0.74%	0.000055	3	0.0501
08-Jan-97	748.41	-0.64%	0.000041	4	0.0498
09-Jan-97	754.85	0.86%	0.000073	5	0.1469
10-Jan-97	759.50	0.61%	0.000038	6	0.0356
13-Jan-97	759.51	0.00%	0.000000	7	0.0678
14-Jan-97	768.86	1.22%	0.000150	8	0.0562
15-Jan-97	767.20	-0.22%	0.000005	9	0.0200
16-Jan-97	769.75	0.33%	0.000011	10	0.0345
17-Jan-97	776.17	0.83%	0.000069	11	0.0483
20-Jan-97	776.70	0.07%	0.000000	12	0.0363
21-Jan-97	782.72	0.77%	0.000060	13	-0.0145
22-Jan-97	786.23	0.45%	0.000020	14	0.0170
23-Jan-97	777.56	-1.11%	0.000123	15	-0.0005
24-Jan-97	770.52	-0.91%	0.000083	16	0.0679
27-Jan-97	765.02	-0.72%	0.000051	17	0.0216
28-Jan-97	765.02	0.00%	0.000000	18	0.0509
29-Jan-97	772.50	0.97%	0.000095	19	0.0595
30-Jan-97	784.17	1.50%	0.000225	20	0.0147
31-Jan-97	786.16	0.25%	0.000006	21	0.0817
03-Feb-97	786.73	0.07%	0.000001	22	0.0261
04-Feb-97	789.26	0.32%	0.000010	23	-0.0011
05-Feb-97	778.28	-1.40%	0.000196	24	0.0321
06-Feb-97	780.15	0.24%	0.000006	25	-0.0043
07-Feb-97	789.56	1.20%	0.000144	26	0.0167
10-Feb-97	785.43	-0.52%	0.000028	27	0.0529
11-Feb-97	789.59	0.53%	0.000028	28	0.0148
				29	0.0085

The autocorrelations of squared returns tend to be positive for short lags and decay exponentially to zero as the number of lags increases.

QUESTION 4

QUESTION 5

Calculating Exponentially Smoothed Variances

Date	Close	Return	Conditional Variance	Conditional St. Deviation
02-Jan-97	737.01			
03-Jan-97	748.03	1.48%	0.000161	1.27%
06-Jan-97	747.65	-0.05%	0.000165	1.28%
07-Jan-97	753.23	0.74%	0.000155	1.24%
08-Jan-97	748.41	-0.64%	0.000149	1.22%
09-Jan-97	754.85	0.86%	0.000142	1.19%
10-Jan-97	759.50	0.61%	0.000138	1.18%
13-Jan-97	759.51	0.00%	0.000132	1.15%
14-Jan-97	768.86	1.22%	0.000124	1.11%
15-Jan-97	767.20	-0.22%	0.000126	1.12%
16-Jan-97	769.75	0.33%	0.000118	1.09%
17-Jan-97	776.17	0.83%	0.000112	1.06%
20-Jan-97	776.70	0.07%	0.000109	1.05%
21-Jan-97	782.72	0.77%	0.000103	1.01%
22-Jan-97	786.23	0.45%	0.000100	1.00%
23-Jan-97	777.56	-1.11%	0.000095	0.98%
24-Jan-97	770.52	-0.91%	0.000097	0.99%
27-Jan-97	765.02	-0.72%	0.000096	0.98%
28-Jan-97	765.02	0.00%	0.000094	0.97%
29-Jan-97	772.50	0.97%	0.000088	0.94%
30-Jan-97	784.17	1.50%	0.000088	0.94%
31-Jan-97	786.16	0.25%	0.000097	0.98%
03-Feb-97	786.73	0.07%	0.000091	0.95%
04-Feb-97	789.26	0.32%	0.000086	0.93%
05-Feb-97	778.28	-1.40%	0.000081	0.90%
06-Feb-97	780.15	0.24%	0.000088	0.94%
07-Feb-97	789.56	1.20%	0.000083	0.91%
10-Feb-97	785.43	-0.52%	0.000087	0.93%

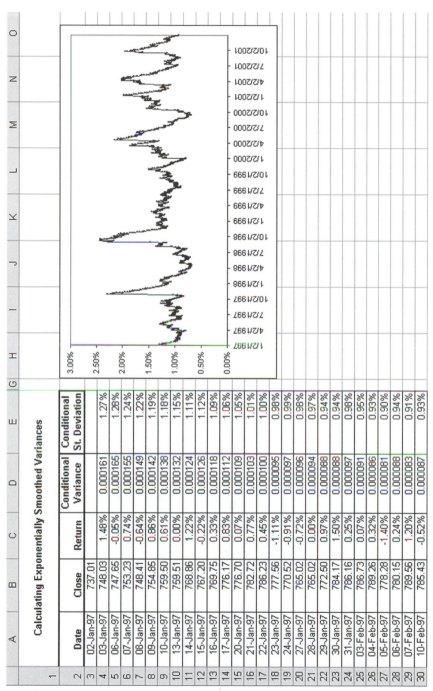

QUESTION 6

Calculating Standardized Returns

Date	Close	Return	σ^2_t	σ_t	Standardized Return
02-Jan-97	737.01				
03-Jan-97	748.03	1.48%	0.000161	1.27%	1.1697
06-Jan-97	747.65	-0.05%	0.000165	1.28%	-0.0396
07-Jan-97	753.23	0.74%	0.000155	1.24%	0.5978
08-Jan-97	748.41	-0.64%	0.000149	1.22%	-0.5264
09-Jan-97	754.85	0.86%	0.000142	1.19%	0.7183
10-Jan-97	759.50	0.61%	0.000138	1.18%	0.5225
13-Jan-97	759.51	0.00%	0.000132	1.15%	0.0011
14-Jan-97	768.86	1.22%	0.000124	1.11%	1.0979
15-Jan-97	767.20	-0.22%	0.000126	1.12%	-0.1928
16-Jan-97	769.75	0.33%	0.000118	1.09%	0.3049
17-Jan-97	776.17	0.83%	0.000112	1.06%	0.7848
20-Jan-97	776.70	0.07%	0.000109	1.05%	0.0653
21-Jan-97	782.72	0.77%	0.000103	1.01%	0.7611
22-Jan-97	786.23	0.45%	0.000100	1.00%	0.4468
23-Jan-97	777.56	-1.11%	0.000095	0.98%	-1.1348
24-Jan-97	770.52	-0.91%	0.000097	0.99%	-0.9228
27-Jan-97	765.02	-0.72%	0.000096	0.98%	-0.7301
28-Jan-97	765.02	0.00%	0.000094	0.97%	0.0000

Moments of Raw and Standardized Returns

Raw		vs.	Standardized	
Mean	0.04%		Mean	0.0100
St. Deviation	1.27%		St. Deviation	1.05
Skewness	-0.238		Skewness	-0.579
Kurtosis	2.662		Kurtosis	2.629

Returns Across Horizons

Date	Close	1-day Return	5-day Return	10-day Return	15-day Return
02-Jan-97	737.01				
03-Jan-97	748.03	1.48%			
06-Jan-97	747.65	-0.05%			
07-Jan-97	753.23	0.74%			
08-Jan-97	748.41	-0.64%			
09-Jan-97	754.85	0.86%	2.39%		
10-Jan-97	759.50	0.61%			
13-Jan-97	759.51	0.00%			
14-Jan-97	768.86	1.22%			
15-Jan-97	767.20	-0.22%			
16-Jan-97	769.75	0.33%	1.95%	4.35%	
17-Jan-97	776.17	0.83%			
20-Jan-97	776.70	0.07%			
21-Jan-97	782.72	0.77%			
22-Jan-97	786.23	0.45%			
23-Jan-97	777.56	-1.11%	1.01%		5.36%
24-Jan-97	770.52	-0.91%			
27-Jan-97	765.02	-0.72%			
28-Jan-97	765.02	0.00%			

1-day Return	
Mean	0.04%
St. Deviation	1.27%
Skewness	-0.238
Kurtosis	2.662

5-day Return	
Mean	0.18%
St. Deviation	2.79%
Skewness	-0.376
Kurtosis	0.332

10-day Return	
Mean	0.35%
St. Deviation	3.44%
Skewness	-0.594
Kurtosis	0.511

15-day Return	
Mean	0.50%
St. Deviation	4.69%
Skewness	-0.262
Kurtosis	-0.006

QUESTION 7

REFERENCES

Allayannis, G., and J. Weston. (2003). "Earnings Volatility, Cash-Flow Volatility and Firm Value," Manuscript, University of Virginia and Rice University.

Berkowitz, J., and J. O'Brien. (2002). "How Accurate Are Value-at-Risk Models at Commercial Banks?" *Journal of Finance*, 57, 1093–1112.

Cont, R. (2001). "Empirical Properties of Asset Returns: Stylized Facts and Statistical Issues," *Quantitative Finance*, 1, 223–236.

Duffie, D., and J. Pan. (1997, Spring)."An Overview of Value at Risk," *Journal of Derivatives*, 4, 7–49.

Dunbar, N. (1999, March). "The New Emperors of Wall Street," *Risk*, 26–33.

JPMorgan/Risk Magazine. (2001). *Guide to Risk Management: A Glossary of Terms*. London: Risk Waters Group.

Marshall, C., and M. Siegel. (1997, Spring). "Value at Risk: Implementing a Risk Measurement Standard," *Journal of Derivatives*, 4, 91–111.

Minton, B., and C. Schrand. (1999). "The Impact of Cash Flow Volatility on Discretionary Investment and the Costs of Debt and Equity Financing," *Journal of Financial Economics*, 54, 423–460.

Smithson, C. (1999, July). "Does Risk Management Work?" *Risk*, 44–45.

Stulz, R. (1996). "Rethinking Risk Management," *Journal of Applied Corporate Finance*, 9(3).

Tufano, P. (1998). "The determinants of stock price exposure: Financial Engineering and the Gold Mining Industry, *Journal of Finance*, 53, 1015–1052.

2

VOLATILITY MODELING

2.1. CHAPTER OVERVIEW

The ultimate goal of this and the following two chapters is to establish a framework for modeling the non-normal conditional distribution of the relatively large number of assets that make up the financial portfolio of a company. This is an ambitious undertaking, and we will proceed cautiously in three steps following what we will call the stepwise distribution modeling approach (SDM). The first step of the SDM is to establish a variance forecasting model for each of the assets individually and to introduce methods for evaluating the performance of these forecasts. The second step is to link the individual variance forecasts with a correlation model. The variance and correlation models together will yield a time-varying covariance model, which can be used to calculate the variance of an aggregate portfolio of assets. Finally, the third step will consider ways to model conditionally non-normal aspects of the assets in our portfolio—that is, aspects that are not captured in the conditional mean and variance.

The second and third steps are analyzed in subsequent chapters, while the first step is covered in this chapter in the following manner:

1. We briefly describe the simplest variance models available including the so-called RiskMetrics or exponential smoothing variance model.
2. We introduce the GARCH variance model and compare it with the RiskMetrics model.
3. We suggest extensions to the basic model, which improve the ability to capture variance persistence and leverage effects. We also consider ways to expand the model to take into account explanatory variables such as volume effects, day-of-week effects, and implied volatility from options.
4. We consider parameter estimation using Quasi Maximum Likelihood and introduce a simple diagnostic check.
5. We describe techniques for assessing the in-sample fit and out-of-sample predictive ability of GARCH models and
6. We suggest how intraday data can be used to enhance daily variance predictability.

2.2. SIMPLE VARIANCE FORECASTING

We begin by establishing some notation and by laying out our underlying assumptions for this chapter. In Chapter 1, we defined the daily asset log-return, R_{t+1}, using the daily closing price, S_{t+1}, as

$$R_{t+1} \equiv \ln \left(S_{t+1} / S_t \right)$$

We will also apply the finding from Chapter 1 that at short horizons such as daily, we can safely assume that the mean value of R_t is zero as it is dominated by the standard deviation of returns. Issues arising at longer horizons will be discussed in Chapter 5. Furthermore, we will assume that the innovations or news hitting the asset return are normally distributed. We hasten to add that the normality assumption is not realistic, and it will be relaxed in Chapters 4 and 5. Normality is simply assumed for now, as it allows us to focus on modeling the conditional variance of the distribution.

Given the assumptions made, we can write the daily return as

$$R_{t+1} = \sigma_{t+1} z_{t+1}, \quad \text{with } z_{t+1} \sim i.i.d. \, N(0, 1)$$

where the abbreviation $i.i.d.$ $N(0, 1)$ stands for "independently and identically normally distributed with mean equal to zero and variance equal to 1."

Together these assumptions imply that once we have established a model of the time-varying variance, σ_{t+1}^2, we will know the entire distribution of the asset, and we can therefore easily calculate any desired risk measure. We are well aware from the stylized facts discussed in Chapter 1 that the assumption of conditional normality that is imposed here is not satisfied in actual data on speculative returns. However, as we will see later on, for the purpose of variance modeling, we are allowed to assume normality even if it is strictly speaking not a correct assumption. This assumption conveniently allows us to postpone discussions of nonnormal distributions to a later chapter.

The sole focus of this chapter then is to establish a model for forecasting tomorrow's variance, σ_{t+1}^2. We know from Chapter 1 that variance, as measured by squared returns, exhibits strong autocorrelation, so that if the recent period was one of high variance, then tomorrow is likely to be a high-variance day as well. The easiest way to capture this phenomenon is by letting tomorrow's variance be the simple average of the most recent m observations, as in

$$\sigma_{t+1}^2 = \frac{1}{m} \sum_{\tau=1}^{m} R_{t+1-\tau}^2 = \sum_{\tau=1}^{m} \frac{1}{m} R_{t+1-\tau}^2$$

Notice that this is a proper forecast in the sense that the forecast for tomorrow's variance is immediately available at the end of today when the daily return is realized. However, the fact that the model puts equal weights (equal to $1/m$) on the past m observations yields unwarranted results. When plotted over time, variance will exhibit box-shaped patterns. An extreme return (either positive or negative) today will bump up variance by $1/m$ times the return squared for exactly m periods after which variance immediately will drop back down. Figure 2.1 illustrates this point for $m = 25$ days. The autocorrelation plot of squared returns in Chapter 1 suggests that a more gradual decline is warranted in the effect of past returns on today's variance. Even if one is content with the box patterns, it is not at all clear how m should be chosen. This is unfortunate as the choice of m is crucial in deciding the patterns of σ_{t+1}: A high m will lead to an excessively smoothly evolving σ_{t+1}, and a low m will lead to an excessively jagged pattern of σ_{t+1} over time.

JP Morgan's RiskMetrics system for market risk management considers the following model, where the weights on past squared returns decline exponentially as we move backward in time. The RiskMetrics variance model, or the exponential smoother as it is sometimes called, is written as

$$\sigma_{t+1}^2 = (1 - \lambda) \sum_{\tau=1}^{\infty} \lambda^{\tau-1} R_{t+1-\tau}^2, \quad \text{for } 0 < \lambda < 1$$

Separating from the sum the squared return term for $\tau = 1$, where $\lambda^{\tau-1} = \lambda^0 = 1$, we get

$$\sigma_{t+1}^2 = (1 - \lambda) \sum_{\tau=2}^{\infty} \lambda^{\tau-1} R_{t+1-\tau}^2 + (1 - \lambda) R_t^2$$

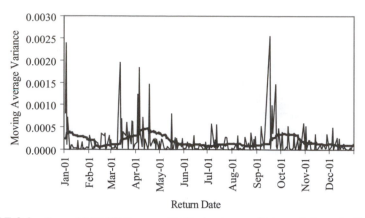

FIGURE 2.1   Squared S&P 500 Returns with Moving Average Variance Estimate (bold) on past 25 observations ($m = 25$).

Applying the exponential smoothing definition again, we can write today's variance, σ_t^2, as

$$\sigma_t^2 = (1 - \lambda) \sum_{\tau=1}^{\infty} \lambda^{\tau-1} R_{t-\tau}^2 = \frac{1}{\lambda} (1 - \lambda) \sum_{\tau=2}^{\infty} \lambda^{\tau-1} R_{t+1-\tau}^2$$

so that tomorrow's variance can be written as

$$\sigma_{t+1}^2 = \lambda \sigma_t^2 + (1 - \lambda) R_t^2$$

The RiskMetrics model's forecast for tomorrow's volatility can thus be seen as a weighted average of today's volatility and today's squared return.

The RiskMetrics model has some clear advantages. First, it tracks variance changes in a way that is broadly consistent with observed returns. Recent returns matter more for tomorrow's variance than distant returns as λ is less than one and therefore gets smaller when the lag, τ, gets bigger. Second, the model only contains one unknown parameter, namely, λ. When estimating λ on a large number of assets, RiskMetrics found that the estimates were quite similar across assets, and they therefore simply set $\lambda = 0.94$ for every asset for daily variance forecasting. In this case, no estimation is necessary, which is a huge advantage in large portfolios. Third, relatively little data need to be stored in order to calculate tomorrow's variance. The weight on today's squared returns is $(1 - \lambda) = 0.06$, and the weight is exponentially decaying to $(1 - \lambda)\lambda^{99} = 0.000131$ on the 100th lag of squared return. After including 100 lags of squared returns, the cumulated weight is $(1 - \lambda) \sum_{\tau=1}^{100} \lambda^{\tau-1} = 0.998$, so that 99.8% of the weight has been included. Therefore it is only necessary to store about 100 daily lags of returns in order to calculate tomorrow's variance, σ_{t+1}^2. Of course, once σ_t^2 is calculated, the past returns are no longer needed.

Given all these advantages of the RiskMetrics model, why not simply end the discussion on variance forecasting here and move on to correlation modeling? Unfortunately, as we will see shortly, the RiskMetrics model does have certain shortcomings, which will motivate us to consider slightly more elaborate models. For example, it does not allow for a leverage effect, which we considered a stylized fact in Chapter 1, and it also provides counterfactual longer-horizon forecasts.

2.3. THE GARCH VARIANCE MODEL

We now introduce a set of models that capture important features of returns data and that are flexible enough to accommodate specific aspects of individual assets. The downside of these models is that they require nonlinear parameter estimation, which will be discussed subsequently.

The simplest generalized autoregressive conditional heteroskedasticity (GARCH) model of dynamic variance can be written as

$$\sigma_{t+1}^2 = \omega + \alpha R_t^2 + \beta \sigma_t^2, \quad \text{with } \alpha + \beta < 1$$

Notice that the RiskMetrics model can be viewed as a special case of the simple GARCH model if we force $\alpha = 1 - \lambda$, $\beta = \lambda$, so that $\alpha + \beta = 1$, and further $\omega = 0$. Thus, the two models appear to be quite similar. However, there is an important difference: We can define the unconditional, or long-run average, variance, σ^2, to be

$$\sigma^2 \equiv E[\sigma_{t+1}^2] = \omega + \alpha E[R_t^2] + \beta E[\sigma_t^2]$$

$$= \omega + \alpha \sigma^2 + \beta \sigma^2, \text{ so that}$$

$$\sigma^2 = \omega/(1 - \alpha - \beta)$$

It is now clear that if $\alpha + \beta = 1$, as is the case in the RiskMetrics model, then the long-run variance, is not well-defined in that model. Thus, an important quirk of the RiskMetrics model emerges: It ignores the fact that the long-run average variance tends to be relatively stable over time. The GARCH model, in turn, implicitly relies on σ^2. This can be seen by solving for ω in the long-run variance equation and substituting it into the dynamic variance equation. We get

$$\sigma_{t+1}^2 = (1 - \alpha - \beta)\sigma^2 + \alpha R_t^2 + \beta \sigma_t^2 = \sigma^2 + \alpha(R_t^2 - \sigma^2) + \beta(\sigma_t^2 - \sigma^2)$$

Thus, tomorrow's variance is a weighted average of the long-run variance, today's squared return, and today's variance. Put differently, tomorrow's variance is the long-run average variance with something added (subtracted) if today's squared return is above (below) its long-run average, and something added (subtracted) if today's variance is above (below) its long-run average.

Our intuition might tell us that ignoring the long-run variance, as the Risk-Metrics model does, is more important for longer-horizon forecasting than for forecasting simply one-day ahead. This intuition is correct, as we will now see.

A key advantage of GARCH models for risk management is that the one-day forecast of variance, $\sigma^2_{t+1|t}$, is given directly by the model as σ^2_{t+1}. Consider now forecasting the variance of the daily return k days ahead, using only information available at the end of today. In GARCH, the expected value of future variance at horizon k is

$$E_t\left[\sigma^2_{t+k}\right] - \sigma^2 = \alpha E_t\left[R^2_{t+k-1} - \sigma^2\right] + \beta E_t\left[\sigma^2_{t+k-1} - \sigma^2\right]$$

$$= \alpha E_t\left[\sigma^2_{t+k-1}z^2_{t+k-1} - \sigma^2\right] + \beta E_t\left[\sigma^2_{t+k-1} - \sigma^2\right]$$

$$= (\alpha + \beta)\left(E_t\left[\sigma^2_{t+k-1}\right] - \sigma^2\right), \text{ so that}$$

$$E_t\left[\sigma^2_{t+k}\right] - \sigma^2 = (\alpha + \beta)^{k-1}\left(E_t\left[\sigma^2_{t+1}\right] - \sigma^2\right) = (\alpha + \beta)^{k-1}\left(\sigma^2_{t+1} - \sigma^2\right)$$

The conditional expectation, $E_t[*]$, refers to taking the expectation using all the information available at the end of day t, which includes the squared return on day t itself.

We will refer to $\alpha + \beta$ as the persistence of the model. A high persistence—that is, an $(\alpha + \beta)$ close to 1—implies that shocks which push variance away from its long-run average will persist for a long time, but eventually the long-horizon forecast will be the long-run average variance, σ^2. Similar calculations for the RiskMetrics model reveal that

$$E_t\left[\sigma^2_{t+k}\right] = \sigma^2_{t+1}, \quad \forall k$$

as $\alpha + \beta = 1$ and σ^2 is undefined. Thus, persistence in this model is 1, which implies that a shock to variance persists forever: An increase in variance will push up the variance forecast by an identical amount for all future forecast horizons. This is another way of saying that the RiskMetrics model ignores the long-run variance when forecasting. If $\alpha + \beta$ is close to one as is typically the case, then the two models might yield similar predictions for short horizons, k, but their longer horizon implications are very different. If today is a high-variance day, then the RiskMetrics model predicts that all future days will be high-variance. The GARCH model more realistically assumes that eventually in the future variance will revert to the average value.

So far we have considered forecasting the variance of daily returns k days ahead. Of more immediate interest is probably the forecast of variance of K–day cumulative returns,

$$R_{t+1:t+k} \equiv \sum_{k=1}^{K} R_{t+k}$$

As we assume that returns have zero autocorrelation, the variance of the cumulative K-day returns is simply

$$\sigma^2_{t+1:t+K} \equiv E_t \left(\sum_{k=1}^{K} R_{t+k} \right)^2 = \sum_{k=1}^{K} E_t \left[\sigma^2_{t+k} \right]$$

So in the RiskMetrics model, we get

$$\sigma^2_{t+1:t+K} = \sum_{k=1}^{K} \sigma^2_{t+1} = K\sigma^2_{t+1}$$

But in the GARCH model, we get

$$\sigma^2_{t+1:t+K} = K\sigma^2 + \sum_{k=1}^{K} (\alpha + \beta)^{k-1} \left(\sigma^2_{t+1} - \sigma^2 \right) \neq K\sigma^2_{t+1}$$

If the RiskMetrics and GARCH model has identical σ^2_{t+1}, and if $\sigma^2_{t+1} < \sigma^2$, then the GARCH variance forecast will be higher than the RiskMetrics forecast. Thus, assuming the RiskMetrics model if the data truly look more like GARCH will give risk managers a false sense of the calmness of the market in the future, when the market is calm today and $\sigma^2_{t+1} < \sigma^2$. Figure 2.2 illustrates this crucial point. We plot $\sigma^2_{t+1:t+K}/K$ for $K = 1, 2, \ldots, 250$ for both the RiskMetrics and the GARCH model starting from a low σ^2_{t+1} and setting $\alpha = 0.05$ and $\beta = 0.90$. The long-run daily variance in the figure is $\sigma^2 = 0.000140$.

An inconvenience shared by the two models is that the multiperiod distribution is unknown even if the one-day ahead distribution is assumed to be normal, as we do in this chapter. Thus, while it is easy to forecast longer-horizon variance in these models, it is not as easy to forecast the entire conditional distribution.

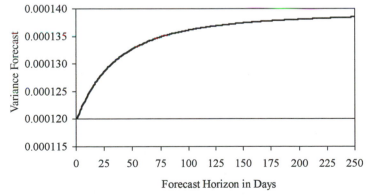

FIGURE 2.2 Variance Forecasts for 1 through 250 Days Ahead Cumulative Returns From GARCH (bold) and RiskMetrics (horizontal line) Models.

We will return to this important issue in Chapter 5 as it is unfortunately often ignored in risk management.

2.4. EXTENSIONS TO THE GARCH MODEL

As we noted earlier, one of the distinct benefits of GARCH models is their flexibility. In this section, we explore this flexibility and present some of the models most useful for risk management.

2.4.1. Long Memory in Variance

The simple GARCH model discussed earlier is often referred to as the GARCH(1,1) model because it relies on only one lag of returns squared and one lag of variance itself. For short-term variance forecasting, this model is often found to be sufficient, but in general we can allow for higher order dynamics by considering the GARCH(p,q) model, which simply allows for longer lags as follows:

$$\sigma_{t+1}^2 = \omega + \sum_{i=1}^{p} \alpha_i R_{t+1-i}^2 + \sum_{j=1}^{q} \beta_j \sigma_{t+1-j}^2$$

The simple GARCH model assumes that the long-term variance is constant over time. The component GARCH model, which is a restricted GARCH(2,2), can be seen as allowing the long-term variance to be time varying and captured by the factor v_{t+1} in

$$\sigma_{t+1}^2 = v_{t+1} + \alpha \left(R_t^2 - v_t \right) + \beta \left(\sigma_t^2 - v_t \right)$$

$$v_{t+1} = \omega + \alpha_v \left(R_t^2 - \sigma_t^2 \right) + \beta_v v_t$$

This model can potentially capture autocorrelation patterns in variance, which die out slower than what is possible in the simple short-memory GARCH(1,1) model.

2.4.2. The Leverage Effect

We argued in Chapter 1 that a negative return increases variance by more than a positive return of the same magnitude. This was referred to as the leverage effect, as a negative return on a stock implies a drop in the equity value, which implies that the company becomes more highly levered and thus more risky (assuming the level of debt stays constant). We can modify the GARCH models so that the weight given to the return depends on whether the return is positive or negative in the following simple manner:

$$\sigma_{t+1}^2 = \omega + \alpha \left(R_t - \theta \sigma_t \right)^2 + \beta \sigma_t^2 = \omega + \alpha \sigma_t^2 \left(z_t - \theta \right)^2 + \beta \sigma_t^2$$

which is sometimes referred to as the NGARCH (nonlinear GARCH) model.

Notice that it is strictly speaking a positive piece of news, $z_t > 0$, rather than raw return R_t, which has less of an impact on variance than a negative piece of news, if $\theta > 0$. The persistence of variance in this model is $\alpha(1 + \theta^2) + \beta$, and the long-run variance is $\sigma^2 = \omega/(1 - \alpha(1 + \theta^2) - \beta)$.

Another way of capturing the leverage effect is to define an indicator variable, I_t, to take on the value 1 if day $t's$ return is negative and zero otherwise. The variance dynamics can now be specified as

$$\sigma_{t+1}^2 = \omega + \alpha R_t^2 + \alpha \theta I_t R_t^2 + \beta \sigma_t^2$$

Thus, a θ larger than zero will again capture the leverage effect. This is sometimes referred to as the GJR-GARCH model.

A different that also captures the leverage is the exponential GARCH model or EGARCH,

$$\ln \sigma_{t+1}^2 = \omega + \alpha \left(\phi R_t + \gamma \left[|R_t| - E |R_t| \right] \right) + \beta \ln \sigma_t^2$$

which displays the usual leverage effect if $\alpha \phi < 0$. The EGARCH model has the advantage that the logarithmic specification ensures that variance is always positive, but it has the disadvantage that the future expected variance beyond one period cannot be calculated analytically.

2.4.3. Explanatory Variables

Because we are considering dynamic models of daily variance, we have to be careful with days where no trading takes place. It is widely recognized that days that followed a weekend or a holiday have higher variance than average days. As weekends and holidays are perfectly predictable, it makes sense so include them in the variance model. Other predetermined variables could be yesterday's trading volume or prescheduled news announcement dates such as company earnings and FOMC meetings dates. As these future events are known in advance, we can model

$$\sigma_{t+1}^2 = \omega + \beta \sigma_t^2 + \alpha \sigma_t^2 z_t^2 + \gamma I T_{t+1}$$

where $I T_{t+1}$ takes on the value 1 if date $t + 1$ is a Monday, for example.

We have not yet discussed option prices, but it is worth mentioning here that so-called implied volatilities from option prices often have quite high predictive value in forecasting next-day variance. Including the variance index (VIX) from the Chicago Board Options Exchange as an explanatory variable can improve the fit of a GARCH variance model of the underlying stock index significantly. Of course, not all underlying market variables have liquid options markets, so the implied volatility variable is not always available for variance forecasting. We will discuss the use of implied volatilities from options further in Chapter 6.

In general, we can write the GARCH variance forecasting model as follows:

$$\sigma_{t+1}^2 = \omega + g(X_t) + \alpha \sigma_t^2 z_t^2 + \beta \sigma_t^2$$

where X_t denote variables known at the end of day t. As the variance is always a positive number, it is important to ensure that the GARCH model always generates a positive variance forecast. In the simple GARCH model, positive coefficients guarantee positivity. In the more general more considered here, positivity of $g(X_t)$ along with positive ω, α, and β will ensure positivity of σ_{t+1}^2.

2.5. MAXIMUM LIKELIHOOD ESTIMATION

In the previous section, we suggested a range of models that we argued should fit the data well, but they contain a number of unknown parameters that must be estimated. In doing so, we face the challenge that the conditional variance, σ_{t+1}^2, is an unobserved variable, which must itself be implicitly estimated along with the parameters of the model, for example, α, β, and ω.

2.5.1. Standard Maximum Likelihood Estimation

We will briefly discuss the method of maximum likelihood estimation, which can be used to find parameter values. Explicitly worked-out examples are included in the answers to the empirical exercises contained on the CD-ROM.

Recall our assumption that

$$R_t = \sigma_t z_t, \quad \text{with } z_t \sim i.i.d.\ N(0, 1)$$

The assumption of $i.i.d.$ normality implies that the probability, or the likelihood, l_t, of R_t is

$$l_t = \frac{1}{\sqrt{2\pi\sigma_t^2}} \exp\left(-\frac{R_t^2}{2\sigma_t^2}\right)$$

and thus the joint likelihood of our entire sample is

$$L = \prod_{t=1}^{T} l_t = \prod_{t=1}^{T} \frac{1}{\sqrt{2\pi\sigma_t^2}} \exp\left(-\frac{R_t^2}{2\sigma_t^2}\right)$$

A natural way to choose parameters to fit the data is then to maximize the joint likelihood of our observed sample. Recall that maximizing the logarithm of a function is equivalent to maximizing the function itself as the logarithm is a monotone, increasing function. Maximizing the logarithm is convenient as it replaces products with sums. Thus, we choose parameters $(\alpha, \beta, ...)$, which solve

$$Max \ln L = Max \sum_{t=1}^{T} \ln(l_t) = Max \sum_{t=1}^{T} \left[-\frac{1}{2} \ln(2\pi) - \frac{1}{2} \ln\left(\sigma_t^2\right) - \frac{1}{2} \frac{R_t^2}{\sigma_t^2} \right]$$

and we refer to the optimal parameters as maximum likelihood estimates or MLEs. The MLEs have the theoretical properties that with infinitely many observations the parameter estimates would converge to their true values and the variance of these estimates would be the smallest possible.

In reality we of course do not have an infinite past of data available. Even if we have a long time series, say, of daily returns on the S&P 500 index available, it is not clear that we should use all that data when estimating the parameters. Sometimes obvious structural breaks such as a new exchange rate arrangement or new rules regulating trading in a particular market can guide in the choice of sample length. But often the dates of these structural breaks are not obvious and the risk manager is left with having to weigh the benefits of a longer sample, which implies more precise estimates (assuming there are no breaks), and a shorter sample, which reduces the risk of estimating across a structural break. When estimating GARCH models, a fairly good general rule of thumb is to use the past 1000 daily observations and to update the sample fairly frequently to allow for the parameters to change over time.

2.5.2. Quasi-Maximum Likelihood Estimation

The skeptical reader will immediately protest that the MLEs rely on the conditional normal distribution assumption, which we argued in Chapter 1 is false. While this protest appears to be valid, a key result in econometrics says that even if the conditional distribution is not normal, MLE will yield estimates of the mean and variance parameters, which converge to the true parameters as the sample gets infinitely large as long as the mean and variance functions are properly specified. This convenient result establishes what is called quasi-maximum likelihood estimation or QMLE, referring to the use of normal MLE estimation even when the normal distribution assumption is false. Notice that QMLE buys us the freedom to worry about the conditional distribution later on (in Chapter 4), but it does come at a price: The QMLE estimates will in general be less precise than those from MLE. Thus, we trade theoretical asymptotic parameter efficiency for practicality.

The operational aspects of parameter estimation will be discussed in the exercises following this chapter. Here we just point out one simple but useful trick, which is referred to as variance targeting. Recall that the simple GARCH model can be written as

$$\sigma_{t+1}^2 = \omega + \alpha R_t^2 + \beta \sigma_t^2 = (1 - \alpha - \beta)\sigma^2 + \alpha R_t^2 + \beta \sigma_t^2$$

Thus, instead of estimating ω by MLE, we can simply set the long-run variance, σ^2, equal to the sample variance, which is easily estimated beforehand as

$$\sigma^2 = \frac{1}{T} \sum_{t=1}^{T} R_t^2$$

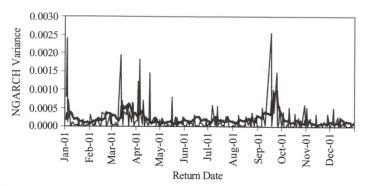

FIGURE 2.3   Squared S&P 500 Returns with NGARCH Variance Estimate (bold). The NGARCH Parameters are Estimated Using Quasi Maximum Likelihood on Daily Returns from January 1, 1997 through December 31, 2001.

Variance targeting has the benefit of imposing the long-run variance estimate on the GARCH model directly. More important, it reduces the number of parameters to be estimated in the model by one. This typically makes estimation much easier.

2.5.3. An Example

Figure 2.3 shows the S&P 500 squared returns from Figure 2.1, but now with an estimated GARCH variance superimposed. The estimated model is the GARCH model with leverage (NGARCH) from above. Using numerical optimization of the likelihood function (see the exercises at the end of the chapter), the optimal parameters imply the following variance dynamics:

$$\sigma_{t+1}^2 = \omega + \alpha \left(R_t - \theta \sigma_t \right)^2 + \beta \sigma_t^2$$
$$= 0.0000099 + 0.0556 \left(R_t - 2.1449\sigma_t \right)^2 + 0.6393\sigma_t^2$$

The parameters have been estimated on the 1257 daily observations from January 2, 1997, through December 31, 2001. The persistence of variance in this model is $\alpha(1 + \theta^2) + \beta = 0.9504$, which is quite a bit lower than in RiskMetrics where it is 1. As illustrated in Figure 2.2, this difference will have important consequences for the variance forecasts for horizons beyond one day.

2.6. VARIANCE MODEL EVALUATION

Before we start using the variance model for risk management purposes, it is appropriate to run the estimated model through some diagnostic checks.

2.6.1. In-Sample Check on the Autocorrelations

In Chapter 1, we studied the behavior of the autocorrelation of returns and squared returns. We found that the raw return autocorrelations did not display any systematic patterns, whereas the squared return autocorrelations were positive for short lags and decreased as the lag order increased.

The objective of variance modeling is essentially to construct a variance measure, σ_t^2, which has the property that the standardized squared returns, R_t^2/σ_t^2 have no systematic autocorrelation patterns. Whether this has been achieved can be assessed in plots such as the top panel of Figure 2.4, where we show the autocorrelation of R_t^2/σ_t^2 from the GARCH model with leverage for the S&P 500 returns along with their standard error bands. The standard errors are calculated simply as $1/\sqrt{T}$, where T is the number of observations in the sample. Usually the autocorrelation is shown along with plus/minus two standard error bands around zero, which simply mean horizontal lines at $-2/\sqrt{T}$ and $2/\sqrt{T}$. These so-called Bartlett standard error bands give the range in which the autocorrelations would fall roughly 95% of the time if the true but unknown autocorrelations of R_t^2/σ_t^2 were all zero.

The bottom panel in Figure 2.4 redraws the autocorrelation of the squared returns from Chapter 1, now with the standard error bands superimposed. Comparing the two panels in Figure 2.4, we see that the GARCH model has been reasonably effective at removing the systematic patterns in the autocorrelation of the squared returns.

2.6.2. Out-of-Sample Check Using Regression

Another traditional method of evaluating a variance model is based on simple regressions where squared returns in the forecast period, $t + 1$, are regressed on the forecast from the variance model, as in

$$R_{t+1}^2 = b_0 + b_1\sigma_{t+1}^2 + e_{t+1}$$

A good variance forecast should be unbiased, that is have an intercept $b_0 = 0$, and be efficient, that is have a slope, $b_1 = 1$. In this regression, the squared returns is used as a proxy for the true but unobserved variance in period $t + 1$. One key question is, how good of a proxy is the squared return?

First of all, notice that it is true that $E_t[R_{t+1}^2] = \sigma_{t+1}^2$, so that the squared return is an unbiased proxy for true variance. But the variance of the proxy is

$$Var_t[R_{t+1}^2] = E_t\left[\left(R_{t+1}^2 - \sigma_{t+1}^2\right)^2\right] = E_t\left[\left(\sigma_{t+1}^2(z_{t+1}^2 - 1)\right)^2\right]$$

$$= \sigma_{t+1}^4 E_t[(z_{t+1}^2 - 1)^2] = \sigma_{t+1}^4(\kappa - 1)$$

where κ is the kurtosis of the innovation, which is 3 under conditional normality but higher in reality. Thus, the squared return is an unbiased but potentially very noisy proxy for the conditional variance.

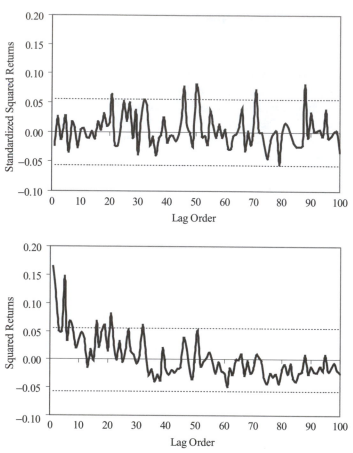

FIGURE 2.4   Autocorrelation of Standardized Squared S&P 500 Returns (top) and of Squared Returns (bottom) with Bartlett Standard Errors (dashed).

Due to the high degree of noise in the squared returns, the fit of the preceding regression as measured by the regression R^2 will be very low, typically around 5 to 10%, even if the variance model used to forecast is indeed the correct one. Thus obtaining a low R^2 in such regressions should not lead one to reject the variance model. The conclusion is just as likely to be that the proxy for true but unobserved variance is simply very inaccurate.

2.7. USING INTRADAY INFORMATION

If the squared return from daily closing prices really is a poor proxy for the true but unobserved daily variance, then we may be able to improve on variance models, which are based purely on squared return, by looking for better variance proxies.

2.7.1. Using Intraday High and Low Prices

One such readily available proxy is the difference between the intraday high and the intraday low log-price, which is often referred to as the range. The intraday high and low prices are often available along with the daily closing prices in standard financial databases. Range-based variance proxies are therefore easily calculated.

Let us define the range of the log-prices to be

$$D_t = \ln\left(S_t^{High}\right) - \ln\left(S_t^{Low}\right)$$

where S_t^{High} and S_t^{Low} are the highest and lowest prices observed during day t.

One can show that the expected value of the squared range is

$$E\left[D_t^2\right] = 4\ln(2)\sigma^2$$

A natural range-based estimate of volatility is therefore

$$\sigma^2 = \frac{1}{4\ln(2)} \frac{1}{T} \sum_{t=1}^{T} D_t^2$$

The range-based estimate of variance is simply a constant times the average squared range. The constant is $\frac{1}{4\ln(2)} \approx 0.361$.

The range-based estimate of unconditional variance suggests that a proxy for the daily variance can be constructed as

$$\sigma_{r,t}^2 = \frac{1}{4\ln(2)} D_t^2 \approx .361 D_t^2$$

The top panel of Figure 2.5 plots $\sigma_{r,t}^2$ for the S&P 500 data. Notice how much less noisy the range is than the daily squared returns, which are shown in the bottom panel. Figure 2.6 shows the autocorrelation of $\sigma_{r,t}^2$ in the top panel. The first-order autocorrelation in the range-based variance proxy is around 0.35 (top panel), whereas it is only half of that in the squared-return proxy (bottom panel). Furthermore, the range-based autocorrelations show more persistence than the squared-return autocorrelations. The range-based autocorrelations are positive and significant from lag 1 through lag 28, whereas the squared-return–based autocorrelations are only significant for the first 5 to 10 lags.

The $\sigma_{r,t}^2$ variance proxy could, of course, be used instead of the squared return for evaluating the forecasts from variance models. Thus, we could run the regression,

$$\sigma_{r,t+1}^2 = b_0 + b_1 \sigma_{t+1}^2 + e_{t+1}$$

which is done in the exercises at the end of the chapter.

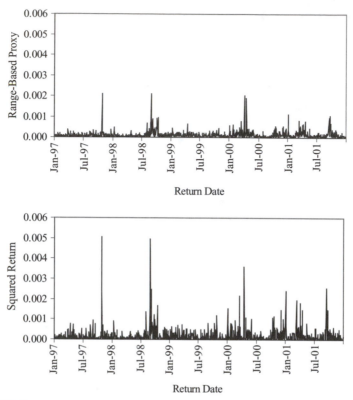

FIGURE 2.5   Range-Based Variance Proxy (top) and Squared Returns (bottom).

It is also interesting to go one step further and use the range as the driving variable in a variance model. At the least, one could use the range as a regressor in the simple GARCH specification as in

$$\sigma_{t+1}^2 = \omega + \alpha R_t^2 + \beta \sigma_t^2 + \gamma D_t^2$$

However, one could go even further and consider the range rather than the squared return to be the fundamental innovation of the variance model.

2.7.2. Using Intraday Returns

Sometimes, the daily high and low prices is not the only intraday information available. Liquid assets are traded many times during a day, and there is potentially useful information in the intraday prices about daily variance.

Consider the case where we have observations every 5 minutes on the price of a liquid asset, for example, the dollar/yen exchange rate. Let m be the number of observations per day. If we have 24-hour trading and 5-minute observations, then

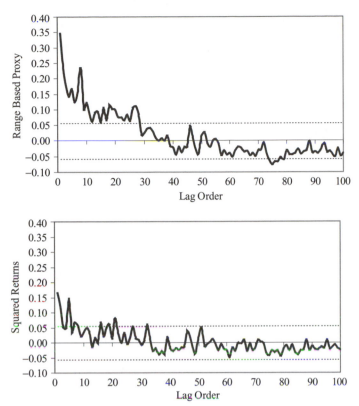

FIGURE 2.6   Autocorrelation of Range-Based Variance Proxy (top) and Autocorrelation of Squared Returns (bottom) with Barlett Standard Errors (dashed).

$m = 24 * 60/5 = 288$. Let the jth observation on day $t + 1$ be denoted $S_{t+j/m}$. Then the closing price on day $t + 1$ is $S_{t+m/m} = S_{t+1}$, and the jth return is

$$R_{t+j/m} = \ln(S_{t+j/m}) - \ln(S_{t+(j-1)/m})$$

Having m observations available within a day, we can calculate an estimate of the daily variance from the intraday squared returns simply as

$$\sigma^2_{m,t+1} = \sum_{j=1}^{m} R^2_{t+j/m}$$

This variance measure could of course also be used instead of the squared return for evaluating the forecasts from variance models. Thus, we could run the regression,

$$\sigma^2_{m,t+1} = b_0 + b_1 \sigma^2_{t+1} + e_{t+1}$$

But again, we want to go further and use the new variance measure directly for variance forecasting.

The so-called realized variance measure noted earlier is, of course, only an estimate of the true variance. Under fairly general conditions it can be shown that as the number of intraday observations, m, gets infinitely large, the realized variance measure will converge to the true variance for day $t+1$. Furthermore, for liquid securities, the distribution of the logarithm of $\sigma^2_{m,t+1}$ across days appears to be very close to the normal distribution. Thus, a very practical and sensible forecasting model of variance based on the realized variance measure would be, for example,

$$\ln \sigma^2_{m,t+1} = \rho \ln \sigma^2_{m,t} + \epsilon_{t+1}, \quad \text{with } \epsilon_{t+1} \sim N(0, \sigma^2_\epsilon)$$

or perhaps

$$\ln \sigma^2_{m,t+1} = \rho \ln \sigma^2_{m,t} + \delta \epsilon_t + \epsilon_{t+1}$$

which are, respectively, an AR(1) and an ARMA(1,1) model in the log-realized volatilities. The AR(1) can be estimated using simple linear regression, while the ARMA(1,1) can be estimated using MLE. The ARMA(1,1) can be viewed as an AR(1) allowing for measurement error in the realized volatilities.

Notice that these simple models are specified in logarithms, while for risk management purposes we are ultimately interested in forecasting the level of variance. As the logarithmic transformation is not linear, we have to be a bit careful when calculating the variance forecast. From the assumption of normality of the error term, we can use the result

$$\epsilon_{t+1} \sim N(0, \sigma^2_\epsilon) \implies E[\exp(\epsilon_{t+1})] = \exp(\sigma^2_\epsilon / 2)$$

Thus, in the AR(1) model, the forecast for tomorrow is

$$\sigma^2_{t+1|t} = E_t[\exp(\rho \ln \sigma^2_{m,t} + \epsilon_{t+1})] = \exp(\rho \ln \sigma^2_{m,t}) E_t[\exp(\epsilon_{t+1})]$$

$$= \left(\sigma^2_{m,t}\right)^\rho \exp(\sigma^2_\epsilon / 2)$$

and for the ARMA(1,1) model, we get

$$\sigma^2_{t+1|t} = E_t[\exp(\rho \ln \sigma^2_{m,t} + \delta \epsilon_t + \epsilon_{t+1})] = \exp(\rho \ln \sigma^2_{m,t} + \delta \epsilon_t) E_t[\epsilon_{t+1}]$$

$$= \left(\sigma^2_{m,t}\right)^\rho \exp(\delta \epsilon_t + \sigma^2_\epsilon / 2)$$

More sophisticated models, such as fractionally integrated ARMA models, can be used to model realized variance. These models may yield better longer horizon variance forecasts than the short-memory ARMA models considered here. For short horizons such as a day or a week, the short-memory ARMA models are likely to perform quite well.

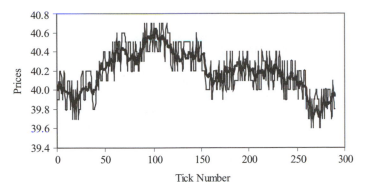

FIGURE 2.7   Fundamental Price (bold) and Quoted Price with Bid-Ask Bounces.

2.7.3. Range-Based versus Realized Variance

There is convincing empirical evidence that for very liquid securities, the realized variance modeling approach is useful for risk management purposes. The intuition is that using the intraday returns gives a very reliable estimate of today's variance, which in turn helps forecasting tomorrow's variance. In standard GARCH models on the other hand, today's variance is implicitly calculated using exponentially declining weights on many past daily squared returns, where the exact weighting scheme depends on the estimated parameters. Thus, the GARCH estimate of today's variance is heavily model dependent, whereas the realized variance for today is calculated exclusively from today's squared intraday returns. When forecasting the future, knowing where you are today is key. Unfortunately in variance forecasting, knowing where you are today is not a trivial matter as variance is not directly observable.

While the realized variance approach has clear advantages, it also has certain shortcomings. First of all, it clearly requires high-quality intraday returns to be feasible. It is very easy to calculate daily realized volatilities from 5-minute returns, but it is not at all a trivial matter to construct at 10-year data set of 5-minute returns. Second, how do we decide on the frequency with which to sample the intraday data? Why 5-minute returns and not 1-minute or 30-minute returns? Clearly, in a perfect world we would sample as often as possible. However, in the real world, the higher the sampling frequency, the bigger the problems arising from market microstructure effects such as bid-ask bounces and discrete tick sizes. Figure 2.7 illustrates this point using simulated data for one trading day. We assume the fundamental asset price, S^{Fund}, follows the dynamics

$$\ln S^{Fund}_{t+j/m} = \ln S^{Fund}_{t+(j-1)/m} + \epsilon_{t+j/m}, \quad \text{with } \epsilon_{t+j/m} \sim N(0, 0.001^2)$$

However, the observed price fluctuates randomly around the bid and ask quotes, which are posted by the market maker. We thus observe

$$S_{t+j/m} = B_{t+j/m} I_{t+j/m} + A_{t+j/m}(1 - I_{t+j/m})$$

where $B_{t+j/m}$ is the bid price, which we take to be the fundamental price rounded down to the nearest \$1/10, and $A_{t+j/m}$ is the ask price, which is the fundamental price rounded up to the nearest \$1/10. $I_{t+j/m}$ is a random variable, which takes the value 1 and 0 with probability 1/2. $I_{t+j/m}$ is thus an indicator variable of whether the observed price is a bid or an ask price.

Figure 2.7 illustrates that the observed intraday price can be quite noisy compared with the fundamental but unobserved price. Therefore, realized variance measures based on intraday returns can be noisy as well. This is especially true for securities with wide bid-ask spreads and infrequent trading. Notice on the other hand that the range-based variance measure discussed earlier is relatively immune to the market microstructure noise. The true maximum can easily be calculated as the observed maximum less one-half of the bid-ask spread, and the true minimum as the observed minimum plus one-half of the bid-ask price. The range-based variance measure thus has clear advantages in less liquid markets.

In the absence of trading imperfections, however, range-based variance proxies can be shown to be only about as useful as 4-hourly intraday returns. Furthermore, as we shall see in the next chapter, the idea of realized variance extends directly to realized covariance and correlation, whereas the range-based covariance and correlation measures are less obvious.

2.8. SUMMARY

This chapter presented a range of variance models that are useful for risk management. Simple equally weighted and exponentially weighted models that require minimal effort in estimation were first introduced. Their shortcomings led us to consider more sophisticated but still simple models from the GARCH family. We highlighted the flexibility of GARCH as a virtue and considered various extensions to account for leverage effects, day-of-week effects, announcement effects, and so on. The powerful and flexible quasi-maximum likelihood estimation technique was presented and will be used in the next chapter as well. In-sample and out-of-sample model validation techniques were introduced subsequently. Standard out-of-sample forecast evaluation regressions make use of the daily squared return as a proxy for observed variance. However, we argued that the daily squared return proxy is a very noisy proxy and considered instead variance proxies based on intraday high and low prices as well as intraday squared returns. Finally, we suggested dynamic variance models, which directly use variance proxies from intraday returns to construct more precise forecasts of future daily variance. Most of the techniques suggested in this chapter are put to use in the empirical exercises that follows.

2.9. FURTHER RESOURCES

The literature on variance modeling has exploded during the past 20 years, and we only present a few papers here. The exponential smoother variance model is studied in JP Morgan (1996). The exponential smoother has been used to forecast a wide range of variables and further discussion of it can be found in Granger and Newbold (1986). The basic GARCH model is introduced in Engle (1982) and Bollerslev (1986), and it is discussed further in Bollerslev, Chou and Kroner (1992) and Engle and Patton (2001). Long memory including fractionally integrated (FIGARCH) models are presented in Baillie, Bollerslev, and Mikkelsen (1996), Bollerslev and Mikkelsen (1999), and Engle and Lee (1999). The leverage effect and other GARCH extensions are described in Ding *et al.* (1993), Glosten *et al.* (1993), Hentschel (1995), and Nelson (1990). Quasi-maximum likelihood estimation of GARCH models is thoroughly treated in Bollerslev and Wooldridge (1992). Taylor (1994) contains a very nice overview of a different class of variance models known as Stochastic Volatility models. This class of models was not included in this chapter due to the relative difficulty of estimating them.

Range-based estimates of static variance models are introduced in Parkinson (1980) with recent developments included in Yang and Zhang (2000). Range-based models of dynamic variance are given in Azalideh *et al.* (2002), Brandt and Jones (2002), and Chou (2001). Brandt and Jones (2002) use the range rather than the squared return as the fundamental innovation in an EGARCH model and find that the range improves the model's variance forecasts significantly. Finally, forecasting with realized variance models is analyzed in Andersen *et al.* (2003).

2.10. EMPIRICAL EXERCISES ON CD-ROM

Open the Chapter2Data.xls file. A number of the exercises in this and the coming chapters rely on the maximum likelihood estimation technique. The general approach to answering these questions is to use the parameter starting values to calculate the log likelihood value of each observation and then compute the sum of these individual log likelihoods. If using Excel, the Solver tool is then activated to maximize the sum of the log likelihoods by changing the cells corresponding to the parameter values. Solver is enabled through Tools, Add-Ins, Solver Add-In. When using Solver, choose the options Use Automatic Scaling and Assume Non-Negative. Set Precision, Tolerance, and Convergence to 0.0000001.

1. Estimate the simple GARCH(1,1) model on the S&P 500 daily log returns using the maximum likelihood estimation (MLE) technique. First estimate

$$\sigma_{t+1}^2 = \omega + \alpha R_t^2 + \beta \sigma_t^2, \quad \text{with } R_t = \sigma_t z_t, \text{ and } z_t \sim N(0, 1)$$

Let the variance of the first observation be equal to the unconditional variance, $Var(R_t)$. Set the starting values of the parameters to $\alpha = 0.1$, $\beta = 0.85$, and $\omega = Var(R_t)(1 - \alpha - \beta) \approx 0.01^2 * 0.05 = .000005$. (*Excel Hint*: The number π is calculated in Excel using the function pi()). Re-estimate the equation using variance targeting, that is, set $\omega = Var(R_t)(1 - \alpha - \beta)$, and use Solver to find

α and β only. Check how the estimated parameters and persistence differ from the variance model in Chapter 1.

2. Include a leverage effect in the variance equation. Estimate

$$\sigma_{t+1}^2 = \omega + \alpha\,(R_t - \theta\sigma_t)^2 + \beta\sigma_t^2, \quad \text{with } R_t = \sigma_t z_t, \text{ and } z_t \sim N(0, 1)$$

Set starting values to $\alpha = 0.1$, $\beta = 0.85$, $\omega = 0.000005$, and $\theta = 0.5$. What is the sign of the leverage parameter? Explain how the leverage effect is captured in this model. Plot the autocorrelations for lag 1 through 100 for R_t^2 as well as R_t^2/σ_t^2, and compare the two. Compare your results with Figure 2.4.

3. Include the option implied volatility VIX series from the Chicago Board Options Exchange (CBOE) as an explanatory variable in the GARCH equation. Use MLE to estimate

$$\sigma_{t+1}^2 = \omega + \alpha\,(R_t - \theta\sigma_t)^2 + \beta\sigma_t^2 + \gamma VIX_t^2/252,$$
$$\text{with } R_t = \sigma_t z_t, \text{ and } z_t \sim N(0, 1)$$

Set starting values to $\alpha = 0.04$, $\beta = 0.5$, $\omega = 0.000005$, $\theta = 2$, and $\gamma = 0.07$.

4. Run a regression of daily squared returns on the variance forecast from the GARCH model with a leverage term. Include a constant term in the regression

$$R_{t+1}^2 = b_0 + b_1\sigma_{t+1}^2 + e_{t+1}$$

(*Excel Hint*: Use the function LINEST.) What is the fit of the regression as measured by the R^2? Is the constant term significantly different from zero? Is the coefficient on the forecast significantly different from one?

5. Run a regression using the range instead of the squared returns as proxies for observed variance—that is, regress

$$\frac{1}{4\ln(2)}D_{t+1}^2 = b_0 + b_1\sigma_{t+1}^2 + e_{t+1}$$

Is the constant term significantly different from zero? Is the coefficient on the forecast significantly different from one? What is the fit of the regression as measured by the R^2? Compare your answer with the R^2 from question 4.

The answers to these exercises can be found in the Chapter2Results.xls file. Previews of the answers follow.

QUESTION 1

Estimating Simple GARCH(1,1) Model with and without Variance Targeting

Date	Close	Return	σ^2_t (without variance targeting)	MLE	σ^2_t (with variance targeting)	MLE
02-Jan-97	737.01					
03-Jan-97	748.03	1.48%	0.000161	2.7640	0.000161	2.7640
06-Jan-97	747.65	-0.05%	0.000167	3.4276	0.000167	3.4293
07-Jan-97	753.23	0.74%	0.000150	3.2988	0.000150	3.2995
08-Jan-97	748.41	-0.64%	0.000142	3.3668	0.000141	3.3678
09-Jan-97	754.85	0.86%	0.000133	3.2677	0.000133	3.2682
10-Jan-97	759.50	0.61%	0.000129	3.4122	0.000129	3.4133
13-Jan-97	759.51	0.00%	0.000122	3.5853	0.000122	3.5868
14-Jan-97	768.86	1.22%	0.000113	2.9625	0.000113	2.9622
15-Jan-97	767.20	-0.22%	0.000120	3.5743	0.000120	3.5763
16-Jan-97	769.75	0.33%	0.000112	3.5819	0.000111	3.5633
17-Jan-97	776.17	0.83%	0.000105	3.3332	0.000105	3.3336
20-Jan-97	776.70	0.07%	0.000106	3.6567	0.000105	3.6581
21-Jan-97	782.72	0.77%	0.000099	3.3901	0.000099	3.3905
22-Jan-97	786.23	0.45%	0.000100	3.5876	0.000099	3.5885
23-Jan-97	777.56	-1.11%	0.000096	3.0664	0.000096	3.0661
24-Jan-97	770.52	-0.91%	0.000104	3.2692	0.000103	3.2696
27-Jan-97	765.02	-0.72%	0.000106	3.4153	0.000105	3.4165
28-Jan-97	765.02	0.00%	0.000104	3.6643	0.000104	3.6366
29-Jan-97	772.50	0.97%	0.000098	3.2133	0.000098	3.2134
30-Jan-97	784.17	1.50%	0.000102	2.5768	0.000102	2.5741
31-Jan-97	786.16	0.25%	0.000119	3.5706	0.000118	3.5743
03-Feb-97	786.73	0.07%	0.000111	3.6314	0.000110	3.6346
04-Feb-97	789.26	0.32%	0.000104	3.6191	0.000103	3.6213

Starting Values		Without Variance Targeting		With Variance Targeting	
α_0	0.1	α	0.1028	α	0.0998
β_0	0.85	β	0.8280	β	0.8282
ω_0	0.000005	ω	0.000012	ω	0.000012
$\alpha_0+\beta_0$	0.95	$\alpha+\beta$	0.9308	$\alpha+\beta$	0.9280
MLE	3722.78	MLE	3748.91	MLE	3748.86

Estimating GARCH(1,1) with Leverage Effect

Close	Return	R^2_t	σ^2_t	R^2_t/σ^2_t	MLE
737.01					
748.03	1.48%	0.000220	0.000161	1.3681	2.7640
747.65	-0.05%	0.000000	0.000121	0.0021	3.5885
753.23	0.74%	0.000055	0.000120	0.4614	3.3651
748.41	-0.64%	0.000041	0.000101	0.4088	3.4778
754.85	0.86%	0.000073	0.000118	0.6234	3.2928
759.50	0.61%	0.000038	0.000097	0.3880	3.5064
759.51	0.00%	0.000000	0.000085	0.0000	3.7701
768.86	1.22%	0.000150	0.000086	1.7501	2.8893
767.20	-0.22%	0.000005	0.000068	0.0689	3.8461
769.75	0.33%	0.000011	0.000075	0.1467	3.7563
776.17	0.83%	0.000069	0.000071	0.9738	3.3717
776.70	0.07%	0.000000	0.000060	0.0077	3.9339
782.72	0.77%	0.000060	0.000063	0.9496	3.4442
786.23	0.45%	0.000020	0.000055	0.3652	3.8042
777.56	-1.11%	0.000123	0.000052	2.3569	2.8331
770.52	-0.91%	0.000083	0.000083	1.0026	3.2811
765.02	-0.72%	0.000051	0.000108	0.4751	3.4101
765.02	0.00%	0.000000	0.000127	0.0000	3.5661
772.50	0.97%	0.000095	0.000124	0.7653	3.1972
784.17	1.50%	0.000225	0.000100	2.2466	2.5626
786.16	0.25%	0.000006	0.000076	0.0843	3.7800
786.73	0.07%	0.000001	0.000073	0.0072	3.8388
789.26	0.32%	0.000010	0.000074	0.1394	3.7675
778.28	-1.40%	0.000196	0.000070	2.8015	2.4634
780.15	0.24%	0.000006	0.000111	0.0517	3.6062

Starting Values

α	0.1000
β	0.8500
ω	0.0000050
θ	0.5000
$\alpha(1+\theta^2)+\beta$	0.9750
MLE	3776.87

With Leverage Effect

α	0.0556
β	0.6393
ω	0.0000099
θ	2.1449
$\alpha(1+\theta^2)+\beta$	0.9504
MLE	3804.14

Calculating Autocorrelations of Squared Raw and Squared Standardized Returns

Lag	Autocorr R^2_t	R^2_t/σ^2_t
1	0.1647	-0.0236
2	0.1187	0.0265
3	0.0501	-0.0134
4	0.0498	0.0088
5	0.1489	0.0263
6	0.0356	-0.0342
7	0.0678	0.0155
8	0.0562	0.0074
9	0.0200	-0.0271
10	0.0345	0.0033
11	0.0483	0.0057
12	0.0363	-0.0091
13	-0.0145	-0.0105
14	0.0170	0.0011
15	-0.0005	-0.0112
16	0.0679	0.0168
17	0.0216	0.0039
18	0.0509	0.0305
19	0.0595	0.0098
20	0.0147	0.0161
21	0.0817	0.0640
22	0.0261	-0.0235
23	-0.0011	-0.0236
24	0.0321	0.0081
25	-0.0043	0.0531
26	0.0167	0.0179

QUESTION 2

Estimating GARCH(1,1) with VIX

	Date	Close	Return	R^2_t	σ^2_t	VIX	MLE		Starting Values		Final Vales with VIX	
1												
2												
3	02-Jan-97	737.01							α	0.0400	α	0.0543
4	03-Jan-97	748.03	1.48%	0.000220	0.000161	19.99%	2.7640		β	0.5000	β	0.4617
5	06-Jan-97	747.65	-0.05%	0.000000	0.000106	20.49%	3.6582		⍵	0.00000500	⍵	0.00000279
6	07-Jan-97	753.23	0.74%	0.000055	0.000102	19.99%	3.4043		θ	2.0000	θ	2.5187
7	08-Jan-97	748.41	-0.64%	0.000041	0.000080	21.18%	3.5394		γ	0.0700	γ	0.0786
8	09-Jan-97	754.85	0.86%	0.000073	0.000099	21.65%	3.3198		MLE	3691.61	MLE	3813.87
9	10-Jan-97	759.50	0.61%	0.000038	0.000078	21.76%	3.5679					
10	13-Jan-97	759.51	0.00%	0.000000	0.000068	21.56%	3.8802					
11	14-Jan-97	768.86	1.22%	0.000150	0.000072	21.43%	2.8107					
12	15-Jan-97	767.20	-0.22%	0.000005	0.000055	21.87%	3.9436					
13	16-Jan-97	769.75	0.33%	0.000011	0.000057	21.96%	3.8067					
14	17-Jan-97	776.17	0.83%	0.000069	0.000065	20.87%	3.3708					
15	20-Jan-97	776.70	0.07%	0.000000	0.000064	20.25%	3.9896					
16	21-Jan-97	782.72	0.77%	0.000060	0.000058	19.51%	3.4447					
17	22-Jan-97	786.23	0.45%	0.000020	0.000048	18.55%	3.8419					
18	23-Jan-97	777.56	-1.11%	0.000123	0.000045	20.77%	2.7226					
19	24-Jan-97	770.52	-0.91%	0.000083	0.000080	20.66%	3.2807					
20	27-Jan-97	765.02	-0.72%	0.000051	0.000107	21.77%	3.4122					
21	28-Jan-97	765.02	0.00%	0.000000	0.000127	22.47%	3.5664					
22	29-Jan-97	772.50	0.97%	0.000095	0.000121	21.77%	3.1997					
23	30-Jan-97	784.17	1.50%	0.000225	0.000091	21.48%	2.4983					
24	31-Jan-97	786.16	0.25%	0.000006	0.000064	20.82%	3.8616					
25	03-Feb-97	786.73	0.07%	0.000001	0.000062	20.54%	3.9174					
26	04-Feb-97	789.26	0.32%	0.000010	0.000065	20.64%	3.8237					
27	05-Feb-97	778.28	-1.40%	0.000196	0.000062	22.13%	2.3392					
28	06-Feb-97	780.15	0.24%	0.000006	0.000109	21.73%	3.6179					
29	07-Feb-97	789.56	1.20%	0.000144	0.000099	20.69%	2.9645					

QUESTION 3

Regression of Daily Squared Returns

Close	Return	R^2_t	σ^2_t
737.01			
748.03	1.48%	0.000220	0.000161
747.65	-0.05%	0.000000	0.000121
753.23	0.74%	0.000055	0.000120
748.41	-0.64%	0.000041	0.000101
754.85	0.86%	0.000073	0.000118
759.50	0.61%	0.000038	0.000097
759.51	0.00%	0.000000	0.000085
768.86	1.22%	0.000150	0.000086
767.20	-0.22%	0.000005	0.000068
769.75	0.33%	0.000011	0.000075
776.17	0.83%	0.000069	0.000071
776.70	0.07%	0.000000	0.000060
782.72	0.77%	0.000060	0.000063
786.23	0.45%	0.000020	0.000055
777.56	-1.11%	0.000123	0.000052
770.52	-0.91%	0.000083	0.000083
765.02	-0.72%	0.000051	0.000108
765.02	0.00%	0.000000	0.000127
772.50	0.97%	0.000095	0.000124
784.17	1.50%	0.000225	0.000100
786.16	0.25%	0.000006	0.000076
786.73	0.07%	0.000001	0.000073
789.26	0.32%	0.000010	0.000074
778.28	-1.40%	0.000196	0.000070
780.15	0.24%	0.000006	0.000111
789.56	1.20%	0.000144	0.000104

GARCH(1,1) coefficients found in Q2

α	0.0556
β	0.6393
ω	0.0000099
θ	2.1449

Results of Regression of Daily Squared Returns received by means of Excel Function LINEST

	Regression R^2 vs. σ^2		
Slope >	1.0133	-0.0000029	< Intercept
Standard Error of Slope >	0.0850	0.0000166	< Standard Error of Intercept
R^2 >	0.1017	0.0003281	< Standard Error of Values
F Statistic >	141.99	1254	< Degrees of Freedom
SS_{xy} >	0.0000153	0.0001350	< SSE

QUESTION 4

QUESTION 5

	Running Regression of Daily Squared Ranges					GARCH(1,1) coefficients found in Q2			Results of Regression of Daily Squared Ranges received by means of Excel Function LINEST					
	B	C	E	F	G	H	I	J	K	L	M	N	O	P
	High	Low	Return	$D^2_t/Ln16$	σ^2_t					Regression D_t vs. σ^2_t				
3	742.81	729.55				α	0.0556		Slope >	0.7507	0.000001	< Intercept		
4	748.24	737.01	1.48%	0.000082	0.000161	β	0.6393		Standard Error of Slope >	0.0407	0.000008	< Standard Error of Intercept		
5	753.31	743.82	-0.05%	0.000058	0.000121	ω	0.0000099		R^2 >	0.2137	0.000157	< Standard Error of Values		
6	753.26	742.18	0.74%	0.000079	0.000120	θ	2.1449		F Statistic >	340.90	1254	< Degrees of Freedom		
7	755.72	747.71	-0.64%	0.000041	0.000101				SS_{xy} >	0.000008	0.000031	< SSE		
8	757.68	748.41	0.86%	0.000055	0.000118									
9	759.65	746.92	0.61%	0.000103	0.000097									
10	762.85	756.69	0.00%	0.000024	0.000085									
11	772.04	759.51	1.22%	0.000097	0.000086									
12	770.95	763.72	-0.22%	0.000032	0.000068									
13	772.05	765.25	0.33%	0.000028	0.000075									
14	776.37	769.72	0.83%	0.000027	0.000071									
15	780.08	774.19	0.07%	0.000021	0.000060									
16	783.72	772.00	0.77%	0.000082	0.000063									
17	786.23	779.56	0.45%	0.000026	0.000055									
18	794.67	776.64	-1.11%	0.000190	0.000052									
19	778.21	768.17	-0.91%	0.000061	0.000083									
20	771.43	764.18	-0.72%	0.000032	0.000108									
21	776.32	761.75	0.00%	0.000129	0.000127									
22	772.70	765.02	0.97%	0.000036	0.000124									
23	784.17	772.50	1.50%	0.000081	0.000100									
24	791.86	784.17	0.25%	0.000034	0.000076									
25	787.14	783.12	0.07%	0.000009	0.000073									
26	789.28	783.68	0.32%	0.000018	0.000074									
27	792.71	773.43	-1.40%	0.000219	0.000070									
28	780.35	774.45	0.24%	0.000021	0.000111									
29	789.72	778.19	1.20%	0.000078	0.000104									

REFERENCES

Andersen, T., T. Bollerslev, F. Diebold, and P. Labys. (2003). "Modeling and Forecasting Realized Volatility," *Econometrica* (In Press).

Azalideh, S., M. Brandt, and F. Diebold. (2002). "Range-Based Estimation of Stochastic Volatility Models," *Journal of Finance*, 57, 1047–1091.

Baillie, R., T. Bollerslev, and H. Mikkelsen. (1996). "Fractionally Integrated Generalized Autoregressive Conditional Heteroskedasticity," *Journal of Econometrics*, 74, 3–30.

Bollerslev, T. (1986). "Generalized Autoregressive Conditional Heteroskedasticity," *Journal of Econometrics*, 31, 307–327.

Bollerslev, T., R. Chou, and K. Kroner. (1992). "ARCH Modeling in Finance: A Review of the Theory and Empirical Evidence," *Journal of Econometrics*, 52, 5–59.

Bollerslev, T., and H. Mikkelsen. (1999). "Long-Term Equity AnticiPation Securities and Stock Market Volatility Dynamics," *Journal of Econometrics*, 92, 75–99.

Bollerslev, T., and J. Wooldridge. (1992). "Quasi-Maximum Likelihood Estimation and Inference in Dynamic Models with Time Varying Covariances," *Econometric Reviews*, 11, 143–172.

Brandt, M., and C. Jones. (2002). "Volatility Forecasting with Range-Based EGARCH Models," Manuscript, the Wharton School.

Chou, R. (2001). "Forecasting Financial Volatilities with Extreme Values: The Conditional Autoregressive Range," Manuscript, Academia Sinica.

Ding, Z., C. W. J. Granger, and R. F. Engle. (1993). "A Long Memory Property of Stock Market Returns and a New Model," *Journal of Empirical Finance*, 83–106.

Engle, R. (1982). "Autoregressive Conditional Heteroskedasticity with Estimates of the Variance of U.K. Inflation," *Econometrica*, 50, 987–1008.

Engle, R., and G. Lee. (1999). "A Permanent and Transitory Component Model of Stock Return Volatility," in R. Engle and H. White, eds., *Cointegration, Causality, and Forecasting: A Festschrift in Honor of Clive W. J. Granger.* Oxford University Press, 475–497.

Engle, R., and A. Patton. (2001). "What Good Is a Volatility Model?" *Quantitative Finance*, 1, 237–245.

Glosten, L., R. Jagannathan, and D. Runkle. (1993). "On the Relation between the Expected Value and the Volatility of the Nominal Excess Return on Stocks," *Journal of Finance*, 48, 1779–1801.

Granger, C. W. J., and P. Newbold. (1986). *Forecasting Economic Time Series*, 2nd ed. New York: Academic Press.

Hentschel, L. (1995). "All in the Family: Nesting Symmetric and Asymmetric GARCH Models," *Journal of Financial Economics*, 39, 71–104.

J P Morgan. (1996). *RiskMetrics—Technical Document*, 4th ed. New York.

Nelson, D. (1990). "Conditional Heteroskedasticity in Asset Pricing: A New Approach," *Econometrica*, 59, 347–370.

Parkinson, M. (1980). "The Extreme Value Method for Estimating the Variance of the Rate of Return," *Journal of Business*, 53, 61–65.

Taylor, S. (1994), "Modelling Stochastic Volatility: A Review and Comparative Study," *Mathematical Finance*, 4, 183–204.

Yang, D., and Q. Zhang. (2000). "Drift-Independent Volatility Estimation Based on High, Low, Open, and Close Prices," *Journal of Business*, 73, 477–491.

3

CORRELATION MODELING

3.1. CHAPTER OVERVIEW

In this chapter, we go through the second part of the stepwise distribution modeling (SDM) approach. The objective is to model the linear dependence, or correlation, between returns on different assets, such as IBM and Microsoft stocks, or on different classes of assets, such as stock indices and Foreign Exchange (FX) rates. Once this is done, we will be able to calculate risk measures on portfolios of securities such as stocks, bonds, and foreign exchange rates.

We start by calculating risk measures such as value at risk for very simple portfolios and discussing how the models of correlation will allow for a quick recalculation of risk measures when the portfolio weights change.

We then present a general model of portfolio risk for large portfolios and consider ways to reduce the problem of dimensionality in such portfolios. Just as the main topic of the previous chapter was modeling the dynamic aspects of variance, the main topic of this chapter is modeling the dynamic aspects of correlation. We consider dynamic correlation models of varying degrees of sophistication, both in terms of their specification and of the information required to calculate them.

3.2. VALUE AT RISK FOR SIMPLE PORTFOLIOS

Value at risk, or VaR, is a simple risk measure that answers the following question: "What dollar loss is such that it will only be exceeded $p \times 100\%$ of the time in the next K trading days?" The $VaR loss is implicitly defined from the probability of getting an even larger loss as in

$$\Pr\left(\$Loss > \$VaR\right) = p$$

We want to map this VaR definition into our model of returns. We can define the portfolio (PF) return as R_{PF} and write the $Loss as

$$\$Loss = -VPF * R_{PF}$$

where VPF is the current market value of the portfolio. Substituting this relationship into the definition of the VaR yields

$$\Pr\left(-VPF * R_{PF} > \$VaR\right) = p$$

Dividing by $-VPF$ on both sides of the inequality, we get

$$\Pr\left(R_{PF} < -\$VaR/VPF\right) = p$$

where the inequality has been switched around because $-VPF$ is a negative number. If we define the VaR relative to the current portfolio value as in

$$VaR \equiv \$VaR/VPF$$

then we have

$$\Pr\left(R_{PF} < -VaR\right) = p$$

This is the definition of VaR we will be using throughout the book. Writing the VaR relative to the current value of the portfolio makes it much easier to think about. Knowing that the $VaR of a portfolio is $500,000 does not mean much unless we know the value of the portfolio. Knowing that the VaR is 50% of the value of the portfolio conveys more information. The appendix to this chapter contains more discussion of the calculation of the VaRs.

If we start by considering a very simple example, namely that our portfolio consists of just one security, say Microsoft stock, then we can use a variance model from the previous chapter to give us a VaR for a portfolio. Let $VaR_{t+1}^{.01}$ denote the 1% VaR for the 1-day ahead return, and assume that returns are normally distributed with zero mean and standard deviation $\sigma_{PF,t+1}$. Then

$$\Pr\left(R_{PF,t+1} < -VaR_{t+1}^{.01}\right) = .01 \Leftrightarrow$$

$$\Pr\left(R_{PF,t+1}/\sigma_{PF,t+1} < -VaR_{t+1}^{.01}/\sigma_{PF,t+1}\right) = .01 \Leftrightarrow$$

$$\Phi\left(-VaR_{t+1}^{.01}/\sigma_{PF,t+1}\right) = .01$$

where $\Phi(*)$ denotes the cumulative density function of the standard normal distribution.

$\Phi(z)$ calculates the probability of being below the number z, and $\Phi_p^{-1} = \Phi^{-1}(p)$ instead calculates the number such that $100 * p\%$ of the probability mass is below Φ_p^{-1}. Taking $\Phi^{-1}(*)$ on both sides of the preceding equation yields the VaR as

$$-VaR_{t+1}^{.01}/\sigma_{PF,t+1} = \Phi^{-1}(0.01) \Leftrightarrow$$

$$VaR_{t+1}^{.01} = -\sigma_{PF,t+1} * \Phi_{.01}^{-1}$$

$$= -.025 * (-2.33)$$

$$= 0.05825$$

where the standard deviation forecast, $\sigma_{PF,t+1}$ for tomorrow's return is assumed to be 2.5% and where we have found $\Phi_{.01}^{-1} = \Phi^{-1}(0.01) = -2.33$ to be the 1% quantile from the standard normal distribution.

Because Φ_p^{-1} is always negative for $p < 0.5$, the minus sign in front of the VaR formula again ensures that the VaR itself is a positive number. The interpretation is thus that the VaR gives a number such that there is a 1% chance of *losing* more than 5.825% of the portfolio value today. If the value of the portfolio today is $2 million, the $VaR would simply be $0.05825 * 2,000,000 = \$116,500$.

Figure 3.1 illustrates the VaR from a normal distribution. Notice that we assume that $K = 1$ and $p = .01$ here. The top panel shows the VaR in the probability distribution function, and the bottom panel shows the VaR in the cumulative distribution function. As we have assumed that returns are normally distributed with a mean of zero, the VaR can be calculated very easily. All we need is a volatility forecast.

VaR has undoubtedly become the industry benchmark for risk calculation. This is because it captures an important aspect of risk, namely how bad things can get with a certain probability, p. Furthermore, it is easily communicated and easily understood.

VaR does, however, have drawbacks. Most important, extreme losses are ignored. The VaR number only tells us that 1% of the time we will get a return below the reported VaR number, but it says nothing about what will happen in those 1% worst cases. Furthermore, the VaR assumes that the portfolio is constant across the next K days, which is unrealistic in many cases when K is larger than a day or a week. Finally, it may not be clear how K and p should be chosen. Later on we will discuss other risk measures that can improve on some of the shortcomings of VaR.

As another simple example, consider a portfolio the value of which consists of 40% Microsoft stocks and 60% GE stocks. One way to calculate the VaR for the portfolio of these two stocks is to directly model the volatility of the portfolio

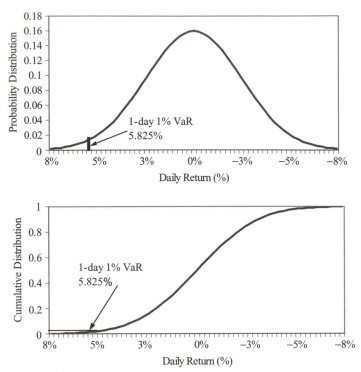

FIGURE 3.1 Value at Risk from the Normal Distribution. Return Probability Distribution (top panel) and Cumulative Return Distribution (bottom panel).

return, $R_{PF,t+1} = 0.4 * R_{MS,t+1} + 0.6 * R_{GE,t+1}$, call it $\sigma_{PF,t+1}$, and then calculate the VaR for the portfolio as

$$VaR_{t+1}^{p} = -\sigma_{PF,t+1} * \Phi_{p}^{-1}$$

where we assume that the portfolio returns are normally distributed.

Notice, however, that this aggregate VaR method is directly dependent on the portfolio allocations (40% and 60%), and it would require us to redo the volatility modeling every time the portfolio is changed or every time we contemplate change and want to study the impact on VaR of changing the portfolio allocations. While modeling the aggregate portfolio return directly may be appropriate for passive portfolio risk measurement, it is not as useful for active risk management. To do sensitivity analysis and assess the benefits of diversification, we need models of the dependence between the return on individual assets or risk factors.

We also hasten to add that the assumption of normality is made for convenience and is not realistic. Important methods for dealing with the nonnormality evident in daily returns will be discussed in Chapters 4 and 5. We simply assume normality now in order to postpone the discussion of the distribution until later. The normality assumption allows us to focus on the modeling of covariance and correlation in this chapter.

3.3. PORTFOLIO VARIANCE

We now establish some notation that is necessary to study the risk of portfolios consisting of an arbitrary number of securities. The return on the portfolio on day $t + 1$ is defined as

$$R_{PF,t+1} = \sum_{i=1}^{n} w_i R_{i,t+1}$$

where the sum is taken over the n securities in the portfolio. w_i denotes the relative weight of security i at the end of day t.

The variance of the portfolio is

$$\sigma_{PF,t+1}^2 = \sum_{i=1}^{n}\sum_{j=1}^{n} w_i w_j \sigma_{ij,t+1} = \sum_{i=1}^{n}\sum_{j=1}^{n} w_i w_j \sigma_{i,t+1}\sigma_{j,t+1}\rho_{ij,t+1}$$

where $\sigma_{ij,t+1}$ and $\rho_{ij,t+1}$ are the covariance and correlation respectively between security i and j on day $t+1$. Notice we have $\sigma_{ij,t+1} = \sigma_{ji,t+1}$, and $\rho_{ij,t+1} = \rho_{ji,t+1}$ for all i and j. We also have $\rho_{ii,t+1} = 1$ and $\sigma_{ii,t+1} = \sigma_{i,t+1}^2$ for all i.

Using vector notation, we will write

$$\sigma_{PF,t+1}^2 = w'\Sigma_{t+1}w$$

where w is the n by 1 vector of portfolio weights, and Σ_{t+1} is the n by n covariance matrix of returns. In the case where $n = 2$, we simply have

$$\sigma_{PF,t+1}^2 = \begin{bmatrix} w_1 & w_2 \end{bmatrix} \begin{bmatrix} \sigma_{1,t+1}^2 & \sigma_{12,t+1} \\ \sigma_{12,t+1} & \sigma_{2,t+1}^2 \end{bmatrix} \begin{bmatrix} w_1 \\ w_2 \end{bmatrix}$$

$$= w_1^2\sigma_{1,t+1}^2 + w_2^2\sigma_{2,t+1}^2 + 2w_1 w_2\sigma_{12,t+1}$$

as $\sigma_{21,t+1} = \sigma_{12,t+1}$.

If we are willing to assume normality, then the VaR of the portfolio is just

$$VaR_{t+1}^p = -\sigma_{PF,t+1} * \Phi_p^{-1}$$

Notice that even if we have already constructed volatility forecasts for each of the securities in the portfolio, then we still have to model and forecast all the correlations. If we have n assets, then we will have $n(n - 1)/2$ different correlations, so if n is 100, then we'll have 4950 correlations to model, which would be a daunting task. We will therefore explicitly be looking for methods that are able to handle large-dimensional portfolios.

3.3.1. Exposure Mappings

A very simple way to reduce the dimensionality of the portfolio variance is to impose a factor structure using observed market returns as factors. In the case of a very well diversified stock portfolio, for example, it may be reasonable to assume that the variance of the portfolio equals that of the S&P 500 market index. This is referred to as index mapping and can be written as

$$\sigma^2_{PF,t+1} = \sigma^2_{Mkt,t+1}$$

In this case, only one volatility—that of the S&P 500 index return—needs to be modeled, and no correlation modeling is necessary. The 1%, 1-day VaR is simply $\sigma_{Mkt,t+1} * 2.33$.

In portfolios that contain systematic risk, but which are diversified enough that the firm-specific idiosyncratic risk can be ignored, one can pose a linear relationship between the portfolio and the market index and use the so-called beta mapping, as in

$$\sigma^2_{PF,t+1} = \beta^2_{PF}\sigma^2_{Mkt,t+1}$$

where β_{PF} is the coefficient from regressing the portfolio return on the market return. In this case, only an estimate of β_{PF} is necessary—no further correlation modeling is needed.

Finally, the risk manager of a large-scale portfolio may consider risk as mainly coming from a relatively small number of different risk factors, say 10. The exact choice of factors depends highly on the particular portfolio at hand, but they could be, for example, country equity indices, FX rates, or commodity price indices. In this case, it makes sense to model the variances and correlations of these risk factors and assign exposures to each factor to get the portfolio variance. This general factor structure can be written

$$\sigma^2_{PF,t+1} = w'_F \Sigma^F_{t+1} w_F$$

where w_F is a vector of exposures to each risk factor and where Σ^F_{t+1} is the covariance matrix of the returns from the risk factors.

3.4. MODELING CONDITIONAL COVARIANCES

Suppose the portfolio under consideration contains n assets. Alternatively, we can think of the risk manager as having chosen n risk factors to be the main drivers of the risk in the portfolio. In either case, an n-dimensional covariance matrix must be estimated where n may be a large number.

We now turn to various methods for constructing the covariance matrix Σ_{t+1} directly, without first modeling the correlations. Arguably the simplest way to model time varying covariances is to rely on plain rolling averages, a method that

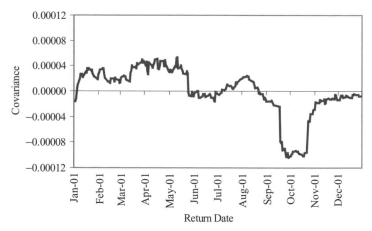

FIGURE 3.2   Rolling Covariance Between S&P 500 and US$/yen Returns.

we considered for volatility in the previous chapter. For the covariance between asset i and j, we can simply estimate

$$\sigma_{ij,t+1} = \frac{1}{m} \sum_{\tau=1}^{m} R_{i,t+1-\tau} R_{j,t+1-\tau}$$

which is easy to do, but which is not necessarily satisfactory due to the dependence on the choice of m. Notice that, as in previous chapters, we assume the average expected return on each asset is simply zero. Figure 3.2 shows the rolling covariance between the S&P 500 and the US$/yen for $m = 25$.

We can instead use a simple exponential smoother on the covariances, and let

$$\sigma_{ij,t+1} = (1 - \lambda) R_{i,t} R_{j,t} + \lambda \sigma_{ij,t}$$

where $\lambda = .94$ as it were for the corresponding volatility model in the previous chapter. Figure 3.3 shows the exponential smoother covariance between the S&P 500 and the US$/yen.

Clearly, the caveats that applied to the exponential smoother volatility model apply to the exponential smoother covariance model as well. The restriction that the coefficient $(1 - \lambda)$ on the cross product of returns $\left(R_{i,t} R_{j,t}\right)$ and the coefficient λ on the past covariance $\left(\sigma_{ij,t}\right)$ sum to one is not necessarily desirable. It implies that there is no mean-reversion in covariance: based on the closing price today; if tomorrow's covariance is high then it will remain high, rather than revert back to its mean.

We can instead consider models with mean reversion in covariance. For example, a GARCH(1,1) specification for covariance would be

$$\sigma_{ij,t+1} = \omega_{ij} + \alpha R_{i,t} R_{j,t} + \beta \sigma_{ij,t}$$

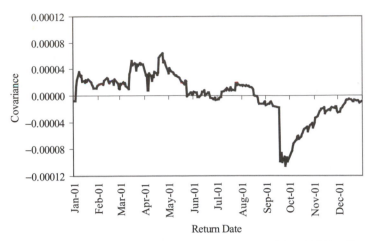

FIGURE 3.3   Exponentially Smoothed Covariance Between S&P 500 and US$/yen Returns.

which will tend to revert to its long run average covariance, which equals

$$\sigma_{ij} = \omega_{ij}/(1 - \alpha - \beta)$$

Notice that so far we have not allowed for the persistence parameters λ, α, and β to vary across securities. This is no coincidence. It must be done to guarantee that the portfolio variance will be positive regardless of the portfolio weights, w. We will say that a covariance matrix, Σ_{t+1}, is internally consistent if for all vectors w:

$$w'\Sigma_{t+1}w \geq 0$$

This corresponds to saying that the covariance matrix is positive-semidefinite. It is ensured by estimating volatilities and covariances in an internally consistent fashion. For example, relying on exponential smoothing using the same λ for every volatility and every covariance will work. Similarly, using a GARCH(1,1) model with α and β identical across variances and covariances and with long-run variances and covariances estimated consistently will work as well.

Unfortunately, it is not clear that the persistence parameters λ, α, and β should be the same for all variances and covariance. We therefore now consider methods that are not subject to this restriction. The estimation of the various parameters introduced earlier and in the following will be discussed subsequently.

3.5. MODELING CONDITIONAL CORRELATIONS

We now turn to the modeling of correlation rather than covariance. This is motivated by the desire to free up the restriction on the persistence across variances and covariances and also by the fact that correlations are easily interpreted as they fall in the interval from minus one to one. Covariances, on the other hand, are a confluence of correlation and variance. For example, the covariance between two assets could be time varying, even though the correlation is constant simply because the variances are time varying. Thus, to truly assess the dynamics in the linear dependence across assets, we need to get a handle on correlation. There is ample empirical evidence that correlations increase during financial turmoil and thereby increase risk even further; therefore, modeling correlation dynamics is crucial to a risk manager.

A simple way to measure correlation is to treat it as the residual from the covariance and the variance models. By definition

$$\sigma_{ij,t+1} = \sigma_{i,t+1}\sigma_{j,t+1}\rho_{ij,t+1}$$

and so

$$\rho_{ij,t+1} = \sigma_{ij,t+1}/(\sigma_{i,t+1}\sigma_{j,t+1})$$

therefore if, for example,

$$\sigma_{ij,t+1} = (1-\lambda)R_{i,t}R_{j,t} + \lambda\sigma_{ij,t}, \quad \text{for all } i,j$$

then

$$\rho_{ij,t+1} = \frac{(1-\lambda)R_{i,t}R_{j,t} + \lambda\sigma_{ij,t}}{\sqrt{((1-\lambda)R_{i,t}^2 + \lambda\sigma_{i,t}^2)((1-\lambda)R_{j,t}^2 + \lambda\sigma_{j,t}^2)}}$$

which, of course, is not particularly intuitive. We therefore now consider models where the dynamic correlation is modeled directly.

We will again rely on the definition

$$\sigma_{ij,t+1} = \sigma_{i,t+1}\sigma_{j,t+1}\rho_{ij,t+1}$$

In matrix notation, we can write

$$\Sigma_{t+1} = D_{t+1}\Gamma_{t+1}D_{t+1}$$

where D_{t+1} is a matrix of standard deviations, $\sigma_{i,t+1}$, on the ith diagonal and zero everywhere else, and where Γ_{t+1} is a matrix of correlations, $\rho_{ij,t+1}$ with ones on the diagonal. In the simple two-by-two case, we have

$$\Sigma_{t+1} = \begin{bmatrix} \sigma_{1,t+1}^2 & \sigma_{12,t+1} \\ \sigma_{12,t+1} & \sigma_{2,t+1}^2 \end{bmatrix}$$

$$= \begin{bmatrix} \sigma_{1,t+1} & 0 \\ 0 & \sigma_{2,t+1} \end{bmatrix} \begin{bmatrix} 1 & \rho_{12,t+1} \\ \rho_{12,t+1} & 1 \end{bmatrix} \begin{bmatrix} \sigma_{1,t+1} & 0 \\ 0 & \sigma_{2,t+1} \end{bmatrix}$$

We will consider the volatilities of each asset to already have been estimated through GARCH or one of the other methods considered in the previous chapter.

We can then standardize each return by its dynamic standard deviation to get the standardized returns,

$$z_{i,t+1} = R_{i,t+1}/\sigma_{i,t+1} \quad \text{for all } i$$

By dividing the returns by their conditional standard deviation, we create variables, $z_{i,t+1}$, $i = 1, 2, .., n$, which all have a conditional standard deviation of one. The conditional covariance of the $z_{i,t+1}$ variables equals the conditional correlation of the raw returns as can be seen from

$$E_t(z_{i,t+1}z_{j,t+1}) = E_t((R_{i,t+1}/\sigma_{i,t+1})(R_{j,t+1}/\sigma_{j,t+1}))$$
$$= E_t(R_{i,t+1}R_{j,t+1})/(\sigma_{i,t+1}\sigma_{j,t+1})$$
$$= \sigma_{ij,t+1}/(\sigma_{i,t+1}\sigma_{j,t+1})$$
$$= \rho_{ij,t+1}, \text{ for all } i, j$$

Thus, modeling the conditional correlation of the raw returns is equivalent to modeling the conditional covariance of the standardized returns.

We first consider simple exponential smoothing correlation models. Let the correlation dynamics be driven by the auxiliary variable $q_{ij,t+1}$, which gets updated by the cross product of the standardized returns, $z_{i,t}$ and $z_{j,t}$ as in

$$q_{ij,t+1} = (1 - \lambda)(z_{i,t}z_{j,t}) + \lambda q_{ij,t}, \quad \text{for all } i, j$$

The exact conditional correlation can now be obtained by normalizing the $q_{ij,t+1}$ variable as in

$$\rho_{ij,t+1} = \frac{q_{ij,t+1}}{\sqrt{q_{ii,t+1}q_{jj,t+1}}}$$

The reason we need to do the normalization is to ensure that the correlation will always fall in the interval from minus one to plus one.

Figure 3.4 shows the exponential smoothed correlations for the S&P 500 and US\$/yen example where λ is estimated to be 0.9828. (Estimation of these models will be discussed shortly.)

Just as we did for volatility models, we may want to consider generalizations of the exponential correlation model, which allow for the correlations to revert to a long-run average correlation, $E[z_{i,t}z_{j,t}]$. We can consider GARCH(1,1)-type specifications of the form

$$q_{ij,t+1} = \bar{\rho}_{ij} + \alpha(z_{i,t}z_{j,t} - \bar{\rho}_{ij}) + \beta(q_{ij,t} - \bar{\rho}_{ij})$$

If we rely on correlation targeting, and set $\bar{\rho}_{ij} = E[z_{i,t}z_{j,t}]$, then we have

$$q_{ij,t+1} = E[z_{i,t}z_{j,t}] + \alpha(z_{i,t}z_{j,t} - E[z_{i,t}z_{j,t}]) + \beta(q_{ij,t} - E[z_{i,t}z_{j,t}])$$

Again we have to normalize to get the conditional correlations

$$\rho_{ij,t+1} = \frac{q_{ij,t+1}}{\sqrt{q_{ii,t+1}q_{jj,t+1}}}$$

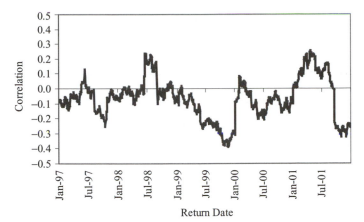

FIGURE 3.4   Exponentially Smoothed Correlation Between S&P 500 and US$/yen Returns.

The key thing to notice about this model is that the correlation persistence parameters α and β are common across i and j. Thus, the model implies that the
persistence of the correlation between any two assets in the portfolio is the same.
It does not, however, imply that the level of the correlations at any time is the same
across pairs of assets. The level of correlation is controlled by $E\left[z_{i,t}z_{j,t}\right]$ and will
thus vary over i and j. It does also not imply that the persistence in correlation
is the same as the persistence in volatility. The persistence in volatility can vary
from asset to asset, and it can vary from the persistence in correlation between
the assets. But the model does imply that the persistence in correlation is constant
across assets. Figure 3.5 shows the GARCH(1,1) correlations for the S&P 500 and
US$/yen example.

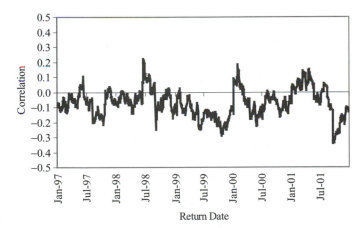

FIGURE 3.5   GARCH Correlation Between S&P 500 and US$/yen Returns.

We can write the models in matrix notation as

$$Q_{t+1} = (1 - \lambda)\left(z_t z_t'\right) + \lambda Q_t$$

for the exponential smoother, and for the GARCH(1,1) we can write

$$Q_{t+1} = E\left[z_t z_t'\right](1 - \alpha - \beta) + \alpha\left(z_t z_t'\right) + \beta Q_t$$

In the two-asset case for the GARCH(1,1) model, we have

$$Q_{t+1} = \begin{bmatrix} q_{11,t+1} & q_{12,t+1} \\ q_{12,t+1} & q_{22,t+1} \end{bmatrix}$$

$$= \begin{bmatrix} 1 & \rho_{12} \\ \rho_{12} & 1 \end{bmatrix}(1 - \alpha - \beta) + \alpha \begin{bmatrix} z_{1,t}^2 & z_{1,t} z_{2,t} \\ z_{1,t} z_{2,t} & z_{2,t}^2 \end{bmatrix}$$

$$+ \beta \begin{bmatrix} q_{11,t} & q_{12,t} \\ q_{12,t} & q_{22,t} \end{bmatrix}$$

where ρ_{12} is the unconditional correlation between the two assets, which can be estimated in advance as

$$\rho_{12} = \frac{1}{T} \sum_{t=1}^{T} z_{1,t} z_{2,t}$$

An important feature of these models is that the matrix Q_{t+1} is positive definite as it is a weighted average of positive semidefinite and positive definite matrices. This will in turn ensure that the correlation matrix Γ_{t+1} and the covariance matrix, Σ_{t+1}, will be positive semidefinite as required.

Another important practical advantage of this model is that we can estimate the parameters in a sequential fashion. First, all the individual variances are estimated one by one using one of the methods from Chapter 2. Second, the returns are standardized and the unconditional correlation matrix is estimated. Third, the correlation persistence parameters α and β are estimated. The key issue is that only very few parameters are estimated simultaneously using numerical optimization. This feature makes the dynamic correlation models considered here extremely tractable for risk management of large portfolios. We now turn to the details of the estimation procedure.

3.6. QUASI-MAXIMUM LIKELIHOOD ESTIMATION

Fortunately, in estimating the dynamic conditional correlation models suggested earlier, we can rely on the quasi-maximum likelihood estimation (QMLE) method, which we used for estimating the GARCH volatility models in Chapter 2.

Although a key benefit of the correlation models suggested here is that they are easy to estimate—even for large portfolios—we will begin by analyzing the case of a portfolio consisting of only two assets. In this case, we can use the bivariate normal distribution function for $z_{1,t}$ and $z_{2,t}$ to write the log likelihood as

$$L_c = -\frac{1}{2} \sum_{t=1}^{T} \left(\ln \left(1 - \rho_{12,t}^2 \right) + \frac{\left(z_{1,t}^2 + z_{2,t}^2 - 2\rho_{12,t} z_{1,t} z_{2,t} \right)}{\left(1 - \rho_{12,t}^2 \right)} \right)$$

where $\rho_{12,t}$ is given from the particular correlation model being estimated and the normalization rule. In the simple exponential smoother example,

$$\rho_{12,t} = \frac{q_{12,t}}{\sqrt{q_{11,t} q_{22,t}}}$$

where

$$q_{11,t} = (1 - \lambda) \left(z_{1,t-1} z_{1,t-1} \right) + \lambda q_{11,t-1}$$

$$q_{12,t} = (1 - \lambda) \left(z_{1,t-1} z_{2,t-1} \right) + \lambda q_{12,t-1}$$

$$q_{22,t} = (1 - \lambda) \left(z_{2,t-1} z_{2,t-1} \right) + \lambda q_{22,t-1}$$

We find the optimal correlation parameter(s), in this case λ, by maximizing the correlation log-likelihood function, L_c. To initialize the dynamics, we set $q_{11,0} = 1$, $q_{22,0} = 1$, and $q_{12,0} = \frac{1}{T} \sum_{t=1}^{T} z_{1,t} z_{2,t}$.

Notice that the variables that enter the likelihood are the rescaled returns, z_t, and not the original raw returns, R_t themselves. We are essentially treating the standardized returns as actual observations here.

In the general case of n assets in the portfolio, we rely on the $n-$dimensional normal distribution function to write the log likelihood as

$$L_c = -\frac{1}{2} \sum_{t} \left(\log |\Gamma_t| + z_t' \Gamma_t^{-1} z_t \right)$$

where $|\Gamma_t|$ denotes the determinant of the correlation matrix, Γ_t.

As before, the QMLE method will give us consistent but inefficient estimates. In theory, we could obtain more precise results by estimating all the volatility models and the correlation model simultaneously. In practice, this is not feasible for large portfolios. In realistic situations, we are forced to rely on the stepwise QMLE method, which gives us decent parameter estimates while avoiding numerical optimization in high dimensions.

3.7. REALIZED AND RANGE-BASED COVARIANCE

At the end of Chapter 2, we considered methods for daily volatility estimation and forecasting that made use of intraday data. These methods can be extended to covariance estimation as well. Consider first daily covariance estimation using, say, 5-minute returns. Again, let the jth observation on day $t + 1$ for asset 1 be denoted, $S_{i,t+j/m}$. Then the jth return on day $t + 1$ is

$$R_{1,t+j/m} = \ln(S_{1,t+j/m}) - \ln(S_{1,t+(j-1)/m}), \quad \text{for } j = 1, 2, \ldots, m$$

Observing m returns within a day for two assets recorded at exactly the same time intervals, we can calculate an estimate of the realized daily covariance from the intraday cross product of returns simply as

$$\sigma_{12,t+1} = \sum_{j=1}^{m} R_{1,t+j/m} R_{2,t+j/m}$$

Given estimates of the two volatilities, the realized correlation can, of course, then easily be calculated as

$$\rho_{12,t+1} = \sigma_{12,t+1}/\left(\sigma_{1,t+1}\sigma_{2,t+1}\right)$$

Treating the realized covariances and correlations as regular time series observations, they can then easily be modeled using standard time series techniques.

While it is straightforward to generalize the idea of realized volatility to realized correlation, extending range-based volatility to range-based correlation is less obvious as the cross product of the ranges is not meaningful. But consider, for example, the case where S_1 is the *US\$/yen* FX rate, and S_2 is the *Euro/US\$* FX rate. If we define S_3 to be the *Euro/yen* FX rate, then by ruling out arbitrage opportunities we can write

$$S_{3,t+1} = S_{1,t+1}S_{2,t+1}$$

Therefore, the log returns can be written

$$R_{3,t+1} = R_{1,t+1} + R_{2,t+1}$$

and the variances as

$$\sigma_{3,t+1}^2 = \sigma_{1,t+1}^2 + \sigma_{2,t+1}^2 + 2\sigma_{12,t+1}$$

Thus, we can rearrange to get the covariance as

$$\sigma_{12,t+1} = \left(\sigma_{3,t+1}^2 - \sigma_{1,t+1}^2 - \sigma_{2,t+1}^2\right)/2$$

If we then use the Parkinson variance proxy from Chapter 2 defined as

$$\tilde{\sigma}_{i,t+1}^2 \approx .361 D_{i,t+1}^2 = .361 \left[\ln \left(S_{i,t+1}^{High} \right) - \ln \left(S_{i,t+1}^{Low} \right) \right]^2$$

then, we have

$$\tilde{\sigma}_{12,t+1} = .185 \left(D_{3,t+1}^2 - D_{1,t+1}^2 - D_{2,t+1}^2 \right)$$

Similar arbitrage arguments can be made between spot and futures prices and between portfolios and individual assets—assuming, of course, that the range prices can be found on all of the involved series.

Finally, as we suggested in the volatility chapter, range-based proxies for covariance can be used as regressors in GARCH covariance models. Consider, for example,

$$\sigma_{ij,t+1} = \omega_{ij} + \alpha R_{i,t} R_{j,t} + \beta \sigma_{ij,t} + \gamma \tilde{\sigma}_{ij,t}$$

At a first glance, we may be worried about a high correlation between $\sigma_{ij,t}$ and $\tilde{\sigma}_{ij,t}$, which in turn may lead to problems in estimating β and γ accurately. However, our main objective is to get a good forecast for $\sigma_{ij,t+1}$ and therefore the individual parameter values are rarely of specific interest. Including the range-based covariance estimate in a GARCH model instead of using it by itself will have the beneficial effect of smoothing out some of the inherent noise in the range-based estimate of covariance.

3.8. SUMMARY

Risk managers who want to calculate risk measures such as value at risk need to construct the matrix of variances and covariances for portfolios consisting of many assets. If the returns are assumed to be normally distributed with a mean of zero, then the covariance matrix is all that is needed to calculate the VaR. This chapter thus considered methods for constructing the covariance matrix. First, we presented simple rolling estimates of covariance, followed by simple exponential smoothing and GARCH models of covariance. We then discussed the important issue of estimating variances and covariances in an internally consistent way so as to ensure that the covariance matrix is positive semidefinite and therefore generates sensible portfolio variances for all possible portfolio weights. This discussion led us to consider modeling the conditional correlation rather than the conditional covariance. We presented a simple framework for dynamic correlation modeling, which is based on standardized returns and which thus relies on preestimated volatility models such as those discussed in Chapter 2. Finally, methods for daily covariance and correlation estimation that make use of intraday information were introduced.

3.9. FURTHER RESOURCES

Bollerslev and Engle (1993) is the standard reference on general multivariate GARCH models, but the simple and practical conditional correlation models in this chapter are taken from Engle (2002) and Engle and Sheppard (2001). See also Tse and Tsui (2002). Range-based covariance estimation is considered in Brandt and Diebold (2002), who also discuss ways to ensure positive semidefiniteness of the covariance matrix. Foreign exchange covariances estimated from intraday returns are shown in Andersen *et al.* (2001). The choice of risk factors may be obvious for some portfolios, but in general it is not. It is therefore useful to let the return data help when deciding on what the factors should look like and how many factors we need. Although not discussed in this chapter, the method of principal components is often helpful in this regard. Frye (1997) contains a neat application to fixed income portfolios and Alexander (2001) suggests multivariate GARCH models, which rely on the idea of principal components. An nice overview of the mechanics of assigning risk factor exposures can be found in Jorion (2000).

3.10. APPENDIX: VaR FROM LOGARITHMIC VERSUS ARITHMETIC RETURNS

The VaR concept used in this book relies on the logarithmic returns as defined in Chapter 1. The $Loss$ definition in the beginning of this chapter is therefore, strictly speaking, an approximation. Assuming a 1-day horizon, we can write

$$\$Loss_{t+1} = -(VPF_{t+1} - VPF_t) \approx -VPF_t * R_{PF,t+1}$$
$$= -VPF_t \ln(VPF_{t+1}/VPF_t)$$

If we want to convert the approximate log-return-based VaR defined is this chapter as

$$\Pr\left(R_{PF,t+1} < -VaR^p_{t+1}\right) = p$$

to one which relies on the exact $Loss_{t+1}$ definition, we can write

$$\Pr\left(R_{PF,t+1} < -VaR^p_{t+1}\right) = p \Leftrightarrow$$
$$\Pr\left(\ln(VPF_{t+1}/VPF_t) < -VaR^p_{t+1}\right) = p \Leftrightarrow$$
$$\Pr\left(VPF_{t+1}/VPF_t < \exp\left(-VaR^p_{t+1}\right)\right) = p \Leftrightarrow$$
$$\Pr\left(VPF_{t+1}/VPF_t - 1 < \exp\left(-VaR^p_{t+1}\right) - 1\right) = p \Leftrightarrow$$
$$\Pr\left(\frac{VPF_{t+1} - VPF_t}{VPF_t} < \exp\left(-VaR^p_{t+1}\right) - 1\right) = p$$

which is now written in terms of the arithmetic return.

    Thus, the conversion of the VaRs is simply

$$\widetilde{VaR}^p_{t+1} = -\left[\exp\left(-VaR^p_{t+1}\right) - 1\right] = 1 - \exp\left(-VaR^p_{t+1}\right)$$

where $\widetilde{VaR}^p_{t+1}$ denotes the VaR from using arithmetic returns. Both are written as a ratio of the current portfolio value and both can be converted to dollars by simply multiplying by today's portfolio value, VPF_t. Notice that if the VaR as a percentage of the total portfolio value is close to zero, then the two VaRs will be close in value.

3.11. EMPIRICAL EXERCISES ON CD-ROM

Open the Chapter3Data.xls file on the CD-ROM.

1. Convert the TSE prices into US$ using the US$/CAD exchange rate. Normalize each time series of closing prices by the first observation and plot them.

2. Calculate daily log returns and plot them on the same scale. How different is the magnitude of variations across the different assets?

3. Construct the unconditional covariance and the correlation matrices for the returns of all assets. What are the determinant values?

4. Calculate the unconditional 1-day, 1% value at risk for a portfolio consisting of 20% in each asset. Calculate also the 1-day, 1% value at risk for each asset individually. Compare the portfolio VaR with the sum individual VaRs. What do you see? (*Excel Hint*: Use the MMULT function to calculate matrix products.)

5. Estimate a Simple GARCH(1,1) model for the variance of the S&P 500, the US$/yen FX rate, and the TSE in US$. Set starting values to $\alpha = 0.06$; $\beta = 0.93$; $\omega = 0.00009$.

6. Standardize each return using its GARCH standard deviation from question 5. Construct the unconditional correlation matrix for the standardized returns of the three assets. This is the constant conditional correlation (CCC) model.

7. Use MLE to estimate λ in the exponential smoother version of the dynamic conditional correlation (DCC) model for the two bivariate systems consisting of the S&P 500 and each of two other series (US$/yen and Toronto Stock Exchange (TSE) index in US$). Set the starting value of λ to 0.94. Calculate and plot the correlations as well as the 1-day, 1% VaRs for the CCC model from question 6 and the exponential smoother DCC model. (Notice that we estimate bivariate systems here simply for convenience of computation in Excel. The models considered can easily be estimated for large sets of assets simultaneously, as is pointed out in the chapter.)

8. Estimate the GARCH DCC model for the bivariate systems from question 7. Set the starting values to $\alpha = 0.05$ and $\beta = 0.9$. Plot the dynamic correlations. Calculate and plot the 1-day, 1% VaRs for the CCC model from question 6 and the GARCH DCC model.

The answers to these exercises can be found in the Chapter3Results.xls file. Previews of the answers follow.

Normalizing and Plotting Raw Data

Date	S&P500	T-Bill	$/Yen	Oil Price	TSE300	S&P500	T-Bill	$/Yen	Oil Price	TSE300
02-Jan-97	100.00	100.00	100.00	100.00	100.00	737.01	130.99	0.00864	25.69	4290.61
03-Jan-97	101.50	100.01	99.36	99.57	100.68	748.03	131.00	0.00859	25.58	4319.85
06-Jan-97	101.44	100.03	99.95	102.06	101.10	747.65	131.03	0.00864	26.22	4337.83
07-Jan-97	102.20	100.05	100.38	101.95	102.16	753.23	131.05	0.00868	26.19	4383.33
08-Jan-97	101.55	100.01	99.85	103.35	102.24	748.41	131.00	0.00863	26.55	4386.73
09-Jan-97	102.42	100.13	99.42	102.18	102.76	754.85	131.16	0.00859	26.25	4409.12
10-Jan-97	103.05	99.95	99.60	100.90	103.42	759.50	130.93	0.00861	25.92	4437.55
13-Jan-97	103.05	99.97	99.32	97.35	103.80	759.51	130.96	0.00859	25.01	4453.46
14-Jan-97	104.32	100.15	98.72	96.77	104.42	768.86	131.18	0.00853	24.86	4480.10
15-Jan-97	104.10	100.17	99.11	100.04	105.37	767.20	131.21	0.00857	25.70	4520.97
16-Jan-97	104.44	100.14	99.24	98.17	106.03	769.75	131.17	0.00858	25.22	4549.54
17-Jan-97	105.31	100.17	98.54	97.63	106.72	776.17	131.21	0.00852	25.08	4578.80
20-Jan-97	105.39	100.21	98.07	96.96	106.47	776.70	131.27	0.00848	24.91	4568.41
21-Jan-97	106.20	100.27	98.04	94.86	105.96	782.72	131.34	0.00848	24.37	4546.19
22-Jan-97	106.68	100.24	97.28	92.84	105.59	786.23	131.31	0.00841	23.85	4530.52
23-Jan-97	105.50	100.21	97.10	91.67	104.68	777.56	131.27	0.00839	23.55	4491.42
24-Jan-97	104.55	100.20	97.29	92.29	104.21	770.52	131.26	0.00841	23.71	4471.31
27-Jan-97	103.80	100.19	96.75	92.02	104.75	765.02	131.24	0.00836	23.64	4494.28
28-Jan-97	103.80	100.31	95.58	92.18	105.16	765.02	131.39	0.00826	23.68	4512.13
29-Jan-97	104.82	100.34	94.77	93.93	105.17	772.50	131.43	0.00819	24.13	4512.29
30-Jan-97	106.40	100.40	94.94	95.29	105.26	784.17	131.52	0.00821	24.48	4516.18
31-Jan-97	106.67	100.54	95.37	92.49	105.71	786.16	131.70	0.00824	23.76	4535.69
03-Feb-97	106.75	100.66	95.05	92.33	106.47	786.73	131.86	0.00822	23.72	4568.12
04-Feb-97	107.09	100.70	94.46	91.94	106.55	789.26	131.91	0.00817	23.62	4571.80
05-Feb-97	105.60	100.66	93.64	91.59	105.89	778.28	131.86	0.00809	23.53	4543.53
06-Feb-97	105.85	100.67	93.37	88.52	104.84	780.15	131.87	0.00807	22.74	4498.36
07-Feb-97	107.13	100.80	93.90	85.01	105.31	789.56	132.03	0.00812	21.84	4518.47
10-Feb-97	106.57	100.82	94.16	84.43	104.63	785.43	132.07	0.00814	21.69	4489.35
11-Feb-97	107.13	100.83	93.70	85.79	105.36	789.59	132.07	0.00810	22.04	4520.38

QUESTION 1

QUESTION 2

Date	Raw Data					Returns				
	S&P500	T-Bill	$/Yen	Oil Price	TSE300	S&P500	T-Bill	$/Yen	Oil Price	TSE300
02-Jan-97	737.01	130.99	0.00864	25.69	4290.61					
03-Jan-97	748.03	131.00	0.00859	25.58	4319.85	1.48%	0.01%	-0.65%	-0.43%	0.68%
06-Jan-97	747.65	131.03	0.00864	26.22	4337.83	-0.05%	0.02%	0.59%	2.47%	0.42%
07-Jan-97	753.23	131.05	0.00868	26.19	4383.33	0.74%	0.01%	0.43%	-0.11%	1.04%
08-Jan-97	748.41	131.00	0.00863	26.55	4386.73	-0.64%	-0.04%	-0.53%	1.37%	0.08%
09-Jan-97	754.85	131.16	0.00859	26.25	4409.12	0.86%	0.12%	-0.44%	-1.14%	0.51%
10-Jan-97	759.50	130.93	0.00861	25.92	4437.55	0.61%	-0.17%	0.18%	-1.27%	0.64%
13-Jan-97	759.51	130.96	0.00869	25.01	4453.46	0.00%	0.02%	-0.28%	-3.57%	0.36%
14-Jan-97	768.86	131.18	0.00863	24.86	4480.10	1.22%	0.17%	-0.61%	-0.60%	0.60%
15-Jan-97	767.20	131.21	0.00857	25.70	4520.97	-0.22%	0.02%	0.39%	3.32%	0.91%
16-Jan-97	769.75	131.17	0.00858	25.22	4549.54	0.33%	-0.03%	0.13%	-1.89%	0.63%
17-Jan-97	776.17	131.21	0.00852	25.08	4578.80	0.83%	0.03%	-0.70%	-0.56%	0.64%
20-Jan-97	776.70	131.27	0.00848	24.91	4568.41	0.07%	0.04%	-0.48%	-0.68%	-0.23%
21-Jan-97	782.72	131.34	0.00848	24.37	4546.19	0.77%	0.06%	-0.03%	-2.19%	-0.49%
22-Jan-97	786.23	131.31	0.00841	23.85	4530.52	0.45%	-0.03%	-0.79%	-2.16%	-0.35%
23-Jan-97	777.56	131.27	0.00839	23.55	4491.42	-1.11%	-0.03%	-0.18%	-1.27%	-0.87%
24-Jan-97	770.52	131.26	0.00841	23.71	4471.31	-0.91%	-0.01%	0.19%	0.68%	-0.45%
27-Jan-97	765.02	131.24	0.00836	23.64	4494.28	-0.72%	-0.01%	-0.56%	-0.30%	0.51%
28-Jan-97	765.02	131.39	0.00826	23.68	4512.13	0.00%	0.11%	-1.21%	0.17%	0.40%
29-Jan-97	772.50	131.43	0.00819	24.13	4512.29	0.97%	0.03%	-0.86%	1.88%	0.00%
30-Jan-97	784.17	131.52	0.00821	24.48	4516.18	1.50%	0.06%	0.18%	1.44%	0.09%
31-Jan-97	786.16	131.70	0.00824	23.76	4535.69	0.25%	0.14%	0.45%	-2.99%	0.43%
03-Feb-97	786.73	131.86	0.00822	23.72	4568.12	0.07%	0.12%	-0.33%	-0.17%	0.71%
04-Feb-97	789.26	131.91	0.00817	23.62	4571.80	0.32%	0.04%	-0.63%	-0.42%	0.08%
05-Feb-97	778.28	131.86	0.00809	23.53	4543.53	-1.40%	-0.04%	-0.87%	-0.38%	-0.62%
06-Feb-97	780.15	131.87	0.00807	22.74	4498.36	0.24%	0.01%	-0.28%	-3.42%	-1.00%
07-Feb-97	789.56	132.03	0.00812	21.84	4518.47	1.20%	0.12%	0.56%	-4.04%	0.45%
10-Feb-97	785.43	132.07	0.00814	21.69	4489.35	-0.52%	0.03%	0.28%	-0.69%	-0.65%
11-Feb-97	789.59	132.07	0.00810	22.04	4520.38	0.53%	0.00%	-0.50%	1.60%	0.69%

Constructing Unconditional Covariance and Correlation Matrices

	S&P500	T-Bill	$/Yen	Oil Price	TSE300		Return S&P500	T-Bill	$/Yen	Oil Price	TSE300
	737.01	130.99	0.00864	25.69	4290.61						
	748.03	131.00	0.00859	25.58	4319.85		1.48%	0.01%	-0.65%	-0.43%	0.68%
	747.65	131.03	0.00864	26.22	4337.83		-0.05%	0.02%	0.59%	2.47%	0.42%
	753.23	131.05	0.00868	26.19	4383.33		0.74%	0.01%	0.43%	-0.11%	1.04%
	748.41	131.00	0.00863	26.55	4386.73		-0.64%	-0.04%	-0.53%	1.37%	0.08%
	754.85	131.16	0.00859	26.25	4409.12		0.86%	0.12%	-0.44%	-1.14%	0.51%
	759.50	130.93	0.00861	25.92	4437.55		0.61%	-0.17%	0.18%	-1.27%	0.64%
	759.51	130.96	0.00859	25.01	4453.46		0.00%	0.02%	-0.28%	-3.57%	0.36%
	768.86	131.18	0.00853	24.86	4480.10		1.22%	0.17%	-0.61%	-0.60%	0.60%
	767.20	131.21	0.00857	25.70	4520.97		-0.22%	0.02%	0.39%	3.32%	0.91%
	769.75	131.17	0.00858	25.22	4549.54		0.33%	-0.03%	0.13%	-1.89%	0.63%
	776.17	131.21	0.00852	25.08	4578.80		0.83%	0.03%	-0.70%	-0.56%	0.64%
	776.70	131.27	0.00848	24.91	4568.41		0.07%	0.04%	-0.48%	-0.68%	-0.23%
	782.72	131.34	0.00848	24.37	4546.19		0.77%	0.06%	-0.03%	-2.19%	-0.49%
	786.23	131.31	0.00841	23.85	4530.52		0.45%	-0.03%	-0.79%	-2.16%	-0.35%
	777.56	131.27	0.00839	23.55	4491.42		-1.11%	-0.03%	-0.18%	-1.27%	-0.87%
	770.52	131.26	0.00841	23.71	4471.31		-0.91%	-0.01%	0.19%	0.68%	-0.45%
	765.02	131.24	0.00836	23.64	4494.28		-0.72%	-0.01%	-0.56%	-0.30%	0.51%
	765.02	131.39	0.00826	23.68	4512.13		0.00%	0.11%	-1.21%	0.17%	0.40%
	772.50	131.43	0.00819	24.13	4512.29		0.97%	0.03%	-0.86%	1.86%	0.00%
	784.17	131.52	0.00821	24.48	4516.18		1.50%	0.06%	0.18%	1.44%	0.09%
	786.16	131.70	0.00824	23.76	4535.69		0.25%	0.14%	0.45%	-2.99%	0.43%
	786.73	131.86	0.00822	23.72	4568.12		0.07%	0.12%	-0.33%	-0.17%	0.71%
	789.26	131.91	0.00817	23.62	4571.80		0.32%	0.04%	-0.63%	-0.42%	0.08%
	778.28	131.86	0.00809	23.53	4543.53		-1.40%	-0.04%	-0.87%	-0.38%	-0.62%
	780.15	131.87	0.00807	22.74	4498.36		0.24%	0.01%	-0.28%	-3.42%	-1.00%
	789.56	132.03	0.00812	21.84	4518.47		1.20%	0.12%	0.56%	-4.04%	0.45%
	785.43	132.07	0.00814	21.69	4489.35		-0.52%	0.03%	0.28%	-0.69%	-0.65%
	789.59	132.07	0.00810	22.04	4520.38		0.53%	0.00%	-0.50%	1.60%	0.69%
	802.77	132.08	0.00805	21.50	4549.42		1.66%	0.01%	-0.67%	-2.48%	0.64%

Both determinants are positive. This means that both matrices are Positive Semi-Definite and are internally consistent

Unconditional Covariance

	S&P500	T-Bill	$/Yen	Oil Price	TSE300
S&P500	1.58E-04	-2.05E-06	-6.31E-06	-1.08E-05	1.17E-04
T-Bill	-2.05E-06	9.59E-07	-4.78E-07	-7.81E-07	-2.12E-06
$/Yen	-6.31E-06	-4.78E-07	6.57E-05	1.44E-05	3.04E-06
Oil Price	-1.08E-05	-7.81E-07	1.44E-05	6.73E-04	1.34E-05
TSE300	1.17E-04	-2.12E-06	3.04E-06	1.34E-05	1.76E-04

Determinant 5.62E-22

Unconditional Correlation

	S&P500	T-Bill	$/Yen	Oil Price	TSE300
S&P500	1.0000	-0.1663	-0.0619	-0.0332	0.7013
T-Bill	-0.1663	1.0000	-0.0602	-0.0307	-0.1631
$/Yen	-0.0619	-0.0602	1.0000	0.0687	0.0283
Oil Price	-0.0332	-0.0307	0.0687	1.0000	0.0389
TSE300	0.7013	-0.1631	0.0283	0.0389	1.0000

Determinant 0.4769

QUESTION 3

Return

	T-Bill	$/Yen	Oil Price	TSE300
	0.01%	-0.65%	-0.43%	0.68%
	0.02%	0.59%	2.47%	0.42%
	0.01%	0.43%	-0.11%	1.04%
	-0.04%	-0.53%	1.37%	0.08%
	0.12%	-0.44%	-1.14%	0.51%
	-0.17%	0.18%	-1.27%	0.64%
	0.02%	-0.28%	-3.57%	0.36%
	0.17%	-0.61%	-0.60%	0.60%
	0.02%	0.39%	3.32%	0.91%
	-0.03%	0.13%	-1.89%	0.63%
	0.03%	-0.70%	-0.56%	0.64%
	0.04%	-0.48%	-0.68%	-0.23%
	0.06%	-0.03%	-2.19%	-0.49%
	-0.03%	-0.79%	-2.16%	-0.35%
	-0.03%	-0.18%	-1.27%	-0.87%
	-0.01%	0.19%	0.68%	-0.45%
	-0.01%	-0.56%	-0.30%	0.51%
	0.11%	-1.21%	0.17%	0.40%
	0.03%	-0.86%	1.88%	0.00%
	0.06%	0.18%	1.44%	0.09%
	0.14%	0.45%	-2.99%	0.43%
	0.12%	-0.33%	-0.17%	0.71%
	0.04%	-0.63%	-0.42%	0.08%
	-0.04%	-0.87%	-0.38%	-0.62%
	0.01%	-0.28%	-3.42%	-1.00%
	0.12%	0.56%	-4.04%	0.45%
	0.03%	0.28%	-0.69%	-0.65%
	0.00%	-0.50%	1.60%	0.69%
	0.01%	-0.67%	-2.48%	0.64%

Unconditional Covariance

	S&P500	T-Bill	$/Yen	Oil Price	TSE300
S&P500	1.58E-04	-2.05E-06	-6.31E-06	-1.08E-05	1.17E-04
T-Bill	-2.05E-06	9.59E-07	-4.78E-07	-7.81E-07	-2.12E-06
$/Yen	-6.31E-06	-4.78E-07	6.57E-05	1.44E-05	3.04E-06
Oil Price	-1.08E-05	-7.81E-07	1.44E-05	6.73E-04	1.34E-05
TSE300	1.17E-04	-2.12E-06	3.04E-06	1.34E-05	1.76E-04

Portfolio weights

S&P500	Short Bond	$/Yen	Oil Price	TSE300
20.00%	20.00%	20.00%	20.00%	20.00%

Number of days	1
Confidence Level	99.00%
VaR S&P500	0.59%
VaR Short Bond	0.05%
VaR Yen/$	0.38%
VaR Oil Price	1.21%
VaR TSE 300	0.62%
VaR Sum	2.83%
VaR Portfolio	1.69%

QUESTION 4

	Return				GARCH Starting Values		Conditional Variance	Likelihood	S&P500 GARCH Final Values	
S&P500	T-Bill	$/Yen	Oil Price	TSE300						
					ω_0	9.00E-05			ω	1.09E-05
1.48%	0.01%	-0.65%	-0.43%	0.68%	α_0	6.00E-02	1.59E-04	2.76	α	9.96E-02
-0.05%	0.02%	0.59%	2.47%	0.42%	β_0	9.30E-01	1.65E-04	3.43	β	8.34E-01
0.74%	0.01%	0.43%	-0.11%	1.04%	$\alpha_0+\beta_0$	9.90E-01	1.49E-04	3.30	$\alpha+\beta$	9.33E-01
-0.64%	-0.04%	-0.53%	1.37%	0.08%			1.40E-04	3.37	MLE	3815.21
0.86%	0.12%	-0.44%	-1.14%	0.51%			1.32E-04	3.27		
0.61%	-0.17%	0.18%	-1.27%	0.64%			1.28E-04	3.41		
0.00%	0.02%	-0.28%	-3.57%	0.36%			1.22E-04	3.59		
1.22%	0.17%	-0.61%	-0.60%	0.60%			1.12E-04	2.96		
-0.22%	0.02%	0.39%	3.32%	0.91%			1.20E-04	3.58		
0.33%	-0.03%	0.13%	-1.89%	0.63%			1.11E-04	3.58		
0.83%	0.03%	-0.70%	-0.56%	0.64%			1.05E-04	3.33		
0.07%	0.04%	-0.48%	-0.68%	-0.23%			1.05E-04	3.66		
0.77%	0.06%	-0.03%	-2.19%	-0.49%			9.85E-05	3.39		
0.45%	-0.03%	-0.79%	-2.16%	-0.35%			9.90E-05	3.59		
-1.11%	-0.03%	-0.18%	-1.27%	-0.87%			9.55E-05	3.07		
-0.91%	-0.01%	0.19%	0.68%	-0.45%			1.03E-04	3.27		
-0.72%	-0.01%	-0.56%	-0.30%	0.51%			1.05E-04	3.42		
0.00%	0.11%	-1.21%	0.17%	0.40%			1.03E-04	3.67		
0.97%	0.03%	-0.86%	1.88%	0.09%			9.72E-05	3.21		
1.50%	0.06%	0.18%	1.44%	0.43%			1.01E-04	2.57		
0.25%	0.14%	0.45%	-2.99%	0.43%			1.18E-04	3.58		
0.07%	0.12%	-0.33%	-0.17%	0.71%			1.10E-04	3.64		
0.32%	0.04%	-0.63%	-0.42%	0.08%			1.03E-04	3.62		
-1.40%	-0.04%	-0.87%	-0.38%	-0.62%			9.75E-05	2.69		
0.24%	0.01%	-0.28%	-3.42%	-1.00%			1.12E-04	3.60		
1.20%	0.12%	0.56%	-4.04%	0.45%			1.05E-04	2.98		
-0.52%	0.03%	0.28%	-0.69%	-0.65%			1.13E-04	3.51		

QUESTION 5

	Standardized Return					Constant Conditional Correlation Matrix						Conditional Variance	Likeli hood	S&P500 GARCH Values	
	S&P500	T-Bill	$/Yen	Oil Price	TSE300		S&P500	T-Bill	$/Yen	Oil Price	TSE300	Conditional Variance	Likeli hood		GARCH Values
4						S&P500	1.0000	-0.1050	-0.0738	-0.0292	0.6990			ω	1.09E-05
5	1.1785	0.1169	-0.7971	-0.1654	0.5123	T-Bill	-0.1050	1.0000	-0.0677	-0.0408	-0.1294	1.59E-04	2.76	α	9.96E-02
6	-0.0395	0.2444	0.7488	1.0133	0.3224	$/Yen	-0.0738	-0.0677	1.0000	0.0668	0.0080	1.65E-04	3.43	β	8.34E-01
7	0.6100	0.1341	0.5580	-0.0463	0.8378	Oil Price	-0.0292	-0.0408	0.0668	1.0000	0.0403	1.49E-04	3.30	α+β	9.33E-01
8	-0.5419	-0.4801	-0.7041	0.5835	0.0627	TSE300	0.6990	-0.1294	0.0080	0.0403	1.0000	1.40E-04	3.37	MLE	3815.21
9	0.7457	1.5279	-0.5968	-0.4968	0.4274							1.32E-04	3.27		
10	0.5421	-1.9009	0.2513	-0.5668	0.5548							1.28E-04	3.41		
11	0.0012	0.1863	-0.3972	-1.6253	0.3152							1.22E-04	2.96		
12	1.1542	1.7058	-0.8997	-0.2426	0.5408							1.12E-04	3.58		
13	-0.1977	0.1972	0.5732	1.4120	0.8392							1.20E-04	3.58		
14	0.3149	-0.2691	0.1900	-0.7425	0.5830							1.11E-04	3.58		
15	0.8120	0.2767	-1.0650	-0.2242	0.6031							1.05E-04	3.33		
16	0.0666	0.4998	-0.7090	-0.2888	-0.2168							1.05E-04	3.66		
17	0.7778	0.6615	-0.0373	-0.9698	-0.4775							9.85E-05	3.39		
18	0.4496	-0.3137	-1.1892	-0.9338	-0.3439							9.90E-05	3.59		
19	-1.1347	-0.3557	-0.2540	-0.5405	-0.8817							9.55E-05	3.07		
20	-0.8971	-0.1448	0.2870	0.2967	-0.4535							1.03E-04	3.27		
21	-0.6995	-0.1297	-0.8550	-0.1342	0.5262							1.05E-04	3.42		
22	0.0000	1.5240	-1.8166	0.0793	0.4121							1.03E-04	3.67		
23	0.9869	0.3788	-1.1180	0.9060	0.0036							9.72E-05	3.21		
24	1.4889	0.7716	0.2309	0.6720	0.0931							1.01E-04	2.57		
25	0.2334	1.6613	0.6094	-1.3908	0.4743							1.18E-04	3.58		
26	0.0692	1.2316	-0.4543	-0.0719	0.7911							1.10E-04	3.64		
27	0.3170	0.3776	-0.8968	-0.1888	0.0886							1.03E-04	3.62		
28	-1.4190	-0.3963	-1.2261	-0.1766	-0.6962							9.75E-05	2.69		
29	0.2270	0.0761	-0.3815	-1.6236	-1.1188							1.12E-04	3.60		
30	1.1719	1.4665	0.7818	-1.6910	0.4842							1.05E-04	2.98		
31	0.4944	0.2721	0.4000	-0.3562	-0.7700							1.13E-04	3.61		

QUESTION 6

REFERENCES

Alexander, C. (2001). "A Primer on the Orthogonal GARCH Model," Manuscript, University of Reading.

Andersen, T., T. Bollerslev, and F. Diebold. (2001). "The Distribution of Realized Exchange Rate Volatility," *Journal of the American Statistical Association*, 96, 42–55.

Bollerslev, T., and R. Engle. (1993). "Common Persistence in Conditional Variances," *Econometrica*, 61, 167–186.

Brandt, M., and F. Diebold. (2002). "A No-Arbitrage Approach to Range-Based Estimation of Return Covariances and Correlations," Manuscript, University of Pennsylvania.

Engle, R. (2002). "Dynamic Conditional Correlation: A Simple Class of Multivariate GARCH Models," *Journal of Business and Economic Statistics*, 20, 339–350.

Engle, R., and K. Sheppard. (2001). "Theoretical and Empirical Properties of Dynamic Conditional Correlation Multivariate GARCH," Manuscript, University of California at San Diego.

Frye, J. (1997). "Principals of Risk: Finding Value-at-Risk through Factor-Based Interest Rate Scenarios," in S. Grayling, ed., *VaR: Understanding and Applying Value-at-Risk*. London: Risk Publications.

Jorion, P. (2000). "Value at Risk, 2nd ed. New York: McGraw-Hill.

Tse, Y., and A. Tsui. (2002). "A Multivariate Generalized Autoregressive Conditional Heteroscedasticity Model with Time-Varying Correlations," *Journal of Business and Economic Statistics*, 20, 351–363.

MODELING THE CONDITIONAL DISTRIBUTION

4.1. CHAPTER OVERVIEW

We now turn to the third and final part of the stepwise distribution modeling (SDM) approach, namely accounting for conditional non-normality in portfolio returns. In Chapter 1, we saw that asset returns are not normally distributed unconditionally. If we construct a simple histogram of past returns on the S&P 500 index, then it will not conform to the density of the normal distribution: The tails of the histogram are fatter than the normal, and the histogram is more peaked around zero. From a risk management perspective, the fat tails, which are driven by relatively few but very extreme observations, are of most interest. These extreme observations can by symptoms of liquidity risk or event risk as defined in Chapter 1.

One motivation for the time-varying variance models discussed in Chapter 2 is that they are capable of accounting for the unconditional non-normality of the data.

For example, a GARCH(1,1) model with normally distributed innovations will imply an unconditionally non-normal distribution, so if one drew a histogram of returns from the GARCH model, they would have fat tails.

Simple normal GARCH models by definition do not capture conditional non-normality in the returns. Returns are conditionally normal if the standardized returns (i.e., returns divided by their time-varying standard deviation) are normally distributed. Unfortunately, histograms from standardized returns typically do not conform to the normal density. Figure 4.1 illustrates this point. The top panel shows the histogram of the raw returns superimposed on the normal distribution, and the bottom panel shows the histogram of the standardized returns superimposed on the normal distribution as well. The volatility model used to standardize the returns is GARCH(1,1) with a leverage effect. Notice that while the bottom histogram conforms more closely to the normal distribution than does the top histogram, there are still some systematic deviations, including fat tails and a more pronounced peak around zero.

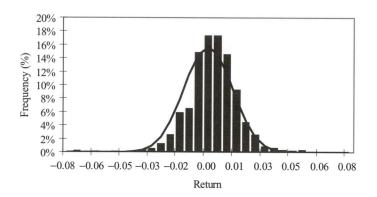

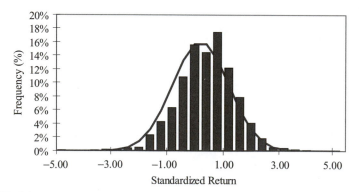

FIGURE 4.1   Histogram of Daily S&P 500 Returns (top) and of Returns Standardized by a GARCH(1,1) Model (bottom). January 1, 1997—December 31, 2001.

We will analyze the conditional nonnormality in several ways:

1. We introduce the quantile-quantile (QQ) plot, which is a graphical tool better at describing tails of distributions than the histogram.
2. We consider a simple Student's $t(d)$ distribution and discuss the estimation of it.
3. We introduce the Cornish-Fisher approximation to value-at-risk in non-normal distributions.
4. We consider extreme value theory for modeling the tail of the conditional distribution.
5. We show the implications for value at risk of the different approaches to distribution modeling. This in turn motivates us to introduce expected shortfall (ES) or TailVaR as a more appropriate risk measure when conditional returns are not normally distributed.

Throughout this chapter we will assume that we are working with a time series of portfolio returns using today's portfolio weights and past returns on the underlying assets in the portfolio. Therefore, we are essentially dealing with a univariate time series. We will assume that the portfolio variance has already been modeled using the methods presented in Chapters 2 and 3. As discussed in the introduction to Chapter 3, working with the univariate time series of portfolio returns has the disadvantage of being conditional on exactly the current set of portfolio weights. If the weights are changed, then the portfolio tail modeling will have to be redone.

4.2. VISUALIZING NON-NORMALITY

We consider the following generic model of the returns on our portfolio:

$$R_{PF,t} = \sum_{i=1}^{n} w_i R_{i,t} = \sigma_{PF,t} z_t, \quad \text{with } z_t \sim D(0, 1)$$

where $\sigma_{PF,t}$ is constructed using the methods in the previous two chapters and where the focus in this chapter is on modeling the distribution of the innovations, $D(0, 1)$, which has a mean of zero and a standard deviation of 1. So far, we have relied on setting $D(0, 1)$ to $N(0, 1)$, but we now want to assess the problems of the normality assumption in risk management, and we want to suggest viable alternatives.

Before we venture into the particular formulas for suitable non-normal distributions, let us first introduce a valuable visual tool for assessing non-normality, which we will also use later on as a diagnostic check on non-normal alternatives. The tool is commonly know as a quantile-quantile (QQ) plot, and the idea is to plot the quantiles of the calculated returns against the quantiles of the normal distribution. If the returns are truly normal, then the graph should look like a straight line on a 45-degree angle. Systematic deviations from the 45-degree line signal that the returns are not well described by the normal distribution. QQ plots are, of course, particularly relevant to risk managers who care about value at risk, which itself is essentially a quantile.

The QQ plot can be constructed as follows: First, sort all standardized returns $z_t = R_{PF,t}/\sigma_{PF,t}$ in ascending order, and call the ith sorted value z_i. Second, calculate the empirical probability of getting a value below the actual as $(i - .5)/T$, where T is the total number of observations. The subtraction of .5 is an adjustment allowing for a continuous distribution.

Calculate the standard normal quantiles as $\Phi^{-1}_{(i-.5)/T}$, where Φ^{-1} denotes the inverse of the standard normal density as before. We can then scatter plot the standardized and sorted returns on the Y-axis against the standard normal quantiles on the X-axis as follows:

$$\{X_i, Y_i\} = \left\{\Phi^{-1}_{(i-.5)/T}, z_i\right\}$$

If the data were normally distributed, then the scatter plot should conform roughly to the the the 45-degree line.

Figure 4.2 shows a QQ plot of the daily S&P 500 returns from Chapter 1. The top panels uses standardized returns from the unconditional standard deviation, σ_{PF}, so that $z_t = R_{PF,t}/\sigma_{PF}$, and the bottom panel works off the returns standardized by a GARCH(1,1) with a leverage effect. Notice that the GARCH model does remove some of the non-normality in the returns, but some still remains. The patterns of deviations from the 45-degree line indicate that large positive returns are captured well by the normal GARCH model but that the model does not allow for a sufficiently fat left tail as compared with the data.

4.3. THE STANDARDIZED t(d) DISTRIBUTION

We now turn to the important task of modeling the non-normality in conditional returns. Perhaps the most important deviations from normality we have seen are the fatter tails and the more pronounced peak in the standardized returns distribution as compared with the normal.

The standardized $t(d)$, call it the $\tilde{t}(d)$, distribution is a relatively simple distribution that is well suited to deal with these features. Conveniently, the distribution has only one parameter, d. The $\tilde{t}(d)$ density is described by the following formula:

$$f_{\tilde{t}(d)}(z; d) = \frac{\Gamma((d + 1)/2)}{\Gamma(d/2)\sqrt{\pi(d - 2)}}(1 + z^2/(d - 2))^{-(1+d)/2}, \quad \text{where } d > 2$$

where z denotes the random variable with mean zero and standard deviation one, and where $\Gamma(*)$ represents the gamma function that can be found in most quantitative software packages. The parameter d must be larger than two for the

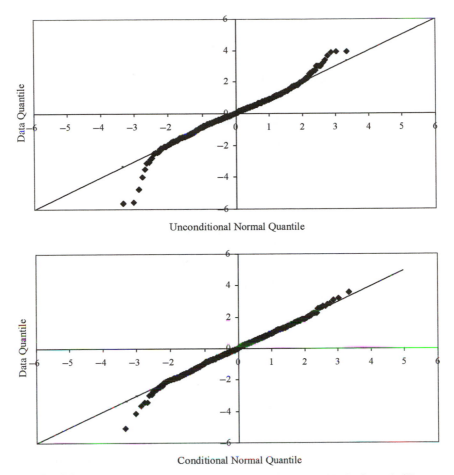

FIGURE 4.2   QQ Plot of daily S&P 500 Returns Against the Normal Distribution and of Returns Standardized by GARCH Against the Normal Distribution.

standardized distribution to be well defined. The key feature of the $\tilde{t}(d)$ distribution is that the random variable, z, is taken to a power, rather than an exponential as in the normal distribution. This will allow for the $\tilde{t}(d)$ distribution to have fatter tails than the normal, that is, higher values of $f(*)$ when z is far from zero.

The distribution is symmetric around zero, and the mean (μ), variance (σ^2), skewness (ζ_1), and excess kurtosis (ζ_2) of the distribution are

$$\mu = 0,$$

$$\sigma^2 = 1,$$

$$\zeta_1 \equiv E[z]^3/\sigma^3 = 0$$

$$\zeta_2 \equiv E[z]^4/\sigma^4 - 3 = 6/(d-4)$$

Thus, notice that d must be higher than four for the kurtosis to be well defined. Notice also that for large values of d, the distribution will have an excess kurtosis of zero and one can show that it converges to the standard normal distribution as d goes to infinity. Indeed, for values of d above 50, the $\tilde{t}(d)$ distribution is difficult to distinguish from the standard normal distribution.

4.3.1. Maximum Likelihood Estimation

Notice that we model our portfolio returns as

$$R_{PF,t} = \sigma_{PF,t}z_t, \quad \text{with } z_t \sim \tilde{t}(d)$$

If we ignore the fact that variance is estimated with error, we can treat the standardized return as a regular random variable, calculated as $z_t = R_{PF,t}/\sigma_{PF,t}$. The d parameter can then be estimated using maximum likelihood by choosing the d which maximizes

$$\ln L_1 = \sum_{t=1}^{T} \ln(f(z_t; d)) = T\left\{\ln(\Gamma((d+1)/2)) - \ln(\Gamma(d/2)) - \ln(\pi)/2\right.$$

$$\left. - \ln(d-2)/2\right\} - \frac{1}{2}\sum_{t=1}^{T}(1+d)\ln(1 + (R_{PF,t}/\sigma_{PF,t})^2/(d-2))$$

Given that we have already modeled and estimated the portfolio variance $\sigma_{PF,t}^2$, and taken it as given, we can maximize $\ln L_1$ with respect to the parameter, d, only. This approach builds again on the quasi-maximum likelihood idea, and it is helpful in that we are only estimating few parameters at a time, in this case only one. The simplicity is potentially important as we are doing numerical optimization.

If we instead want to estimate the variance parameters and the d parameter simultaneously, we must adjust the distribution to take into account the variance, $\sigma_{PF,t}^2$, and we get

$$f(R_{PF,t}; d) = \frac{\Gamma((d+1)/2)}{\Gamma(d/2)\sqrt{\pi(d-2)\sigma_{PF,t}^2}}(1 + (R_{PF,t}/\sigma_{PF,t})^2/(d-2))^{-(1+d)/2}$$

To estimate all the parameters together, we must maximize the log-likelihood of the sample of returns, which can be written

$$\ln L_2 = \sum_{t=1}^{T} \ln(f(R_{PF,t}; d)) = \ln L_1 - \sum_{t=1}^{T} \ln(\sigma_{PF,t}^2)/2$$

If we can maximize $\ln L_2$ over all the parameters simultaneously, including those needed to define $\sigma_{PF,t}^2$, then we will get more precise parameter estimates in general.

As a simple univariate example of the difference between quasi maximum likelihood estimation (QMLE) and maximun likelihood estimation (MLE), consider the GARCH(1,1)-$\tilde{t}(d)$ model with leverage. We have

$$R_{PF,t+1} = \sigma_{PF,t+1}z_{t+1}, \quad \text{with } z_{t+1} \sim \tilde{t}(d), \text{ where}$$

$$\sigma_{PF,t+1}^2 = \omega + \alpha \left(R_{PF,t} - \theta\sigma_{PF,t}\right)^2 + \beta\sigma_{PF,t}^2$$

We can either estimate all the parameters, i.e. $\{\omega, \alpha, \beta, \theta, d\}$ in one step using $\ln L_2$ noted earlier, which would correspond to exact MLE, or we can first estimate the GARCH parameters $\{\omega, \alpha, \beta, \theta\}$ using the QMLE method in Chapter 2, which assumes the likelihood from a normal distribution, and then estimate the conditional distribution parameter, d, from $\ln L_1$. In this simple example, exact MLE is clearly feasible as the total number of parameters is only five. The empirical exercises at the end of the chapter contain a comparison of the two estimates for the GARCH(1,1)-$\tilde{t}(d)$ model, which has been found to be a very good statistical model of asset returns.

4.3.2. An Easy Estimate

While the quasi-maximum likelihood estimation procedure as noted here is in line with the suggestions made in previous chapters, there is a very simple alternative estimation procedure available in this case. If the conditional variance model has already been estimated, then we are only estimating one parameter, namely d. As there is a simple closed-form relationship between d and the excess kurtosis, ζ_2, this suggests first simply calculating ζ_2 from the z_t variable and then calculating d from

$$\zeta_2 = 6/(d-4) \Rightarrow d = 6/\zeta_2 + 4$$

Thus, if excess kurtosis is found to be 1, for example, then the estimate of d is 10. This is a simple method-of-moments estimate, where we match the fourth moment of the data to that of the distribution.

4.3.3. QQ Plots

We can generalize the preceding QQ plot to assess the appropriateness of non-normal distributions as well. In particular, we would like to assess if the returns standardized by the GARCH model conform to the $\tilde{t}(d)$ distribution.

However, the quantile of the standardized $\tilde{t}(d)$ distribution is usually not easily found, whereas the quantile from the conventional Student's $t(d)$ distribution is. We therefore need the relationship

$$\Pr\left(z_t\sqrt{\frac{d}{d-2}} < t_p^{-1}(d)\right) = p$$

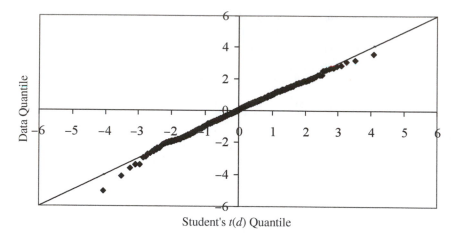

FIGURE 4.3   QQ Plot of Daily S&P 500 Returns Against the $\tilde{t}(d)$ Distribution.

$$\Leftrightarrow \Pr(z_t < t_p^{-1}(d)\sqrt{\frac{d-2}{d}}) = p$$

$$\Leftrightarrow \tilde{t}_p^{-1}(d) = \sqrt{\frac{d-2}{d}}t_p^{-1}(d)$$

where $t_p^{-1}(d)$ is the pth quantile of the conventional Student's $t(d)$ distribution.
We are now ready to construct the QQ plot as

$$\{X_i, Y_i\} = \left\{\sqrt{\frac{d-2}{d}}t_{(i-.5)/T}^{-1}(d), z_i\right\}$$

where z_i again denotes the ith sorted standardized return.

Figure 4.3 shows the QQ plot of the standardized returns from the GARCH-$\tilde{t}(d)$ with leverage, estimated using QMLE; d is estimated to be 12.6. Notice that the model now fits the left tail better, but this happens partly at the cost of fitting the right tail worse. The symmetry of the $\tilde{t}(d)$ distribution appears to be somewhat constraining.

4.3.4. Calculating Value at Risk

Once d is estimated, we can calculate the value at risk for the portfolio return:

$$R_{PF,t+1} = \sigma_{PF,t+1}z_{t+1}, \quad \text{with } z_{t+1} \sim \tilde{t}(d)$$

as

$$VaR_{t+1}^p = -\sigma_{PF,t+1}\tilde{t}_p^{-1}(d)$$

where $\tilde{t}_p^{-1}(d)$ is the pth quantile of the $\tilde{t}(d)$ distribution.

Thus, we have

$$VaR_{t+1}^p = -\sigma_{PF,t+1}\sqrt{\frac{d-2}{d}}\tilde{t}_p^{-1}(d)$$

where we have used the preceding result relating the quantiles of the standardized $\tilde{t}(d)$ distribution to that of the conventional student's $t(d)$.

We round off this section by stressing again that so far we have analyzed the conditional distribution of the aggregate portfolio return only. Thus, the distribution is dependent on the particular set of portfolio weights, and the distribution must be recalculated when the weights change.

4.4. THE CORNISH-FISHER APPROXIMATION TO VAR

The $t(d)$ distribution is arguably the most used tool for allowing for conditional nonnormality in portfolio returns. However, it is somewhat restrictive in that it builds on only one parameter and it does not, for example, allow for conditional skewness. We now consider a simple alternative way of calculating value-at-risk, which has certain advantages. First, it does allow for skewness as well as excess kurtosis. Second, it is easily calculated from the empirical skewness and excess kurtosis estimates from the standardized returns. Third, it can be viewed as an approximation to the value at risk from a wide range of conditionally non-normal distributions.

We again start by defining standardized portfolio returns by

$$z_{t+1} = R_{PF,t+1}/\sigma_{PF,t+1} \sim D(0,1)$$

The Cornish-Fisher VaR with coverage rate, p, can then be calculated as

$$VaR_{t+1}^p = -\sigma_{PF,t+1}CF_p^{-1}$$

where

$$CF_p^{-1} = \Phi_p^{-1} + \frac{\zeta_1}{6}\left[(\Phi_p^{-1})^2 - 1\right] + \frac{\zeta_2}{24}\left[(\Phi_p^{-1})^3 - 3\Phi_p^{-1}\right]$$
$$- \frac{\zeta_1^2}{36}\left[2(\Phi_p^{-1})^3 - 5\Phi_p^{-1}\right]$$

Again, ζ_1 is the skewness and ζ_2 is the excess kurtosis of the standardized returns, z_t. The Cornish-Fisher quantile can be viewed as a Taylor expansion around the normal distribution. Notice that if we have neither skewness nor excess kurtosis so that $\zeta_1 = \zeta_2 = 0$, then we simply get the quantile of the normal distribution back:

$$CF_p^{-1} = \Phi_p^{-1}, \quad \text{for } \zeta_1 = \zeta_2 = 0.$$

Consider now, for example, the 1% VaR, where $\Phi_{.01}^{-1} \approx -2.33$. Allowing for skewness and kurtosis, we can calculate the Cornish-Fisher 1% quantile as

$$CF_p^{-1} \approx -2.33 + 0.74\zeta_1 - 0.24\zeta_2 - 0.38\zeta_1^2$$

and the portfolio VaR can be calculated as

$$VaR_{t+1}^{.01} = -(-2.33 + 0.74\zeta_1 - 0.24\zeta_2 - 0.38\zeta_1^2)\sigma_{PF,t+1}$$

Thus, for example, if skewness equals -1 and excess kurtosis equals 4, then we get

$$VaR_{t+1}^{.01} = -(-2.33 - 0.74 - 0.24 * 4 - 0.38)\sigma_{PF,t+1} = 4.41\sigma_{PF,t+1}$$

which is almost twice as high as the VaR number from a normal distribution, which equals $2.33\sigma_{PF,t+1}$.

The Cornish-Fisher approach constructs approximations to quantiles from estimates of skewness and kurtosis. These estimates are in turn constructed from the sample of all standardized returns. These estimates may be influenced excessively by standardized returns close to zero, which risk managers care little about. We therefore now turn to an approach that only makes use of extreme data points.

4.5. EXTREME VALUE THEORY (EVT)

Typically, the biggest risks to a portfolio is the sudden occurrence of a single large negative return. Having an as-precise-as-possible knowledge of the probabilities of such extremes is therefore at the essence of financial risk management. Consequently, risk managers perhaps should focus attention explicitly on modeling the tails of the returns distribution. Fortunately, a branch of statistics is devoted exactly to the modeling of these extreme values.

The central result in extreme value theory states that the extreme tail of a wide range of distributions can approximately be described by a relatively simple distribution, the so-called generalized Pareto distribution.

Virtually all results in extreme value theory (EVT) assume that returns are *i.i.d.* and are therefore not very useful unless modified to the asset return environment. Asset returns appear to approach normality at long horizons, thus EVT is more important at short horizons, such as daily. Unfortunately, the *i.i.d.* assumption is the least appropriate at short horizons due to the time-varying variance patterns. We therefore need to get rid of the variance dynamics before applying EVT. Consider therefore again the standardized portfolio returns

$$z_{t+1} = R_{PF,t+1}/\sigma_{PF,t+1} \sim i.i.d. \; D(0,1)$$

Fortunately, it is in many cases reasonable to assume that these standardized returns are *i.i.d.* Thus, we will proceed to apply EVT to the standardized returns and then combine EVT with the variance models estimated in Chapter 2 in order to calculate VaRs.

4.5.1. Defining EVT

Let us first introduce some notation. Consider the probability of standardized returns z less a threshold u being below a value x given that the standardized return itself is beyond the threshold, u. We write

$$F_u(x) \equiv \Pr\{z - u \le x | z > u\}, \quad \text{where } x > u$$

We are thus working with the standardized returns in excess of a threshold, and the distribution, $F_u(*)$, depends on the choice of threshold, which we will discuss next. Using the general definition of a conditional probability, we can write

$$F_u(x) = \frac{\Pr\{u < z \le x + u\}}{\Pr\{z > u\}} = \frac{F(x + u) - F(u)}{1 - F(u)}$$

Thus, we can write the distribution of the standardized returns in excess of the threshold as a function of the distribution of the standardized returns themselves, $F(*)$, which is our ultimate object of interest.

The key result in extreme value theory states that as you let the threshold, u, get large, in almost any distribution you can think of, $F_u(x)$, converges to the generalized Pareto (GP) distribution, $G(x; \xi, \beta)$, where

$$G(x; \xi, \beta) = \begin{cases} 1 - (1 + \xi x/\beta)^{-1/\xi} & \text{if } \xi \ne 0 \\ 1 - \exp(-x/\beta) & \text{if } \xi = 0 \end{cases}$$

with $\beta > 0$, and

$$\begin{cases} x \ge u & \text{if } \xi \ge 0 \\ u \le x \le u - \beta/\xi & \text{if } \xi < 0 \end{cases}$$

Standard distributions that are covered by the EVT result include those that are heavy tailed, for example the Student's $t(d)$ distribution, where the tail parameter, ξ, is positive. This is, of course, the case of most interest in financial risk management, where returns tend to have fat tails.

The normal distribution is also covered. We noted earlier that a key difference between the Student's $t(d)$ distribution and the normal distribution is that the former has power tails and the latter has exponential tails. Thus, for the normal distribution we have that the tail parameter, ξ, equals zero.

Finally, short tailed distributions, which are of less interest in financial risk management, are covered with tail parameter $\xi < 0$.

4.5.2. Parameter Estimation

Consider points, x with $x > u$, in the tail of the distribution, and let $y = x + u$, then we can rearrange

$$F_u(x) = \frac{F(x + u) - F(u)}{1 - F(u)}$$

to get

$$F(y) = 1 - [1 - F(u)][1 - F_u(y - u)]$$

Let T denote the total sample size and let T_u denote the number of observations beyond the threshold, u. The term $1 - F(u)$ can then be estimated simply by the proportion of data point beyond the threshold, u, call it T_u/T. $F_u(*)$ can be estimated by MLE on the standardized observations in excess of the chosen threshold. Assuming $\xi \neq 0$, we then have the distribution

$$F(y) = 1 - T_u/T \left(1 + \xi \left(y - u\right)/\beta\right)^{-1/\xi}$$

4.5.3. An Easy Estimate

If we are willing to assume that the tail parameter, ξ, is positive, as is typically the case in finance, then a very easy estimator exists, namely the so-called Hill estimator. We can write

$$\Pr(z > y) = 1 - F(y) = L(y)y^{-1/\xi} \approx cy^{-1/\xi}, \quad \text{for } y > u$$

The approximation builds on the fact that $L(y)$ is a slowly varying function of y for most distributions and is thus set to a constant, c. Given this approximation and using the definition of a conditional distribution, we can define the likelihood function for all observations y_i larger than the threshold, u, as

$$L = \prod_{i=1}^{T_u} f(y_i)/(1 - F(u)) = \prod_{i=1}^{T_u} -\frac{1}{\xi}cy_i^{-1/\xi-1}/(cu^{-1/\xi}), \quad \text{for } y_i > u$$

so that the log likelihood function is

$$\ln L = -\sum_{i=1}^{T_u} -\ln(\xi) - (1/\xi + 1)\ln(y_i) + \frac{1}{\xi}\ln(u)$$

Taking the derivative with respect to ξ and setting it to zero yields the simple Hill estimator

$$\xi = \frac{1}{T_u}\sum_{i=1}^{T_u}\ln(y_i/u)$$

We can estimate the c parameter by ensuring that the fraction of observations beyond the threshold is accurately captured by the density as in

$$F(u) = 1 - T_u/T$$

From the definition of $F(u)$, we can write

$$1 - cu^{-1/\xi} = 1 - T_u/T$$

Solving this equation for c yields the estimate

$$c = \frac{T_u}{T} u^{1/\xi}$$

Our estimate of the cumulative density function for observations beyond u is therefore

$$F(y) = 1 - cy^{-1/\xi} = 1 - \frac{T_u}{T}(y/u)^{-1/\xi}$$

Notice that our estimates are available in closed form—they do not require numerical optimization. They are therefore extremely easy to calculate.

So far we have implicitly referred to extreme returns as being large gains. Of course, as risk managers we are more interested in extreme negative returns corresponding to large losses. To this end, we simply do the EVT analysis on the negative of returns instead of returns themselves.

4.5.4. Choosing the Threshold

Until now, we have focused on the benefits of the EVT methodology, such as the explicit focus on the tails and the ability to study each tail separately, thereby avoiding unwarranted symmetry assumptions. The EVT methodology does have an Achilles' heel, however, namely the choice of threshold u. When choosing u, one must balance two evils: bias and variance. If u is set too large, then only very few observations are left in the tail and the estimate of the tail parameter, ξ, will be very uncertain. If on the other hand u is set too small, then the EVT theory may not hold, meaning that the data to the right of the threshold do not conform sufficiently well to the generalized Pareto distribution to generate unbiased estimates of ξ.

For samples of around 1000 observations, corresponding to about 5 years of daily data, a good rule of thumb is to set the threshold so as to keep the largest 5% of the observations for estimating ξ—that is, we set $T_u = 50$. The threshold u will then simply be the 95th percentile of the data set.

4.5.5. Constructing the QQ Plot from EVT

We next want to show the QQ plot of the large losses using the EVT distribution. Define y to be a standardized loss, that is,

$$y_i = -R_i/\sigma_i$$

The first step is to estimate ξ and c from the losses, y_i, using the Hill estimator noted earlier.

Next we need to compute the inverse cumulative distribution function, which gives us the quantiles. Recall the EVT cumulative density function from before:

$$F(y) = 1 - cy^{-1/\xi} = 1 - \frac{T_u}{T}(y/u)^{-1/\xi}$$

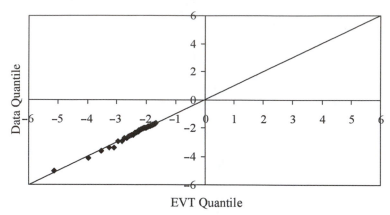

FIGURE 4.4   QQ Plot of Daily S&P 500 Returns Against the EVT Distribution.

The third step is to set the estimated cumulative probability function equal to $1 - p$ so that there is only a p probability of getting a standardized loss worse than the quantile, F_{1-p}^{-1}, which is implicitly defined by

$$F(F_{1-p}^{-1}) = 1 - p$$

from the definition of $F(*)$, we can solve for the quantile to get

$$F_{1-p}^{-1} = u \left[p / (T_u / T) \right]^{-\xi}$$

We are now ready to construct the QQ plot from EVT using the relationship

$$\{X_i, Y_i\} = \left\{ u \left[\{(i - .5)/T\}/(T_u/T) \right]^{-\xi}, y_i \right\}$$

where y_i is the ith sorted in descending order standardized loss.

Figure 4.4 shows the QQ plots of the EVT tails for large losses from the standardized S&P 500 returns. For this data, ξ is estimated to be 0.23. Notice how closely the EVT quantiles fit the data.

4.5.6. Calculating VaR from the EVT Quantile

We are, of course, ultimately interested not in QQ plots but rather in portfolio risk measures such as value at risk. Using again the loss quantile F_{1-p}^{-1} defined earlier by

$$F_{1-p}^{-1} = u \left[p / (T_u / T) \right]^{-\xi}$$

The VaR from the EVT combined with the variance model is now easily calculated as

$$VaR^p_{t+1} = \sigma_{PF,t+1} F^{-1}_{1-p} = \sigma_{PF,t+1} u \left[p/(T_u/T) \right]^{-\xi}$$

The reason for using the $(1-p)$th quantile from the EVT loss distribution in the VaR with coverage rate p is that the quantile such that $(1-p)*100\%$ of *losses* are smaller than it is the same as minus the quantile such that $p*100\%$ of *returns* are smaller than it.

We usually calculate the VaR taking Φ^{-1}_p to be the pth quantile from the standardized *return* so that

$$VaR^p_{t+1} = -\sigma_{PF,t+1} \Phi^{-1}_p$$

But we now take F^{-1}_{1-p} to be the $(1-p)$th quantile of the standardized *loss* so that

$$VaR^p_{t+1} = \sigma_{PF,t+1} F^{-1}_{1-p}$$

4.6. THE EXPECTED SHORTFALL RISK MEASURE

The upshot of the discussion in this chapter so far is that the normal versus EVT distribution may lead to similar 1% VaRs but very different 0.1% or 0.01% VaRs due to the different tail shapes. That is to say that standard VaR calculations based on a 1% coverage rate may conceal the fact that the tail shape of the distribution does not conform to the normal distribution. Figure 4.5 illustrates this point. It shows the left tail of a normal distribution as well as an EVT distribution, with a tail parameter $\xi = 0.5$. The figure is constructed so that the two distributions have the same 1% VaRs, but clearly very different tail shapes. The tail of the normal distribution very quickly converges to zero, whereas the EVT distribution has a long and fat tail. The figure thus shows that underlying two similar 1% VaR numbers can be two very different tail risk profiles. In the example given, the portfolio with the EVT distribution is arguably much more risky than the portfolio with the normal distribution in that it implies non-negligable probabilities of very large losses.

We previously discussed a key shortcoming of VaR, namely that it is concerned only with the number of losses that exceed the VaR and not the magnitude of these losses. The magnitude, however, should be of serious concern to the risk manager. Large VaR exceedences are much more likely to cause financial distress, such as bankruptcy, than are small exceedences, and we therefore want to consider a risk measure that accounts for the magnitude of large losses as well as their probability of occurring.

The most complete measure of large losses is no doubt the entire shape of the tail of the distribution of losses beyond the VaR. The tail of the portfolio return

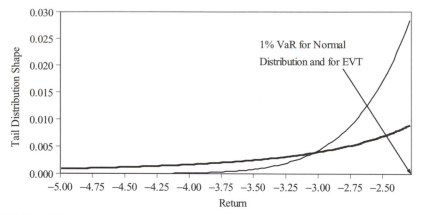

FIGURE 4.5   Tail Shapes of the Normal Distribution and EVT (bold) with $\xi = 0.5$. For Comparison, the 1% VaR is Fixed at 2.33 in the EVT Distribution.

distribution, when modeled correctly, tells the risk manager everything about the future losses. Reporting the entire tail of the return distribution corresponds to reporting VaRs for many different coverage rates, say p ranging from .001% to 1% in increments of .001%. It may, however, be less effective as a reporting tool to senior management than is a single VaR number. Arguably, the vast popularity of VaR as a risk measurement tool is due to its simple interpretation as "What's the loss so that only 1% of potential losses tomorrow will be worse?"

The challenge is to come up with a portfolio risk measure that retains the simplicity of the VaR but conveys information regarding the shape of the tail. Expected shortfall (ES), or TailVaR as it is sometimes called, does exactly this.

ES is defined as

$$ES_{t+1}^{p} = -E_t[R_{t+1}|R_{t+1} < -VaR_{t+1}^{p}]$$

where the negative signs in front of the expectation and the VaR are needed because the ES and the VaR are defined as positive numbers. The expected shortfall tells us the expected value of tomorrow's return, conditional on it being worse than the VaR. In line with our VaR definition in Chapter 3, the ES measure is defined in terms of log return rather than dollar loss.

The distribution tail shape is a two-dimensional object that gives us information on the range of possible losses on the x-axis and the probability associated with each outcome on the y-axis. The expected shortfall measure aggregates these two dimensions into a single number by computing the average of the tail outcomes weighted by their probabilities. So where VaR tells us the loss so that only 1% of potential losses will be worse, the ES tells us the expected loss given that we actually get a loss from the 1% tail. So while we are not conveying all the information in the shape of the tail when using ES, the key is that the shape of the tail beyond the VaR measure now is important for determining the risk number.

To gain more insight into the ES as a risk measure, let's first consider the normal distribution. The expected value of a normal variable with zero mean return truncated at the VaR is

$$ES_{t+1}^p = -E_t\left[R_{t+1}|R_{t+1} \le -VaR_{t+1}^p\right] = \sigma_{PF,t+1}\frac{\phi\left(-VaR_{t+1}^p/\sigma_{PF,t+1}\right)}{\Phi\left(-VaR_{t+1}^p/\sigma_{PF,t+1}\right)}$$

where $\phi(*)$ denotes the density function and $\Phi(*)$ the cumulative density function of the standard normal distribution. Of course, in the normal case we know that

$$VaR_{t+1}^p = -\sigma_{PF,t+1}\Phi_p^{-1}$$

Thus, we have

$$ES_{t+1}^p = \sigma_{PF,t+1}\frac{\phi\left(\Phi_p^{-1}\right)}{p}$$

which has a structure very similar to the VaR measure. The ratio of the expected shortfall to the VaR is

$$\frac{ES_{t+1}^p}{VaR_{t+1}^p} = -\frac{\phi\left(\Phi_p^{-1}\right)}{p\Phi_p^{-1}}$$

When, for example, $p = .01$, we have $\Phi_p^{-1} \approx -2.33$, and the ratio

$$\frac{ES_{t+1}^{.01}}{VaR_{t+1}^{.01}} \approx -\frac{(2\pi)^{-1/2}\exp(-(-2.33)^2/2)}{.01(-2.33)} \approx 1.15$$

In the normal case, one can show that as the VaR coverage probability p gets close to zero, the ratio of the ES to the VaR goes to 1.

In general, the ratio of ES to VaR for fat-tailed distribution will be higher than that of the normal. For the EVT distribution, when p goes to zero, the ES to VaR ratio converges to

$$\frac{ES_{t+1}^{p\approx 0}}{VaR_{t+1}^{p\approx 0}} \approx \frac{1}{1-\xi}$$

So that for fat-tailed distributions where $\xi > 0$, the fatter the tail, the larger the ratio of ES to VaR. For example, in Figure 4.5 where $\xi = 0.5$, the ES to VaR ratio is roughly 2, even though the 1% VaR is the same in the two distributions. Thus, the ES measure is more revealing than the VaR about the magnitude of losses larger than the VaR.

4.7. SUMMARY

Time-varying variance models help explain non-normal features of financial returns data. However, even the distribution of returns standardized by a dynamic variance tends to be fat tailed and maybe skewed. This chapter has considered methods for modeling the non-normality of portfolio returns by building on the variance and correlation models established in earlier chapters and using the same maximum likelihood estimation techniques.

We first considered a graphical tool for visualizing non-normality in the data, the so-called QQ plot. This tool was used to assess the appropriateness of alternative distributions. We first considered the normal distribution, which showed large deviations from the data in the tails. Second, we defined the standardized $t(d)$ distribution, which allows for fatter tails than the normal, but which also assumes that the distribution is symmetric around zero. While the $t(d)$ distribution fits the data better in the tails, it appeared to be restricted by the symmetry assumption.

In light of the evidence of asymmetry, we introduced the Cornish Fisher approximation to the value-at-risk calculation, which allows for asymmetry through a nonzero skewness. We next considered extreme value theory, which models each tail of the distribution individually and therefore also allows for asymmetry. The simple Hill estimator was used to find the parameters of the EVT distribution. The estimation of EVT has the intuitive appeal that only data in the tail of interest is used to estimate that particular tail.

Finally, in light of the mounting evidence of non-normality in financial returns, we discussed the shortcomings of the value-at-risk measure and considered expected shortfall as a viable alternative.

4.8. FURTHER RESOURCES

Extensions to the basic symmetric $t(d)$ distribution considered here can be found in Hansen (1994), and Fernandez and Steel (1998). The GARCH-$\tilde{t}(d)$ model was introduced by Bollerslev (1987). Applications of extreme value theory to financial risk management is discussed in McNeil (2000). The choice of threshold value in the GARCH-EVT model is discussed in McNeil and Frey (2000). Huisman *et al.* (2001) explore improvements to the simple Hill estimator considered here. Multivariate extensions to the univariate EVT analysis considered here can be found in Longin (2000), Longin and Solnik (2001), and Poon *et al.* (2001).

Artzner *et al.* (1999) define the concept of a coherent risk measure and show that expected shortfall (ES) is coherent whereas VaR is not. Studying dynamic portfolio management based on ES and VaR, Basak and Shapiro (2001) find that when a large loss does occur, ES risk management leads to lower losses than VaR risk management. Cuoco, He, and Issaenko (2001) argue instead that VaR and ES risk management lead to equivalent results as long as the VaR and ES risk measures are recalculated often. Both Basak and Shapiro (2001) and Cuoco *et al.* (2001) assume that returns are normally distributed. Finally, notice that the ES expression in this chapter relies on log-returns and is therefore an approximation to the standard dollar loss definition. See the appendix to Chapter 3 for details.

4.9. EMPIRICAL EXERCISES ON CD-ROM

Open the Chapter4Data.xls file on the CD-ROM.

1. Construct a QQ plot of the S&P 500 returns divided by the unconditional standard deviation. Use the normal distribution. Compare your result with the top panel of Figure 4.2. (*Excel Hint*: Use the NORMSINV function to calculate the standard normal quantiles.)

2. Copy and paste the estimated GARCH(1,1) volatilities from Chapter 2, question 2.

3. Standardize the returns using the volatilities from question 2. Construct a QQ plot for the standardized returns using the normal distribution. Compare your result with the bottom panel of Figure 4.2.

4. Using QMLE, estimate the GARCH(1,1)-$\tilde{t}(d)$ model. Fix the variance parameters at their values from question 3. Set the starting value of d equal to 10. (*Excel Hint*: Use the GAMMALN function for the log-likelihood function of the standardized $t(d)$ distribution.)

    Construct a QQ plot for the standardized returns using the standardized $t(d)$ distribution. Compare your result with Figure 4.3. (*Hint*: Excel contains a two-sided quantile from the $t(d)$ distribution. To compute one-sided quantiles from the standardized $t(d)$ distribution, we use the relationship

$$\tilde{t}_p^{-1}(d) = \begin{cases} -|\text{tinv}(2p, d)| \sqrt{(d-2)/d}, & \text{if } p \le 0.5 \\ |\text{tinv}(2(1-p), d)| \sqrt{(d-2)/d} & \text{if } p > 0.5 \end{cases}$$

where TINV is the function in Excel, and where $\tilde{t}_p^{-1}(d)$ is the standardized one-sided quantile we need for the QQ plot.)

5. Estimate the GARCH(1.1)-$\tilde{t}(d)$ model using MLE instead of QMLE. Set the starting values of all parameters equal to the final values from question 4. Skip this question if you are working on a slow computer.

6. Estimate the EVT model on the standardized portfolio returns using the Hill estimator. Use the 5% largest losses to estimate EVT. (*Excel Hint*: Use the PERCENTILE function to calculate the pth quantile of a series.) Calculate the 0.01% standardized return quantile implied by each of the following models: normal, $t(d)$, EVT, and Cornish-Fisher. Notice how different the 0.01% VaRs would be from these four models.

7. Construct the QQ plot using the EVT distribution for the 5% largest losses. Compare your result with Figure 4.4.

    The answers to these exercises can be found in the Chapter4Results.xls file. Previews of the answers follow.

QUESTION I

Constructing Normal QQ-plot for the Returns Standardized by Unconditional Standard Deviation

	Date	Close	Return	Sorted Return	Standardized Return	Rank	Normal Quantiles
3	02-Jan-97	737.01					
4	03-Jan-97	748.03	1.48%	-7.11%	-5.6056	1	-3.3542
5	06-Jan-97	747.65	-0.05%	-7.04%	-5.5512	2	-3.0371
6	07-Jan-97	753.23	0.74%	-6.00%	-4.7322	3	-2.8797
7	08-Jan-97	748.41	-0.64%	-5.05%	-3.9774	4	-2.7719
8	09-Jan-97	754.85	0.86%	-4.41%	-3.4788	5	-2.6891
9	10-Jan-97	759.50	0.61%	-3.91%	-3.0835	6	-2.6214
10	13-Jan-97	759.51	0.00%	-3.91%	-3.0814	7	-2.5639
11	14-Jan-97	768.86	1.22%	-3.69%	-2.9095	8	-2.5138
12	15-Jan-97	767.20	-0.22%	-3.50%	-2.7582	9	-2.4694
13	16-Jan-97	769.75	0.33%	-3.19%	-2.5059	10	-2.4293
14	17-Jan-97	776.17	0.83%	-3.16%	-2.4867	11	-2.3928
15	20-Jan-97	776.70	0.07%	-3.10%	-2.4423	12	-2.3592
16	21-Jan-97	782.72	0.77%	-3.08%	-2.4311	13	-2.3281
17	22-Jan-97	786.23	0.45%	-3.06%	-2.4093	14	-2.2991
18	23-Jan-97	777.56	-1.11%	-3.01%	-2.3732	15	-2.2720
19	24-Jan-97	770.52	-0.91%	-2.85%	-2.2429	16	-2.2463
20	27-Jan-97	765.02	-0.72%	-2.84%	-2.2408	17	-2.2221
21	28-Jan-97	765.02	0.00%	-2.80%	-2.2085	18	-2.1992
22	29-Jan-97	772.50	0.97%	-2.78%	-2.1941	19	-2.1773
23	30-Jan-97	784.17	1.50%	-2.77%	-2.1801	20	-2.1564
24	31-Jan-97	786.16	0.25%	-2.73%	-2.1478	21	-2.1364
25	03-Feb-97	786.73	0.07%	-2.66%	-2.0958	22	-2.1173
26	04-Feb-97	789.26	0.32%	-2.63%	-2.0688	23	-2.0989
27	05-Feb-97	778.28	-1.40%	-2.62%	-2.0640	24	-2.0811
28	06-Feb-97	780.15	0.24%	-2.62%	-2.0634	25	-2.0641
29	07-Feb-97	789.56	1.20%	-2.60%	-2.0463	26	-2.0475
30	10-Feb-97	785.43	-0.52%	-2.58%	-2.0365	27	-2.0316

Descriptive Statistics

Number of observ.	1256
Mean	0.0004
Standard Deviation	0.0127
Kurtosis	2.6624
Skewness	-0.2377

NORMSINV returns the inverse of the standard normal cumulative distribution. The distribution has a mean of zero and a standard deviation of one. In order to avoid obtaining infinity while using NORMSINV, the argument should be as follows: (Rank-0.5)/n

Estimated GARCH(1,1) model from Chapter 2, Question 2

Date	Close	Return	Squared Return	Conditional Variance	Likelihood		Starting Values		Maximum Likelihood	
02-Jan-97	737.01						α	0.1000	α	0.0556
03-Jan-97	748.03	1.48%	0.000220	0.000161	2.7640		β	0.8500	β	0.6393
06-Jan-97	747.65	-0.05%	0.000000	0.000121	3.5885		ω	0.0000050	ω	0.0000099
07-Jan-97	753.23	0.74%	0.000055	0.000120	3.3651		θ	0.5000	θ	2.1449
08-Jan-97	748.41	-0.64%	0.000041	0.000101	3.4778		$\alpha(1+\theta^2)+\beta$	0.9750	$\alpha(1+\theta^2)+\beta$	0.9504
09-Jan-97	754.85	0.86%	0.000073	0.000118	3.2928		MLE	3776.87	MLE	3804.14
10-Jan-97	759.50	0.61%	0.000038	0.000097	3.5064					
13-Jan-97	759.51	0.00%	0.000000	0.000085	3.7701					
14-Jan-97	768.86	1.22%	0.000150	0.000086	2.8893					
15-Jan-97	767.20	-0.22%	0.000005	0.000068	3.8461					
16-Jan-97	769.75	0.33%	0.000011	0.000075	3.7563					
17-Jan-97	776.17	0.83%	0.000069	0.000071	3.3717					
20-Jan-97	776.70	0.07%	0.000000	0.000060	3.9339					
21-Jan-97	782.72	0.77%	0.000060	0.000063	3.4442					
22-Jan-97	786.23	0.45%	0.000020	0.000055	3.6042					
23-Jan-97	777.56	-1.11%	0.000123	0.000052	2.8331					
24-Jan-97	770.52	-0.91%	0.000083	0.000083	3.2811					
27-Jan-97	765.02	-0.72%	0.000051	0.000108	3.4101					
28-Jan-97	765.02	0.00%	0.000000	0.000127	3.5661					
29-Jan-97	772.50	0.97%	0.000095	0.000124	3.1972					
30-Jan-97	784.17	1.50%	0.000225	0.000100	2.5626					
31-Jan-97	786.16	0.25%	0.000006	0.000076	3.7800					
03-Feb-97	786.73	0.07%	0.000001	0.000073	3.8388					
04-Feb-97	789.26	0.32%	0.000010	0.000074	3.7675					
05-Feb-97	778.28	-1.40%	0.000196	0.000070	2.4634					
06-Feb-97	780.15	0.24%	0.000006	0.000111	3.6062					
07-Feb-97	789.56	1.20%	0.000144	0.000104	2.9754					

QUESTION 2

	Conditional Variance	Standardized Return	Likelihood	Rank	Sorted Standardized Return	Standard Normal Quantiles		Starting Values		Maximum Likelihood	
3								α	0.1000	α	0.0556
4	0.000161	1.1697	2.7640	1	-5.0658	-3.3542		β	0.8500	β	0.6393
5	0.000121	-0.0461	3.5885	2	-4.1344	-3.0371		ω	0.0000050	ω	0.0000099
6	0.000120	0.6793	3.3651	3	-3.6416	-2.8797		θ	0.5000	θ	2.1449
7	0.000101	-0.6394	3.4778	4	-3.4000	-2.7719		$\alpha(1+\theta^2)+\beta$	0.9750	$\alpha(1+\theta^2)+\beta$	0.9504
8	0.000118	0.7895	3.2928	5	-3.3900	-2.6891		MLE	3776.87	MLE	3804.14
9	0.000097	0.6229	3.5064	6	-2.9606	-2.6214		**Descriptive Statistics**			
10	0.000085	0.0014	3.7701	7	-2.9406	-2.5639		Number of observ.	1256		
11	0.000086	1.3229	2.8893	8	-2.7361	-2.5138		Mean	0.0169		
12	0.000068	-0.2625	3.8461	9	-2.7230	-2.4694		Standard Deviation	0.9985		
13	0.000075	0.3830	3.7563	10	-2.6140	-2.4293		Kurtosis	0.9012		
14	0.000071	0.9868	3.3717	11	-2.5668	-2.3928		Skewness	-0.2433		
15	0.000060	0.0878	3.9339	12	-2.5035	-2.3592					
16	0.000063	0.9745	3.4442	13	-2.4969	-2.3281					
17	0.000055	0.6044	3.8042	14	-2.3697	-2.2991					
18	0.000052	-1.5352	2.8331	15	-2.3572	-2.2720					
19	0.000083	-1.0013	3.2811	16	-2.3491	-2.2463					
20	0.000108	-0.6892	3.4101	17	-2.2627	-2.2221					
21	0.000127	0.0000	3.5661	18	-2.1904	-2.1992					
22	0.000124	0.8748	3.1972	19	-2.1708	-2.1773					
23	0.000100	1.4989	2.5626	20	-2.1279	-2.1564					
24	0.000076	0.2904	3.7800	21	-2.1124	-2.1364					
25	0.000073	0.0847	3.8388	22	-2.0704	-2.1173					
26	0.000074	0.3734	3.7675	23	-2.0647	-2.0989					
27	0.000070	-1.6738	2.4634	24	-2.0395	-2.0811					
28	0.000111	0.2273	3.6062	25	-2.0227	-2.0641					

QUESTION 3

QUESTION 4

Squared Return	Conditional Variance	Standardized Return	Likelihood	Rank	Sorted Standardized Return	Student t(d) Quantiles		Starting Values		Final Values	
									0.0556		0.0556
								α		α	
0.000220	0.000161	1.1697	-1.6779	1	-5.0658	-4.0792		β	0.6393	β	0.6393
0.000000	0.000121	-0.0461	-0.8537	2	-4.1344	-3.5142		ω	0.0000099	ω	0.0000099
0.000055	0.000120	0.6793	-1.1421	3	-3.6416	-3.2578		θ	2.1449	θ	2.1449
0.000041	0.000101	-0.6394	-1.1097	4	-3.4000	-3.0905		α(1+θ²)+β	0.9504	α(1+θ²)+β	0.9504
0.000073	0.000118	0.7895	-1.2409	5	-3.3900	-2.9661		d	10.0000	d	12.5922
0.000038	0.000097	0.6229	-1.0968	6	-2.9606	-2.8670		MLE	-1772.00	MLE	-1771.60
0.000000	0.000085	0.0014	-0.8523	7	-2.9406	-2.7845					
0.000150	0.000086	1.3229	-1.8915	8	-2.7361	-2.7139					
0.000005	0.000068	-0.2625	-0.8964	9	-2.7230	-2.6621					
0.000011	0.000075	0.3830	-0.9458	10	-2.6140	-2.5971					
0.000069	0.000071	0.9868	-1.4500	11	-2.5668	-2.5476					
0.000000	0.000060	0.0878	-0.8572	12	-2.5035	-2.5026					
0.000060	0.000063	0.9745	-1.4356	13	-2.4969	-2.4613					
0.000020	0.000055	0.6044	-1.0827	14	-2.3597	-2.4231					
0.000123	0.000052	-1.5352	-2.2177	15	-2.3572	-2.3875					
0.000083	0.000083	-1.0013	-1.4669	16	-2.3491	-2.3543					
0.000051	0.000108	-0.6892	-1.1505	17	-2.2627	-2.3232					
0.000000	0.000127	0.0000	-0.8523	18	-2.1904	-2.2938					
0.000095	0.000124	0.8746	-1.3264	19	-2.1708	-2.2660					
0.000225	0.000100	1.4989	-2.1596	20	-2.1279	-2.2396					
0.000006	0.000076	0.2904	-0.9062	21	-2.1124	-2.2145					
0.000001	0.000073	0.0847	-0.8669	22	-2.0704	-2.1905					
0.000010	0.000074	0.3734	-0.9412	23	-2.0647	-2.1676					
0.000196	0.000070	-1.6738	-2.4471	24	-2.0395	-2.1457					
0.000006	0.000111	0.2273	-0.8854	25	-2.0227	-2.1246					

	E	F	G	H	I	J	K	L	M	N	O
								Starting Values		Final Values	
2	Conditional Variance	Standardized Return	Likelihood	Rank	Sorted Standardized Return	Student t(d) Quantiles					
3								α	0.0556	α	0.0472
4	0.000161	1.1697	2.6892	1	-5.2011	-4.0792		β	0.6393	β	0.6569
5	0.000124	-0.0456	3.6429	2	-4.1965	-3.5142		ω	0.0000099	ω	0.0000085
6	0.000123	0.6709	3.3672	3	-3.7651	-3.2579		θ	2.1449	θ	2.3143
7	0.000105	-0.6268	3.4814	4	-3.4703	-3.0906		$\alpha(1+\theta^2)+\beta$	0.9507	$\alpha(1+\theta^2)+\beta$	0.9570
8	0.000120	0.7812	3.2798	5	-3.4686	-2.9661		d	10.0000	d	12.5926
9	0.000101	0.6113	3.5127	6	-3.0203	-2.8670		MLE	3812.10	MLE	3812.64
10	0.000089	0.0014	3.8131	7	-2.8864	-2.7845					
11	0.000089	1.2957	2.8103	8	-2.7584	-2.7139					
12	0.000071	-0.2556	3.8789	9	-2.7095	-2.6521					
13	0.000078	0.3762	3.7882	10	-2.6469	-2.5971					
14	0.000073	0.9692	3.3298	11	-2.5324	-2.5476					
15	0.000063	0.0860	3.9787	12	-2.5169	-2.5026					
16	0.000065	0.9595	3.4038	13	-2.4631	-2.4613					
17	0.000057	0.5943	3.8138	14	-2.4227	-2.4231					
18	0.000054	-1.5132	2.7337	15	-2.3731	-2.3875					
19	0.000081	-1.0108	3.2326	16	-2.3231	-2.3543					
20	0.000104	-0.7025	3.4238	17	-2.1916	-2.3232					
21	0.000122	0.0000	3.6553	18	-2.1841	-2.2938					
22	0.000119	0.8915	3.1737	19	-2.1834	-2.2660					
23	0.000098	1.5133	2.4319	20	-2.1368	-2.2396					
24	0.000076	0.2907	3.8360	21	-2.1276	-2.2145					
25	0.000073	0.0847	3.9045	22	-2.1089	-2.1905					
26	0.000074	0.3738	3.8159	23	-2.0859	-2.1676					
27	0.000070	-1.6730	2.3369	24	-2.0303	-2.1457					
28	0.000107	0.2317	3.6835	25	-2.0263	-2.1246					

QUESTION 5

	Sorted Loss		EVT_loss	1-day 1% VaRs				Hill Estimator			Quantiles	
	y_{jt}	$Lnf(y_{jt}/u)$		Normal	t-Student	Cornish-Fisher		Threshold	-1.6753		EVT	2.4321
4	5.0658	1.1065	0.030860	0.029518	0.031200	0.029639		T_u	63		Normal	2.3263
5	4.1344	0.9034	0.026790	0.025625	0.027085	0.025730		Tail Parametr	0.2312		t Student	2.4589
6	3.6416	0.7764	0.026624	0.025466	0.026917	0.025570		Cut-off (EVT)	95.00%		Cornish-Fisher	2.3359
7	3.4000	0.7078	0.024419	0.023357	0.024688	0.023453		Quantile (p)	1.00%		Skewness	-0.2433
8	3.3900	0.7049	0.026393	0.025245	0.026684	0.025349		degree of freedom	12.5926		Kurtosis	0.9012
9	2.9606	0.5694	0.023979	0.022936	0.024243	0.023030						
10	2.9406	0.5626	0.022364	0.021391	0.022610	0.021479						
11	2.7361	0.4906	0.022494	0.021516	0.022742	0.021604						
12	2.7230	0.4858	0.020026	0.019155	0.020246	0.019233						
13	2.6140	0.4449	0.021073	0.020157	0.021305	0.020239						
14	2.5668	0.4267	0.020471	0.019580	0.020696	0.019661						
15	2.5035	0.4017	0.018913	0.018090	0.019121	0.018164						
16	2.4969	0.3991	0.019270	0.018432	0.019482	0.018507						
17	2.3597	0.3426	0.018006	0.017223	0.018204	0.017293						
18	2.3572	0.3415	0.017567	0.016803	0.017760	0.016872						
19	2.3491	0.3381	0.022092	0.021131	0.022335	0.021218						
20	2.2627	0.3006	0.025278	0.024179	0.025556	0.024278						
21	2.1904	0.2681	0.027427	0.026234	0.027729	0.026341						
22	2.1708	0.2591	0.027050	0.025874	0.027348	0.025980						
23	2.1279	0.2392	0.024329	0.023271	0.024597	0.023366						
24	2.1124	0.2318	0.021230	0.020306	0.021463	0.020389						
25	2.0704	0.2118	0.020804	0.019899	0.021033	0.019981						
26	2.0647	0.2090	0.020912	0.020003	0.021142	0.020085						
27	2.0395	0.1967	0.020357	0.019471	0.020581	0.019551						
28	2.0227	0.1884	0.025675	0.024559	0.025958	0.024669						
29	2.0178	0.1860	0.024793	0.023714	0.025066	0.023811						

QUESTION 6

QUESTION 7

Constructing QQ-plot for EVT		Edit Formula	Sorted Losses		EVT Tail Quantile			Hill Estimator		
Date	R_t/σ_t	Rank	$R_t/\sigma_{t,loss}$	ABS($R_t/\sigma_{t,loss}$)	Loss	ABS Loss		u		-1.6753
02-Jan-97								T_u		63
03-Jan-97	1.1697	1	-5.0658	5.0658	-5.1241	5.1241		ξ		0.2312
06-Jan-97	-0.0461	2	-4.1344	4.1344	-3.9749	3.9749		Cut-off (EVT)		0.95
07-Jan-97	0.6793	3	-3.6416	3.6416	-3.5322	3.5322		Quantile (p)		0.01
08-Jan-97	-0.6394	4	-3.4000	3.4000	-3.2679	3.2679				
09-Jan-97	0.7895	5	-3.3900	3.3900	-3.0834	3.0834				
10-Jan-97	0.6229	6	-2.9606	2.9606	-2.9437	2.9437				
13-Jan-97	0.0014	7	-2.9406	2.9406	-2.8321	2.8321				
14-Jan-97	1.3229	8	-2.7361	2.7361	-2.7400	2.7400				
15-Jan-97	-0.2625	9	-2.7230	2.7230	-2.6618	2.6618				
16-Jan-97	0.3830	10	-2.6140	2.6140	-2.5943	2.5943				
17-Jan-97	0.9868	11	-2.5668	2.5668	-2.5349	2.5349				
20-Jan-97	0.0878	12	-2.5035	2.5035	-2.4822	2.4822				
21-Jan-97	0.9745	13	-2.4969	2.4969	-2.4348	2.4348				
22-Jan-97	0.6044	14	-2.3597	2.3597	-2.3919	2.3919				
23-Jan-97	-1.5352	15	-2.3572	2.3572	-2.3527	2.3527				
24-Jan-97	-1.0013	16	-2.3491	2.3491	-2.3167	2.3167				
27-Jan-97	-0.6892	17	-2.2627	2.2627	-2.2835	2.2835				
28-Jan-97	0.0000	18	-2.1904	2.1904	-2.2526	2.2526				
29-Jan-97	0.8748	19	-2.1708	2.1708	-2.2239	2.2239				
30-Jan-97	1.4989	20	-2.1279	2.1279	-2.1970	2.1970				

REFERENCES

Artzner, P., F. Delbaen, J. Eber, and D. Heath. (1999). "Coherent Measures of Risk," *Mathematical Finance*, 9, 203–228.

Basak, S., and A. Shapiro. (2001). "Value-at-Risk Based Risk Management: Optimal Policies and Asset Prices," *Review of Financial Studies*, 14, 371–405.

Bollerslev, T. (1987). "A Conditionally Heteroskedastic Time Series Model for Speculative Prices and Rates of Return," *Review of Economics and Statistics*, 69, 542–547.

Cuoco, D., H. He, and S. Issaenko. (2001). "Optimal Dynamic Trading Strategies with Risk Limits," Manuscript, The Wharton School, University of Pennsylvania.

Fernandez, C., and M. F. J. Steel. (1998). "On Bayesian Modeling of Fat Tails and Skewness," *Journal of the American Statistical Association*, 93, 359–371.

Hansen, B. (1994). "Autoregressive Conditional Density Estimation," *International Economic Review*, 35, 705–730.

Huisman, R., K. Koedijk, C. Kool, and F. Palm. (2001). "Tail-Index Estimates in Small Samples," *Journal of Business and Economic Statistics*, 19, 208–216.

Longin, F. (2000). "From Value at Risk to Stress Testing: The Extreme Value Approach," *Journal of Banking and Finance*, 24, 1097–1130.

Longin, F., and B. Solnik. (2001). "Extreme Correlation of International Equity Markets," *Journal of Finance*, 56, 649–676.

McNeil, A. (2000). "Extreme Value Theory for Risk Managers," in Paul Embrechts, ed., *Extremes and Integrated Risk Management*. London: Risk Books.

McNeil, A., and R. Frey. (2000). "Estimation of Tail-Related Risk Measures for Heteroskedastic Financial Time Series: An Extreme Value Approach," *Journal of Empirical Finance*, 7, 271–300.

Poon, S.-H., M. Rockinger, and J. Tawn. (2001). "New Extreme-Value Dependence Measures and Finance Applications," Manuscript, HEC Paris.

5

SIMULATION-BASED METHODS

5.1. CHAPTER OVERVIEW

The main objectives of this chapter are twofold. First, we want to introduce methods for forecasting the distribution of portfolio returns, which are very popular in practice but which we argue have some key flaws, namely the so-called historical simulation methods. Second, we want to consider ways in which the daily risk models we have constructed in previous chapters can be used for risk forecasting at multiple horizons. While most risk models are estimated on daily data and therefore automatically forecast 1 day ahead, risk managers are typically interested in the risk across longer horizons as well.

    The chapter is organized as follows:

1. We introduce the historical simulation (HS) method and discuss its pros and particularly its cons.
2. We consider an extension of HS, often referred to as weighted historical simulation (WHS).
3. We show how Monte Carlo simulation (MCS) can be used to generate multiday forecasts from the conditional daily risk models constructed in Chapters 2 through 4.
4. We argue the advantages of combining the conditional variance and correlation models from Chapters 2 and 3 with a modified version of HS, which

we refer to as filtered historical simulation (FHS). FHS can be used to generate daily as well as multiday forecasts from daily models. The FHS method has been found to perform well, and it can be seen as a model-free alternative to the model-based conditional distribution methods suggested in Chapter 4.

5.2. HISTORICAL SIMULATION (HS)

Before defining exactly what we mean by historical simulation, let us recap some notation and ideas from previous chapters. This will help us in comparing HS with the previously suggested methods.

5.2.1. Background

First, return on the portfolio on day $t + 1$ is defined as

$$R_{PF,t+1} = \sum_{i=1}^{n} w_i R_{i,t+1}$$

where the sum is taken over the n securities in the portfolio. w_i denotes the relative weight of security i at the end of day t.

We have previously written the variance of the portfolio return as

$$\sigma^2_{PF,t+1} = \sum_{i=1}^{n}\sum_{j=1}^{n} w_i w_j \sigma_{ij,t+1} = \sum_{i=1}^{n}\sum_{j=1}^{n} w_i w_j \sigma_{i,t+1}\sigma_{j,t+1}\rho_{ij,t+1}$$

where $\sigma_{ij,t+1}$ is the covariance and $\rho_{ij,t+1}$ is the correlation between security i and j on day $t + 1$. We have $\rho_{ii,t+1} = 1$, and we write $\sigma_{ii,t+1} = \sigma^2_{i,t+1}$ for all i.

In Chapter 2, we considered univariate variance models, which can be used to estimate the portfolio variance, $\sigma^2_{PF,t+1}$, directly from the time series of past hypothetical portfolio returns. Alternatively, the variance models can be used to model the individual asset variances, $\sigma^2_{i,t+1}$, which in conjunction with the correlation models for $\rho_{ij,t+1}$ in Chapter 3 can be used to form the portfolio variance by summing over all the assets as in the preceding equation. While the latter approach clearly requires more effort, its advantage is that it can be used for active asset allocation purposes. The former aggregate portfolio approach simply provides a risk measurement tool.

In either of these variance modeling approaches, the VaR of the portfolio is simply

$$VaR^p_{t+1} = -\sigma_{PF,t+1} * F_p^{-1}$$

where F_p^{-1} is the pth quantile of the rescaled portfolio returns.

5.2.2. Defining Historical Simulation

Against this backdrop we are now ready to define the historical simulation approach to risk management. The HS techniques is deceptively simple. Consider again the definition of portfolio returns

$$R_{PF,t+1} = \sum_{i=1}^{n} w_i R_{i,t+1}$$

and consider the availability of a past sequence of m daily hypothetical portfolio returns, calculated using past returns on the underlying assets of the portfolio, but using today's portfolio weights. We write

$$\left\{R_{PF,t+1-\tau}\right\}_{\tau=1}^{m} \equiv \left\{\sum_{i=1}^{n} w_i R_{i,t+1-\tau}\right\}_{\tau=1}^{m}$$

The HS technique simply assumes that the distribution of tomorrow's portfolio returns, $R_{PF,t+1}$, is well approximated by the empirical distribution of the past m observations—that is, $\left\{R_{PF,t+1-\tau}\right\}_{\tau=1}^{m}$. Put differently, the distribution of $R_{PF,t+1}$ is captured by the histogram of $\left\{R_{PF,t+1-\tau}\right\}_{\tau=1}^{m}$. The value at risk (VaR) with coverage rate, p, is then simply calculated as $100p$th percentile of the sequence of past portfolio returns. We write

$$VaR_{t+1}^{p} = -Percentile\left\{\left\{R_{PF,t+1-\tau}\right\}_{\tau=1}^{m}, 100p\right\}$$

Thus, we simply sort the returns in $\left\{R_{PF,t+1-\tau}\right\}_{\tau=1}^{m}$ in ascending order and choose the VaR_{t+1}^{p} to be the number such that only $100p\%$ of the observations are smaller than the VaR_{t+1}^{p}. As the VaR typically falls in between two observations, linear interpolation can be used to calculate the exact number. Standard quantitative software packages will have the *Percentile* or similar functions built in so that the linear interpolation is performed automatically.

5.2.3. Pros and Cons of Historical Simulation

Historical simulation is widely used in practice. The main reasons are (1) the ease with which is it implemented and (2) its model-free nature.

The first advantage is difficult to argue with. The HS technique clearly is very easy to implement. No parameters have to be estimated by maximum likelihood or any other method. Therefore, no numerical optimization has to be performed.

The second advantage is more contentious, however. The HS technique is model-free in the sense that it does not rely on any particular parametric model such as a GARCH(1,1) for variance and a normal distribution for the standardized returns. HS lets the past m data points speak fully about the distribution of tomorrow's return without imposing any further assumptions. This has the obvious advantage compared with the approach taken in Chapters 2 to 4, that relying on modeling assumptions can be misleading if the model is poor.

The model-free nature of the HS model also has serious drawbacks, however.

Consider the choice of the data sample length, m. How large should m be? This drawback is very similar in nature to the model-free estimates of variance and covariance from daily returns, which were discussed at the beginning of Chapters 2 and 3, respectively. If m is too large, then the most recent observations, which presumably are the most relevant for tomorrow's distribution, will carry very little weight, and the VaR will tend to look very smooth over time. If m is chosen to be too small, then the sample may not include enough large losses to enable the risk manager to calculate, say, a 1% VaR with any precision. Conversely, the most recent past may be very unusual, so that tomorrow's VaR will be too extreme. The upshot is that the choice of m is very ad hoc, and, unfortunately, the particular choice of m matters a lot for the magnitude and dynamics of VaR from the HS technique. Typically m is chosen in practice to be between 250 and 1000 days corresponding to approximately 1 to 4 years. Figure 5.1 shows VaRs from HS $m = 250$ and $m = 1000$, respectively, using daily returns on the S&P 500 for 2001. Notice the curious box-shaped patterns that arise from the abrupt inclusion and exclusion of large losses in the moving sample. Notice also how the dynamic patterns of the HS VaRs are crucially dependent on m. The lack of properly specified dynamics in the HS methodology causes it to ignore well-established stylized facts on return dependence—most importantly variance clustering. The result is highly curious-looking patterns in the VaR over time, as witnessed by Figure 5.1.

As a reasonably large m is needed in order to calculate 1% VaRs with any degree of precision, the HS technique has a serious drawback when it comes to calculating the VaR for the next say 10 days rather than the next day. Ideally, the 10-day VaR should be calculated from 10-day nonoverlapping past returns, which

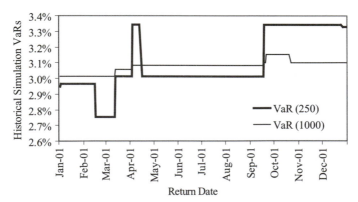

FIGURE 5.1 VaRs from Historical Simulation Using a Moving Sample of 250 Days (bold) and 1000 Days. Daily S&P 500 Returns, 2001.

would entail coming up with 10 times as many past daily returns. This is often not feasible. Thus, the model-free advantage of the HS technique is simultaneously a serious drawback. As the HS method does not rely on a well-specified dynamic model, we have no theoretically correct way of extrapolating from the 1-day distribution to get the 10-day distribution other than finding more past data. While it may be tempting to simply multiply the 1-day VaR from HS by $\sqrt{10}$ to obtain a 10-day VaR, doing so is only valid under the assumption of normality, which the HS approach is explicitly tailored to avoid. If the data were truly normally distributed, then HS would not be an attractive method at all.

In contrast, the daily dynamic return models suggested in Chapters 2 to 4 can be generalized to provide distributions at any horizon. We will consider methods to do so later in the chapter.

5.3. WEIGHTED HISTORICAL SIMULATION (WHS)

We have discussed the inherent tension in the HS approach regarding the choice of sample size, m. If m is too small, then we do not have enough observations in the left tail to calculate a precise VaR measure, and if m is too large, then the VaR will not be sufficiently responsive to the most recent returns, which presumably have the most information about tomorrow's distribution.

We now consider a modification of the HS technique, which is designed to relieve the tension in the choice of m by assigning relatively more weight to the most recent observations and relatively less weight to the returns further in the past. This technique is referred to as weighted historical simulation (WHS).

WHS is implemented as follows:

1. Our sample of m past hypothetical returns, $\{R_{PF,t+1-\tau}\}_{\tau=1}^{m}$, is assigned probability weights declining exponentially through the past as follows:

$$\eta_\tau = \left\{ \eta^{\tau-1}(1-\eta)/\left(1-\eta^m\right) \right\}_{\tau=1}^{m}$$

   so that, for example, today's observation is assigned the weight $\eta_1 = (1-\eta)/(1-\eta^m)$. Note that η_τ goes to zero as τ get large, and that the weights from $\tau = 1, 2 \ldots, m$ sum to 1. Typically, η is assumed to be a number between 0.95 and 0.99.

2. The observations, along with their assigned weights, are sorted in ascending order.

3. The $100p\%$ VaR is calculated by accumulating the weights of the ascending returns until $100p\%$ is reached. Again, linear interpolation can be used to calculate the exact VaR number between the two sorted returns with cumulative probability weights surrounding p.

Notice that once η is chosen, the WHS technique still does not require estimation and thus retains the ease of implementation, which is the hallmark of

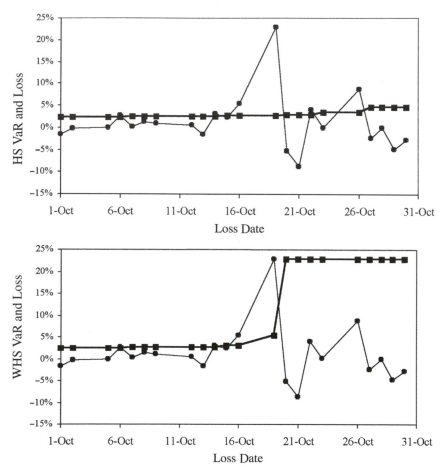

FIGURE 5.2   VaRs (bold with squares) and Daily Losses from **Long** S&P 500 Position, October 1987. Historical Simulation VaR (top panel) and Weighted Historical Simulation VaR (bottom panel).

simple HS. It has the added advantage that the weighting function builds in some conditionality in the technique: Today's market conditions matter more as today's return gets weighted much more than past returns. The weighting function also makes the choice of m somewhat less crucial.

An obvious downside of the WHS approach is that no guidance is given on how to choose η. A more subtle, but also much more important downside is the effect on the weighting scheme of positive versus negative past returns, a downside that WHS shares with HS. We illustrate this with a somewhat extreme example drawing on the month surrounding the October 19, 1987, crash in the stock market. Figure 5.2 contains two panels both showing in dots the daily losses on a portfolio consisting of a $1 long position in the S&P 500 index. Notice how the returns are relatively calm before October 19, when a more than 20% loss from the crash set off a dramatic increase in market variance.

The squares in the top panel show the VaR from the simple HS technique, using an m of 250. The key thing to notice of course is how the simple HS technique responds slowly and relatively little to the dramatic loss on October 19. The HS's lack of response to the crash is due to its unconditional nature: Once the crash occurs, it simply becomes another observation in the sample, which carries the same weight as the other 250 past observation. The VaR from the WHS method in the bottom panel shows a much more rapid and large response to the VaR forecast from the crash. As soon as the large portfolio loss from the crash is recorded, it gets assigned a large weight in the weighting scheme, which in turn increases the VaR dramatically. The WHS estimate in Figure 5.2 assumes a η of 0.99.

Thus, apparently the WHS performs its task sublimely. The conditionality of the weighting scheme kicks in to lower the VaR exactly when our intuition says it should. Unfortunately, all is not well. Consider Figure 5.3, which in both panels shows the daily losses from a short $1 position in the S&P 500 index. Thus, we have simply flipped the losses from before around the x-axis. The top panel shows the VaR from HS, which is even more sluggish than before: As we are short the S&P, the market crash corresponds to a large gain rather than a large loss. Consequently, it has no impact on the VaR, which is calculated from the largest losses only. Consider now the WHS VaR instead. The bottom panel of Figure 5.3 shows that as we are short the market, the October 19 crash has no impact on our VaR, only the subsequent market rebound, which corresponds to a loss for us, increases the VaR.

Thus, the upshot is that while WHS responds quickly to large losses, it does not respond to large gains. Arguably it should. The market crash sets off an increase in market variance, which the WHS only picks up if the crash is bad for our portfolio position. To put it bluntly, the WHS treats a large loss as a signal that risk has increased, but a large gain is chalked up to the portfolio managers being clever. This is not a prudent risk management approach.

Notice that a simple GARCH model estimated on portfolio returns would have picked up the increase in market variance from the crash regardless of whether the crash meant a gain or a loss to us. In the simple GARCH model, returns are squared and losses and gains are treated as having the same impact on tomorrow's variance and therefore on the portfolio risk.

Finally, a serious downside of WHS, and one which it shares with the simple HS approach, is that the multiday value at risk requires a large amount of past daily return data, which is often not easy to obtain. We now turn to exactly this issue of multiperiod risk calculations and consider risk management methods in which multiday value at risk easily can be calculated.

5.4. MULTI-PERIOD RISK CALCULATIONS

So far we have mostly considered calculating value at risk and other risk measures for the 1-day horizon. However, risk managers are typically also interested in the risk of their holdings at horizons beyond 1 day. In the simplistic case, where portfolio returns are normally distributed with a constant variance, σ_{PF}^2, the

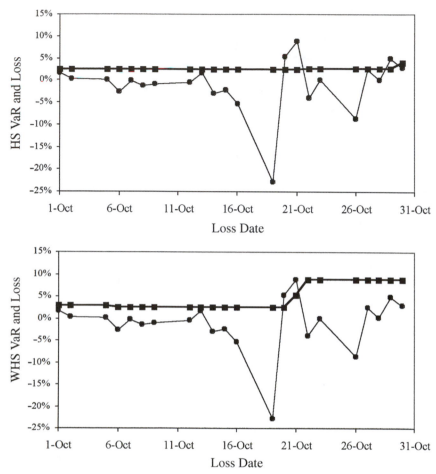

FIGURE 5.3   VaRs (bold with squares) and Daily Losses from **Short** S&P 500 Position, October 1987. Historical Simulation VaR (top panel) and Weighted Historical Simulation VaR (bottom panel).

returns over the next K days are also normally distributed, but with variance $K\sigma_{PF}^2$. In that case, we can easily calculate the VaR for returns over the next K days calculated on day t, as

$$VaR_{t+1:t+K}^p = \sqrt{K}\sigma_{PF}\Phi_p^{-1} = \sqrt{K}VaR_{t+1}^p$$

In the much more realistic case where the portfolio variance is time varying, going from 1 day ahead to K days ahead VaR is not so simple. As we saw in Chapter 2, the variance of K-day returns in general is

$$\sigma_{t+1:t+K}^2 \equiv E_t\left(\sum_{k=1}^{K} R_{t+k}\right)^2 = \sum_{k=1}^{K} E_t\left[\sigma_{t+k}^2\right]$$

where we have omitted the portfolio, PF, subscripts.

In the simple RiskMetrics variance model, where $\sigma_{t+1}^2 = \lambda \sigma_t^2 + (1 - \lambda) R_t^2$, we get

$$\sigma_{t+1:t+K}^2 = \sum_{k=1}^{K} \sigma_{t+1}^2 = K \sigma_{t+1}^2$$

so that variances actually do scale by K in the RiskMetrics model. However, we argued in Chapter 2 that the absence of mean reversion in variance, which is underlying the simply scaling rule in the RiskMetrics model, will imply counterfactual variance forecasts at longer horizons. Furthermore, although the variance is scaled by K in this model, the returns at horizon K are no longer normally distributed. In fact, one can show that the RiskMetrics model implies that returns get further away from normality as the horizon increases, which is counterfactual as we discussed in Chapter 1.

In the symmetric GARCH(1,1) model, where $\sigma_{t+1}^2 = \omega + \alpha R_t^2 + \beta \sigma_t^2$, we instead get

$$\sigma_{t+1:t+K}^2 = K \sigma^2 + \sum_{k=1}^{K} (\alpha + \beta)^{k-1} \left(\sigma_{t+1}^2 - \sigma^2 \right) \neq K \sigma_{t+1}^2$$

where

$$\sigma^2 = \frac{\omega}{1 - \alpha - \beta}$$

is the unconditional, or average, long-run variance. Notice that conveniently in GARCH models, tomorrow's variance, σ_{t+1}^2, can be calculated at the end of today once R_t is realized.

In this case, the variance does mean revert and it therefore does not scale by the horizon K, and again the returns over the next K days are not normally distributed, even if the 1-day returns are assumed to be. However, a nice feature of mean-reverting GARCH models is that as K gets large, the return distribution does approach the normal. This appears to be a common feature of real-life return data as we argued in Chapter 1.

The upshot is that we are faced with the challenge of computing risk measures such as VaR at multiple horizons, without knowing the analytical form for the distribution of returns at those horizons. Fortunately, this challenge can be met through the use of Monte Carlo simulation techniques.

In Chapter 1 we discussed two stylized facts regarding the mean or average daily return—first, that it is very difficult to forecast, and, second, that it is very small relative to the daily standard deviation. At a longer horizon, it is still fairly difficult to forecast the mean, but the relative importance of the mean increases with horizon. Consider a simple example where daily returns are normally distributed with a constant mean and variance as in

$$R_{t+1} \sim i.i.d. \ N \left(\mu, \sigma^2 \right)$$

The 1-day VaR is thus

$$VaR^p_{t+1} = -\left(\mu + \sigma \Phi^{-1}_p\right) \approx -\sigma \Phi^{-1}_p$$

where the approximation holds as the daily mean is typically orders of magnitude smaller than the standard deviation.

The K-day returns in this case is distributed

$$R_{t+1:t+K} \sim N\left(K\mu, K\sigma^2\right)$$

and the K-day VaR is thus

$$VaR^p_{t+1:t+K} = -\left(K\mu + \sqrt{K}\sigma \Phi^{-1}_p\right) \not\approx -\sqrt{K}\sigma \Phi^{-1}_p$$

As the horizon, K, gets large, the relative importance of the mean increases and the zero-mean approximation no longer holds.

Although the mean return is potentially important at longer horizons in order to save on notation, we will still assume that the mean is zero in the sections that follow. However, it is easy to generalize the analysis to include a nonzero mean.

5.5. MONTE CARLO SIMULATION (MCS)

We illustrate the power of Monte Carlo simulation (MCS) through a simple example. Consider our GARCH(1,1)-normal model of returns, where

$$R_{t+1} = \sigma_{t+1} z_{t+1}, \quad \text{with } z_{t+1} \sim N(0, 1)$$

and

$$\sigma^2_{t+1} = \omega + \alpha R^2_t + \beta \sigma^2_t$$

As mentioned earlier, at the end of day t we obtain R_t and we can calculate σ^2_{t+1}, which is tomorrow's variance in the GARCH model.

Using random number generators, which are standard in most quantitative software packages, we can generate a set of artificial random numbers

$$\breve{z}_{i,1}, \quad i = 1, 2, \ldots, MC$$

drawn from the standard normal distribution, $N(0, 1)$. MC denotes the number of draws, which could be, for example, 1000. To confirm that the random numbers do indeed conform to the standard normal distribution, a histogram of the random numbers can be constructed and compared with the theoretical normal probability distribution function.

From these random numbers we can calculate a set of hypothetical returns for tomorrow as

$$\check{R}_{i,t+1} = \sigma_{t+1}\check{z}_{i,1}$$

Given these hypothetical returns, we can update the variance to get a set of hypothetical variances for the day after tomorrow, $t + 2$, as follows:

$$\check{\sigma}_{i,t+2}^2 = \omega + \alpha \check{R}_{i,t+1}^2 + \beta \sigma_{t+1}^2$$

Given a new set of artificial random numbers drawn from the $N(0, 1)$ distribution,

$$\check{z}_{i,2}, \quad i = 1, 2, \ldots, MC$$

we can calculate the hypothetical return on day $t + 2$ as

$$\check{R}_{i,t+2} = \check{\sigma}_{i,t+2}\check{z}_{i,2}$$

and variance is now updated by

$$\check{\sigma}_{i,t+3}^2 = \omega + \alpha \check{R}_{i,t+2}^2 + \beta \check{\sigma}_{i,t+2}^2$$

Graphically, we can illustrate the simulation of hypothetical daily returns from day $t + 1$ to day $t + K$ as

Each row corresponds to a so-called Monte Carlo simulation path, which branches out from σ_{t+1}^2 on the first day, but which does not branch out after that. On each day a given branch gets updated with a new random number, which is different from the one used any of the days before. We end up with MC sequences of hypothetical daily returns for day $t + 1$ through day $t + K$. From these hypothetical future daily returns, we can easily calculate the hypothetical K-day return from each Monte Carlo path as

$$\check{R}_{i,t+1:t+K} = \sum_{k=1}^{K} \check{R}_{i,t+k}, \quad \text{for } i = 1, 2, \ldots, MC$$

If we collect these MC hypothetical K-day returns in a set $\left\{ \check{R}_{i,t+1:t+K} \right\}_{i=1}^{MC}$, then we can calculate the K-day value at risk simply by calculating the $100p$ percentile as in

$$VaR_{t+1:t+K}^{p} = -Percentile\left\{ \left\{ \check{R}_{i,t+1:t+K} \right\}_{i=1}^{MC}, 100p \right\}$$

Notice that in contrast to the HS and WHS techniques introduced earlier, the GARCH-MCS method outlined here is truly conditional in nature as it builds on today's estimate of tomorrow's variance, σ_{t+1}^2.

Another key advantage of the MCS technique is its flexibility. We can use MCS for any assumed distribution of standardized returns—normality is not required. If we think the standardized $t(d)$ distribution with $d = 12$, for example, describes the data better, then we simply draw from this distribution. Commercial software packages typically contain the regular $t(d)$ distribution, but we can standardize these draws by multiplying by $\sqrt{(d-2)/d}$ as we saw in Chapter 4. Furthermore, the MCS technique can be used for any fully specified dynamic variance model.

5.6. FILTERED HISTORICAL SIMULATION (FHS)

So far in this chapter, we have discussed methods that take very different approaches: historical simulation (HS) is a completely model-free approach, which imposes virtually no structure on the distribution of returns: the historical returns calculated with today's weights are used directly to calculate a percentile. The Monte Carlo simulation (MCS) approach takes the opposite view and assumes parametric models for variance, correlation (if a disaggregate model is estimated), and the distribution of standardized returns. Random numbers are then drawn from this distribution to calculate the desired risk measure.

Both of these extremes in the model-free/model-based spectrum have pros and cons. Taking a model-based approach (MCS, for example) is good if the model is a fairly accurate description of reality. Taking a model-free approach (HS, for example) is sensible in that the observed data may capture features of the returns distribution that are not captured by any standard parametric model.

The filtered historical simulation approach (FHS), which we present next, attempts to combine the best of the model-based with the best of the model-free approaches in a very intuitive fashion. FHS combines model-based methods of variance with model-free methods of distribution in the following way.

Assume we have estimated a GARCH-type model of our portfolio variance. Although we are comfortable with our variance model, we are not comfortable making a specific distributional assumption about the standardized returns, such as a normal or a $\tilde{t}(d)$ distribution. Instead, we would like the past returns data to tell us about the distribution directly without making further assumptions.

To fix ideas, consider again the simple example of a GARCH(1,1) model:

$$R_{t+1} = \sigma_{t+1} z_{t+1}$$

where

$$\sigma_{t+1}^2 = \omega + \alpha R_t^2 + \beta \sigma_t^2$$

Given a sequence of past returns, $\{R_{t+1-\tau}\}_{\tau=1}^{m}$, we can estimate the GARCH model and calculate past standardized returns from the observed returns and from the estimated standard deviations as

$$\hat{z}_{t+1-\tau} = R_{t+1-\tau}/\sigma_{t+1-\tau}, \quad \text{for } \tau = 1, 2, \ldots, m$$

We will refer to the set of standardized returns as $\left\{\hat{z}_{t+1-\tau}\right\}_{\tau=1}^{m}$.

Moving forward now, at the end of day t we obtain R_t and we can calculate σ_{t+1}^2, which is day $t + 1$'s variance in the GARCH model. Instead of drawing random $\hat{z}$s from a random number generator, which relies on a specific distribution, we can draw with replacement from our own database of past standardized residuals, $\left\{\hat{z}_{t+1-\tau}\right\}_{\tau=1}^{m}$. The random drawing can be operationalized by generating a discrete uniform random variable distributed from 1 to m. Each draw from the discrete distribution then tells us which τ and thus which $\hat{z}_{t+1-\tau}$ to pick from the set $\left\{\hat{z}_{t+1-\tau}\right\}_{\tau=1}^{m}$.

We again build up a distribution of hypothetical future returns as

$$\sigma_{t+1}^2 \longrightarrow \begin{array}{llll} \hat{z}_{1,1} \to \hat{R}_{1,t+1} \to \hat{\sigma}_{1,t+2}^2 & \hat{z}_{1,2} \to \hat{R}_{1,t+2} \to \hat{\sigma}_{1,t+3}^2 & \cdots & \hat{z}_{1,K} \to \hat{R}_{1,t+K} \\ \hat{z}_{2,1} \to \hat{R}_{2,t+1} \to \hat{\sigma}_{2,t+2}^2 & \hat{z}_{2,2} \to \hat{R}_{2,t+2} \to \hat{\sigma}_{2,t+3}^2 & \cdots & \hat{z}_{2,K} \to \hat{R}_{2,t+K} \\ \cdots & \cdots & \cdots & \cdots \\ \cdots & \cdots & \cdots & \cdots \\ \hat{z}_{FH,1} \to \hat{R}_{FH,t+1} \to \hat{\sigma}_{FH,t+2}^2 & \hat{z}_{FH,2} \to \hat{R}_{FH,t+2} \to \hat{\sigma}_{FH,t+3}^2 & \cdots & \hat{z}_{FH,K} \to \hat{R}_{FH,t+K} \end{array}$$

where FH is the number of times we draw from the standardized residuals on each future date, for example, 1000, and where K is the horizon of interest measured in number of days.

We end up with FH sequences of hypothetical daily returns for day $t + 1$ through day $t + K$. From these hypothetical daily returns, we calculate the hypothetical K-day returns as

$$\hat{R}_{i,t+1:t+K} = \sum_{k=1}^{K} \hat{R}_{i,t+k}, \quad \text{for } i = 1, 2, \ldots, FH$$

If we collect the FH hypothetical K-day returns in a set $\left\{\hat{R}_{i,t+1:t+K}\right\}_{i=1}^{FH}$, then we can calculate the K-day value at risk simply by calculating the $100p$ percentile as in

$$VaR_{t+1:t+K}^{p} = -Percentile\left\{\left\{\hat{R}_{i,t+1:t+K}\right\}_{i=1}^{FH}, 100p\right\}$$

In the case where $K = 1$, the variance is known and sampling is not necessary. We can simply calculate the 1-day VaR using the percentile of the database of standardized residuals as in

$$VaR_{t+1}^{p} = -\sigma_{t+1}Percentile\left\{\left\{\hat{z}_{t+1-\tau}\right\}_{\tau=1}^{m}, 100p\right\}$$

At the end of Chapter 4, we introduced expected shortfall (ES) as an alternative risk measure to VaR. ES is defined as a the expected return given that the return falls below the VaR. For the K-day horizon, we have

$$ES^p_{t+1:t+K} = -E_t\left[R_{t+1:t+K}|R_{t+1:t+K} < -VaR^p_{t+1:t+K}\right]$$

The ES measure can be calculated from the simulated returns by simply taking the average of all the $\hat{R}_{i,t+1:t+K}$s that fall below the $-VaR^p_{t+1:t+K}$ number— that is

$$ES^p_{t+1:t+K} = \frac{-1}{p*FH} * \sum_{i=1}^{FH} \hat{R}_{i,t+1:t+K} * \mathbf{1}\left(\hat{R}_{i,t+1:t+K} < -VaR^p_{t+1:t+K}\right)$$

where the indicator function $\mathbf{1}(*)$ returns a one if the argument is true and zero if not. The ES risk measure can be calculated from Monte Carlo simulation in a similar fashion. Notice that it is, however, not obvious how to calculate ES from historical simulation or weighted historical simulation.

Another interesting and useful feature of FHS as compared with simple HS is that it can generate large losses in the forecast period, even without having observed a large loss in the recorded past returns. Consider the case where we have a relatively large negative z in our database, which occurred on a relatively low variance day. If this z gets combined with a high-variance day in the simulation period, then the resulting hypothetical loss will be large.

We close this section by reemphasizing that the FHS method suggested here combines a conditional model for variance with a historical simulation method for the standardized returns. FHS thus retains the key conditionality feature through σ_{t+1} but relieves us from having to make assumptions about the tail distribution. Building on the variance and correlation models from Chapters 2 and 3, FHS thus represents a viable alternative to the model-based distributional models in Chapter 4. Finally and most important, the FHS method has been found to perform very well in several studies, and it should be given serious consideration by any risk management team.

5.7. SUMMARY

Risk managers have a variety of methods to choose from when building a risk management system. The purpose of this chapter has been to introduce a variety of simulation-based methods ranging from completely model-free approaches such as historical simulation to completely model-based approaches such as Monte Carlo simulation. We have underscored the benefits of conditional approaches, which use all the relevant information available at any given time. Such considerations have motivated the introduction of filtered historical simulation, which combines conditional variance models with historical simulation of the standardized returns.

As an added advantage, FHS can easily be used to calculate risk measures for any given horizon of interest.

5.8. FURTHER RESOURCES

Useful overviews of the various approaches to value at risk calculation can be found in Duffie and Pan (1997) and Manganelli (2000).

Bodoukh, Richardson, and Whitelaw (1998) introduce the weighted historical simulation approach. They find that it compares favorably with both the HS approach and the RiskMetrics model.

Christoffersen, Diebold, and Schuermann (1998) elaborate on the issues involved in calculating VaRs at different horizons. Diebold, Hickman, Inoue, and Schuermann (1998) study the problems arising from simple scaling rules of variance across horizons. Christoffersen and Diebold (2000) investigate the usefulness of dynamic variance models for risk management at various forecast horizons.

Hull and White (1998) and Barone-Adesi, Giannopoulos, and Vosper (1999) introduce the filtered historical simulation approach, and Barone-Adesi, Giannopoulos, and Vosper (2000) consider an application of FHS to portfolios of options and futures. Figures 5.2 and 5.3 follow Pritsker (2001), who finds that the FHS approach compares favorably with the HS and WHS approaches.

Finally, Engle and Manganelli (1999) suggest an interesting alternative method for VaR calculation based on conditional quantile regression, which was not discussed.

5.9. EMPIRICAL EXERCISES ON CD-ROM

Open the Chapter5data.xls file on the CD-ROM. Use sheet 1 for questions 1 and 2, and sheet 2 for questions 3 and 4.

1. Assume you are long \$1 of the S&P 500 index on each day. Calculate the 1-day, 1% VaRs on each day in October 1987 using historical simulation and weighted historical simulation. You can ignore the linear interpolation part of WHS. Use a weighting parameter of $\eta = 0.99$ in WHS. Use a 250-day moving sample size for both HS and WHS. (*Excel Hint*: Sort the returns along with their weights by selecting both columns in Excel and sorting by returns.) Plot losses and VaRs from HS and losses and VaRs from WHS in two different figures. Compare your result with Figure 5.2. Note that we are comparing losses (i.e., negative returns) with VaRs denoted as positive numbers.

2. Redo question 1, assuming instead that you are short \$1 of the S&P 500 each day. Compare your result with Figure 5.3.

3. For each day in 2001, calculate the 1-day, 1% VaRs using the following methods: (a) RiskMetrics, that is, normal distribution with an exponential smoother on variance using the weight, $\lambda = 0.94$; (b) GARCH(1,1)-$\tilde{t}(d)$ with parameters estimated in Chapter 4, question 5; (c) historical simulation; and (d) filtered historical simulation (*Excel Hint*: Use the sampling tool in data analysis.) Use a 251-day moving sample. Plot the VaRs along with the return.

4. Estimate 10-day, 1% VaRs on December 29, 2000, using FHS (with 1000 simulations), RiskMetrics scaling the daily VaRs by $\sqrt{10}$ (although it is incorrect), and GARCH(1,1)-$\tilde{t}(d)$ with parameters estimated in Chapter 4, question 5. (*Excel Hint*: To simulate returns, generate uniformly distributed random numbers from 0.000001 to 0.999999. To obtain $\tilde{t}(d)$ distributed random numbers for the standardized returns in the GARCH model, use the TINV function in Excel the same way it was used in Chapter 4.)

The answers to these exercises can be found in the Chapter5Results.xls file. Previews of the answers follow.

Calculating 1-day 1% VaRs HS and WHS for October 1987, assuming being long S&P500

	Date	Close	Return	Minus Return	Past Horizon	Daily Weights	VaR (HS)	VaR (WHS)		
									Constant	0.99
									Cut off	0.01
									Number of observations	250
250	24-Sep-87	319.72	-0.46%	0.46%	5	0.0105				
251	25-Sep-87	320.16	0.14%	-0.14%	4	0.0106				
252	28-Sep-87	323.20	0.95%	-0.95%	3	0.0107				
253	29-Sep-87	321.69	-0.47%	0.47%	2	0.0108				
254	30-Sep-87	321.83	0.04%	-0.04%	1	0.0109				
255	01-Oct-87	327.33	1.69%	-1.69%			2.37%	2.37%		
256	02-Oct-87	328.07	0.23%	-0.23%			2.37%	2.37%		
257	05-Oct-87	328.08	0.00%	0.00%			2.37%	2.37%		
258	06-Oct-87	319.22	-2.74%	2.74%			2.37%	2.37%		
259	07-Oct-87	318.54	-0.21%	0.21%			2.43%	2.74%		
260	08-Oct-87	314.16	-1.38%	1.38%			2.43%	2.74%		
261	09-Oct-87	311.07	-0.99%	0.99%			2.43%	2.74%		
262	12-Oct-87	309.39	-0.54%	0.54%			2.43%	2.74%		
263	13-Oct-87	314.52	1.64%	-1.64%			2.43%	2.74%		
264	14-Oct-87	305.23	-3.00%	3.00%			2.43%	2.74%		
265	15-Oct-87	298.08	-2.37%	2.37%			2.58%	3.00%		
266	16-Oct-87	282.70	-5.30%	5.30%			2.58%	3.00%		
267	19-Oct-87	224.84	-22.90%	22.90%			2.71%	5.30%		
268	20-Oct-87	236.83	5.20%	-5.20%			2.87%	22.90%		
269	21-Oct-87	258.38	8.71%	-8.71%			2.87%	22.90%		
270	22-Oct-87	248.25	-4.00%	4.00%			2.87%	22.90%		
271	23-Oct-87	248.22	-0.01%	0.01%			3.51%	22.90%		
272	26-Oct-87	227.67	-8.64%	8.64%			3.51%	22.90%		
273	27-Oct-87	233.19	2.40%	-2.40%			4.66%	22.90%		
274	28-Oct-87	233.28	0.04%	-0.04%			4.66%	22.90%		
275	29-Oct-87	244.77	4.81%	-4.81%			4.66%	22.90%		

QUESTION 1

Calculating 1-day 1% VaRs HS and WHS for October 1987, assuming being short S&P500

	Date	Close	Return	Minus Return	Past Horizon	Daily Weights	VaR (HS)	VaR (WHS)			
1									Constant	0.99	
2									Cut off	0.01	
3									Number of observations	250	
251	25-Sep-87	320.16	-0.14%	0.14%	4	0.0106					
252	28-Sep-87	323.20	-0.95%	0.95%	3	0.0107					
253	29-Sep-87	321.69	0.47%	-0.47%	2	0.0108					
254	30-Sep-87	321.83	-0.04%	0.04%	1	0.0109					
255	01-Oct-87	327.33	-1.69%	1.69%			2.36%	2.84%			
256	02-Oct-87	328.07	-0.23%	0.23%			2.36%	2.84%			
257	05-Oct-87	328.08	0.00%	0.00%			2.36%	2.84%			
258	06-Oct-87	319.22	2.74%	-2.74%			2.36%	2.43%			
259	07-Oct-87	318.54	0.21%	-0.21%			2.36%	2.43%			
260	08-Oct-87	314.16	1.38%	-1.38%			2.36%	2.43%			
261	09-Oct-87	311.07	0.99%	-0.99%			2.36%	2.43%			
262	12-Oct-87	309.39	0.54%	-0.54%			2.36%	2.43%			
263	13-Oct-87	314.52	-1.64%	1.64%			2.36%	2.43%			
264	14-Oct-87	305.23	3.00%	-3.00%			2.36%	2.43%			
265	15-Oct-87	298.08	2.37%	-2.37%			2.36%	2.43%			
266	16-Oct-87	282.70	5.30%	-5.30%			2.36%	2.43%			
267	19-Oct-87	224.84	22.90%	-22.90%			2.36%	2.43%			
268	20-Oct-87	236.83	-5.20%	5.20%			2.36%	2.43%			
269	21-Oct-87	258.38	-8.71%	8.71%			2.42%	5.20%			
270	22-Oct-87	248.25	4.00%	-4.00%			2.64%	8.71%			
271	23-Oct-87	248.22	0.01%	-0.01%			2.64%	8.71%			
272	26-Oct-87	227.67	8.64%	-8.64%			2.64%	8.71%			
273	27-Oct-87	233.19	-2.40%	2.40%			2.64%	8.71%			
274	28-Oct-87	233.28	-0.04%	0.04%			2.64%	8.71%			
275	29-Oct-87	244.77	-4.81%	4.81%			2.64%	8.71%			
276	30-Oct-87	251.79	-2.83%	2.83%			3.85%	8.71%			

QUESTION 2

Calculating 1-day 1% VaRs for 2001 using HS, Risk Metrics, GARCH-t and FHS models

Close	Return	Risk Metrics Conditional	GARCH-t Conditional	Returns / Standard Deviation	VaR			
					HS	Risk Metrics	GARCH-t	FHS
1455.22								
1399.42	-3.91%	0.000196	0.000196	-2.7893				
1402.11	0.19%	0.000276	0.000379	0.0986				
1403.45	0.10%	0.000260	0.000346	0.0514				
1441.47	2.67%	0.000245	0.000319	1.4963				
1457.60	1.11%	0.000273	0.000228	0.7365				
1436.56	-1.31%	0.000264	0.000185	-0.9659				
1432.25	-0.44%	0.000258	0.000224	-0.2934				
1449.68	1.21%	0.000244	0.000228	0.8010				
1465.15	1.06%	0.000238	0.000183	0.7847				
1455.14	-0.69%	0.000231	0.000149	-0.5617				
1455.90	0.05%	0.000220	0.000165	0.0407				
1445.57	-0.71%	0.000206	0.000157	-0.5686				
1441.36	-0.29%	0.000197	0.000173	-0.2217				
1401.53	-2.80%	0.000186	0.000175	-2.1195				
1410.03	0.60%	0.000222	0.000286	0.3578				
1404.09	-0.42%	0.000211	0.000248	-0.2682				
1398.56	-0.39%	0.000199	0.000249	-0.2499				
1360.16	-2.78%	0.000188	0.000250	-1.7617				
1394.46	2.49%	0.000223	0.000369	1.2973				
1409.28	1.06%	0.000247	0.000269	0.6450				
1409.12	-0.01%	0.000239	0.000220	-0.0076				
1424.97	1.12%	0.000225	0.000209	0.7730				
1424.37	-0.04%	0.000219	0.000170	-0.0323				
1424.24	-0.01%	0.000206	0.000164	-0.0071				
1441.72	1.22%	0.000193	0.000158	0.9704				

Risk Metrics

λ	0.94
$1-\lambda$	0.06
Persistence	1.00

GARCH-t

α	0.0472
β	0.6669
ω	0.0000085
θ	2.3143
d	12.5926
Persistence	0.9570
Cut off	0.01

QUESTION 3

QUESTION 4

Estimating 10-day 1% VaRs for FHS, GARCH-t and Risk Metrics models

Date	Close	Return	Risk Metrics Conditional	GARCH-t Condition	Retuns / Standard
03-Jan-00	1455.22				
04-Jan-00	1399.42	-3.91%	0.000197	0.000197	-2.7866
05-Jan-00	1402.11	0.19%	0.000277	0.000360	0.0985
06-Jan-00	1403.45	0.10%	0.000260	0.000346	0.0514
07-Jan-00	1441.47	2.67%	0.000245	0.000320	1.4954
10-Jan-00	1457.60	1.11%	0.000273	0.000229	0.7361
11-Jan-00	1438.56	-1.31%	0.000264	0.000186	-0.9653
12-Jan-00	1432.25	-0.44%	0.000259	0.000225	-0.2933
13-Jan-00	1449.68	1.21%	0.000244	0.000228	0.8007
14-Jan-00	1465.15	1.06%	0.000238	0.000183	0.7843
18-Jan-00	1455.14	-0.69%	0.000231	0.000149	-0.5614
19-Jan-00	1455.90	0.05%	0.000220	0.000165	0.0407
20-Jan-00	1445.57	-0.71%	0.000207	0.000157	-0.5684
21-Jan-00	1441.36	-0.29%	0.000197	0.000173	-0.2216
24-Jan-00	1401.53	-2.80%	0.000186	0.000175	-2.1188
25-Jan-00	1410.03	0.60%	0.000222	0.000286	0.3577
26-Jan-00	1404.09	-0.42%	0.000211	0.000248	-0.2681
27-Jan-00	1398.56	-0.39%	0.000199	0.000249	-0.2499
28-Jan-00	1360.16	-2.78%	0.000188	0.000250	-1.7613
31-Jan-00	1394.46	2.49%	0.000223	0.000369	1.2971
01-Feb-00	1409.28	1.06%	0.000247	0.000269	0.6449
02-Feb-00	1409.12	-0.01%	0.000239	0.000220	-0.0076
03-Feb-00	1424.97	1.12%	0.000225	0.000209	0.7729
04-Feb-00	1424.37	-0.04%	0.000219	0.000170	-0.0323
07-Feb-00	1424.24	-0.01%	0.000206	0.000164	-0.0071
08-Feb-00	1441.72	1.22%	0.000193	0.000158	0.9703
09-Feb-00	1411.71	-2.10%	0.000191	0.000126	-1.8750

Risk Metrics

λ	0.9400
$1-\lambda$	0.0600

GARCH-t

α	0.0472
β	0.6569
ω	0.0000085
θ	2.3143
d	12.5926

10-day VaR on 12/29/00

Risk Metrics	9.79%
GARCH-t	12.49%
FHS	14.41%
Cut off	1.00%

REFERENCES

Barone-Adesi, G., K. Giannopoulos, and L. Vosper. (1999). "VaR without Correlations for nonlinear Portfolios," *Journal of Futures Markets*, 19, 583–602.

Barone-Adesi, G., K. Giannopoulos, and L. Vosper. (2000). "Backtesting Derivative Portfolios with FHS," Manuscript, USI and City Business School.

Bodoukh, J., M. Richardson, and R. Whitelaw. (1998). "The Best of Both Worlds," *Risk*, 11, May, 64–67.

Christoffersen, P., and F. Diebold. (2000). "How Relevant Is Volatility Forecasting for Financial Risk Management?" *Review of Economics and Statistics*, 82, 1–11.

Christoffersen, P., F. Diebold, and T. Schuermann. (1998, October). "Horizon Problems and Extreme Events in Financial Risk Management," *Economic Policy Review*, Federal Reserve Bank of New York, 109–118.

Diebold, F. X., A. Hickman, A. Inoue, and T. Schuermann. (1998). "Scale Models," *Risk*, 11, 104–107.

Duffie, D., and J. Pan. (1997). "An Overview of Value at Risk," *Journal of Derivatives*, 4, 7–49.

Engle, R., and S. Manganelli. (1999). "CAViaR: Conditional Value at Risk by Quantile Regression," Manuscript, NYU Stern.

Hull, J., and A. White. (1998). "Incorporating Volatility Updating into the Historical Simulation Method for VaR," *Journal of Risk*, 1, 5–19.

Manganelli, S. (2000). "Value at Risk Models in Finance," Manuscript, European Central Bank.

Pritsker, M. (2001). "The Hidden Dangers of Historical Simulation," Manuscript, Federal Reserve Board.

6

OPTION PRICING

6.1. CHAPTER OVERVIEW

The previous chapters have established a framework for constructing the distribution of a portfolio of assets with simple linear payoffs—for example, stocks, bonds, foreign exchange, forwards, futures, and commodities. This chapter is devoted to the pricing of options. An option derives its value from an underlying asset but its payoff is not a linear function of the underlying asset price, and so the option price is not a linear function of the underlying asset price either. This nonlinearity adds complications to pricing and risk management.

In this chapter we will do the following:

1. Provide some basic definitions.
2. Establish an option pricing formula under the simplistic assumption that daily returns on the underlying asset follow an independent normal distribution with constant variance. We will refer to this as the Black-Scholes-Merton (BSM) formula. While the BSM model provides a useful benchmark, it systematically misprices observed options. We therefore consider the following alternatives.

3. Extend the normal distribution model by allowing for skewness and kurtosis in returns. We will rely on the Gram-Charlier expansion around the normal distribution to derive an option pricing formula in this case.

4. Extend the model by allowing for time-varying variance relying on the GARCH models from Chapter 2. Two GARCH option pricing models are considered: one allows for general variance specifications but requires Monte Carlo simulation or another numerical technique; the other assumes a specific variance dynamic but provides a closed form solution for the option price.

5. Introduce the ad hoc implied volatility function (IVF) approach to option pricing. The IVF method is not derived from any coherent theory but it works well in practice.

In this chapter, we will restrict attention to the pricing of European options, which can only be exercised on the maturity date. The following chapter will describe in detail the risk management techniques available when the portfolio contains options. At the end of the next chapter we will also provide the key references to pricing methods for American options, which can be exercised on any day up until the maturity date.

There is enough material in this chapter to fill an entire book, so needless to say the discussion will be brief. We will simply provide an overview of different available option pricing models and suggest further readings at the end of the chapter. This chapter thus assumes that the reader is already familiar with option pricing, including risk-neutral valuation.

6.2. BASIC DEFINITIONS

A European call option gives the owner the right but not the obligation (that is the *option*) to *buy* a unit of the underlying asset $\tilde{T}$ days from now at the price X. We refer to $\tilde{T}$ as the days to maturity and X as the strike price of the option. We denote the price of the European call option today by c, the price of the underlying asset today by S_t, and at maturity of the option by $S_{t+\tilde{T}}$.

A European put option gives the owner of the option the right to *sell* a unit of the underlying asset $\tilde{T}$ days from now at the price X. We denote the price of the European put option today by p. The European option restricts the owner from exercising the option before the maturity date. American options can be exercised any time before the maturity date.

We note that the number of days to maturity, $\tilde{T}$, is counted in calendar days and not in trading days. A standard year of course has 365 calendar days but only around 252 trading days. In previous chapters we have been using trading days for returns and value-at-risk (VaR) horizons, for example, referring to a two-week VaR as a 10-day VaR. In this chapter it is therefore important to note that we are using 365 days per year when calculating volatilities and interest rates.

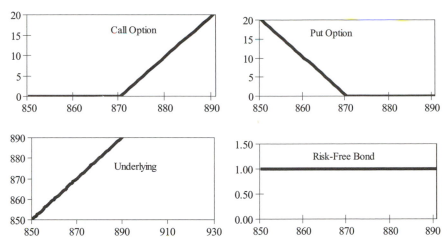

FIGURE 6.1 Payoffs as a Function of the Value of the Underlying Asset at Maturity. Call Option, Put Option, Underlying asset, Risk-Free Bond.

The payoff function is the option's defining characteristic. Figure 6.1 contains four panels. The top left panel shows the payoff from a call option and the top right panel shows the payoff of a put option both with a strike price of 870. The payoffs are drawn as a function of the hypothetical price of the underlying asset at maturity of the option, $S_{t+\tilde{T}}$. Mathematically, the payoff function for a call option is

$$Max\left\{S_{t+\tilde{T}} - X, 0\right\}$$

and for a put option is

$$Max\left\{X - S_{t+\tilde{T}}, 0\right\}$$

The bottom left panel of Figure 6.1 shows the payoff function of the underlying asset itself, which is simply a straight line with a slope of one. The bottom right-hand panel shows the value at maturity of a risk-free bond, which pays the face value 1, at maturity $t + \tilde{T}$ regardless of the future price of the underlying risky asset and indeed regardless of any other assets. Notice the linear payoffs of stocks and bonds and the nonlinear payoffs of options.

6.3. OPTION PRICING UNDER THE NORMAL DISTRIBUTION

We start off by going back to the most simple assumptions we made about asset returns. Let daily returns on an asset be independently and identically distributed according to the normal distribution,

$$R_{t+1} = \ln(S_{t+1}) - \ln(S_t) \sim N(\mu, \sigma^2)$$

Then the aggregate return over $\tilde{T}$ days will also be normally distributed with the mean and variance appropriately scaled as in

$$R_{t+1:t+\tilde{T}} = \ln(S_{t+\tilde{T}}) - \ln(S_t) \sim N(\tilde{T}\mu, \tilde{T}\sigma^2)$$

and the future asset price can of course be written as

$$S_{t+\tilde{T}} = S_t \exp\left(R_{t+1:t+\tilde{T}}\right)$$

The so-called risk-neutral valuation principle calculates the option price as the discounted expected payoff, where discounting is done using the risk-free rate and where the expectation is taken using the risk-neutral distribution:

$$c = \exp\left(-r\tilde{T}\right)E_t^*\left[Max\left\{S_{t+\tilde{T}} - X, 0\right\}\right]$$

where $Max\left\{S_{t+\tilde{T}} - X, 0\right\}$ as before is the payoff function and where r is the risk-free interest rate per day. The expectation $E_t^*[*]$ is taken using the risk-neutral distribution where all assets earn an expected return equal to the risk-free rate. In this case, the option price can be written as

$$c = \exp\left(-r\tilde{T}\right)\int_{-\infty}^{\infty} Max\left\{S_t \exp\left(x^*\right) - X, 0\right\} f(x^*)\,dx^*$$

$$= \exp\left(-r\tilde{T}\right)\int_{\ln(X/S_t)}^{\infty} S_t \exp\left(x^*\right)f(x^*)\,dx^* - \int_{\ln(X/S_t)}^{\infty} Xf(x^*)\,dx^*$$

where x^* is the risk-neutral variable corresponding to the underlying asset return between now and the maturity of the option. $f(x^*)$ denotes the risk-neutral distribution, which we take to be the normal so that $x^* \sim N(\tilde{T}r, \tilde{T}\sigma^2)$. The second integral is easily evaluated whereas the first requires several steps. In the end, one obtains the call option price

$$c_{BSM} = \exp\left(-r\tilde{T}\right)\left[S_t \exp\left(r\tilde{T}\right)\Phi(d) - X\Phi\left(d - \sigma\sqrt{\tilde{T}}\right)\right]$$

$$= S_t\Phi(d) - \exp\left(-r\tilde{T}\right)X\Phi\left(d - \sigma\sqrt{\tilde{T}}\right)$$

where $\Phi(z)$ is the cumulative density of a standard normal variable, and where

$$d = \frac{\ln\left(S_t/X\right) + \tilde{T}\left(r + \sigma^2/2\right)}{\sigma\sqrt{\tilde{T}}}$$

We will refer to this as the Black-Scholes-Merton (BSM) model. Black, Scholes, and Merton derived this pricing formula in the early 1970s using a model where trading takes place in continuous time. Assuming continuous trading only the absence of arbitrage opportunities is needed to derive the formula.

It is worth emphasizing that to stay consistent with the rest of the book, the volatility and risk-free interest rates are both denoted in daily terms, and option maturity is denoted in number of calendar days, as this is market convention.

The elements in the option pricing formula have the following interpretation:

- $\Phi\left(d - \sigma\sqrt{\tilde{T}}\right)$ is the risk-neutral probability of exercise.

- $X\Phi\left(d - \sigma\sqrt{\tilde{T}}\right)$ is the expected risk-neutral payout at exercise.

- $S_t\Phi(d)\exp(r\tilde{T})$ is the risk-neutral expected value of the stock acquired through exercise of the option.

- $\Phi(d)$ measures the sensitivity of the option price to changes in the underlying asset price, S_t, and is referred to as the delta of the option, where $\delta_{BSM} \equiv \frac{\partial c_{BSM}}{\partial S_t}$ is the first derivative of the option with respect to the underlying asset price. This and other sensitivity measures are discussed in detail in the next chapter.

To get the price of a European put option, p, we invoke the put-call parity, which is a simple no-arbitrage condition that does not rely on any particular option pricing model. It states

$$S_t + p = c + X\exp(-r\tilde{T})$$

It can be derived from considering two portfolios: One consists of the underlying asset and the put option, and another consists of the call option and a cash position equal to the discounted value of the strike price. Whether the underlying asset price at maturity, $S_{t+\tilde{T}}$, ends up below or above the strike price X, both portfolios will have the same value, namely $Max\left\{S_{t+\tilde{T}}, X\right\}$, at maturity and therefore they must have the same value today for the no-arbitrage condition to hold. The portfolio values underlying this argument are shown in the following table:

Time t	Time $t+\tilde{T}$	
Portfolio I	If $S_{t+\tilde{T}} \leq X$	If $S_{t+\tilde{T}} > X$
S_t	$S_{t+\tilde{T}}$	$S_{t+\tilde{T}}$
p	$X - S_{t+\tilde{T}}$	0
$S_t + p$	X	$S_{t+\tilde{T}}$
Portfolio II	If $S_{t+\tilde{T}} \leq X$	If $S_{t+\tilde{T}} > X$
c	0	$S_{t+\tilde{T}} - X$
$X\exp(-r\tilde{T})$	X	X
$c + X\exp(-r\tilde{T})$	X	$S_{t+\tilde{T}}$

The put-call parity also suggests how options can be used in risk management. Suppose an investor who has an investment horizon of $\tilde{T}$ days owns a stock with current value S_t. The value of the of the stock at the maturity of the option is $S_{t+\tilde{T}}$, which in the worst case could be zero. But an investor who owns the stock along with a put option with a strike price of X is guaranteed the future portfolio value $Max\left\{S_{t+\tilde{T}}, X\right\}$, which is at least X. The downside of the stock portfolio including this so-called protective put is thus limited, where as the upside is still unlimited. The protection is not free however as buying the put option requires paying the current put option price or premium, p.

Using the put-call parity result and the formula for c_{BSM}, we can get the put price formula as

$$p_{BSM} = c_{BSM} + X \exp(-r\tilde{T}) - S_t$$

$$= e^{-r\tilde{T}} \left\{ X \left[1 - \Phi\left(d - \sigma\sqrt{\tilde{T}}\right) \right] - S_t \left[1 - \Phi(d) \right] e^{r\tilde{T}} \right\}$$

$$= e^{-r\tilde{T}} X \Phi\left(\sigma\sqrt{\tilde{T}} - d\right) - S_t \Phi(-d)$$

where the last line comes from the symmetry of the normal distribution, which implies that $[1 - \Phi(z)] = \Phi(-z)$.

In the case where cash flows such as dividends accrue to the underlying asset, we discount the current asset price to account for the cash flows by replacing S_t by $S_t \exp(-q\tilde{T})$ everywhere, where q is the expected rate of cash flow per day until maturity of the option. This adjustment can be made to both the call and the put price formula, and in both cases the formula for d will then be

$$d = \frac{\ln(S_t/X) + \tilde{T}(r - q + \sigma^2/2)}{\sigma\sqrt{\tilde{T}}}$$

The adjustment is made because the option holder at maturity receives only the underlying asset on that date and not the cash flow that has accrued to the asset during the life of the option. This cash flow is retained by the owner of the underlying asset.

We now want to use the Black-Scholes pricing model to price a European call option written on the S&P 500 index. On August 29, 2002, the value of the index was 917.80. The European call option has a strike price of 890 and 23 days to maturity. The risk-free interest rate for a 23 day holding period is found from the T-bill rates to be 0.004521% per day (that is, 0.00004521) and the dividend accruing to the index over the next 23 days is expected to be 0.004360% per day. For now we assume the volatility of the index is 1.341285% per day. Thus, we have

$$S_t = 917.80$$

$$X = 890$$

$$\tilde{T} = 23$$

$$r = 0.004521\%$$

$$q = 0.004360\%$$

$$\sigma = 1.341285\%$$

and we can calculate

$$d = \frac{\ln(S_t/X) + \tilde{T}(r - q + \sigma^2/2)}{\sigma\sqrt{\tilde{T}}} = 0.510896, \quad \text{and } d - \sigma\sqrt{\tilde{T}} = 0.446570$$

which gives

$$\Phi(d) = 0.695288, \quad \text{and} \quad \Phi\left(d - \sigma\sqrt{\tilde{T}}\right) = 0.672407$$

from which we can calculate the BSM call option price as

$$c_{BSM} = S_t \exp\left(-q\tilde{T}\right)\Phi(d) - \exp\left(-r\tilde{T}\right)X\Phi\left(d - \sigma\sqrt{\tilde{T}}\right) = 39.68$$

6.3.1. Model Implementation

The simple model considered earlier implies that a European option price can be written as a nonlinear function of six variables,

$$c_{BSM} = c(S_t, r, X, \tilde{T}, q; \sigma)$$

The stock price is readily available, and a Treasury bill rate with maturity $\tilde{T}$ can be used as the risk-free interest rate. The strike price and time to maturity are known features of any given option contract, thus only one parameter needs to be estimated—namely, the volatility, σ. As the option pricing formula is nonlinear, volatility can be estimated from a sample of n options on the same underlying asset, minimizing the mean-squared dollar pricing error (MSE)

$$MSE_{BSM} = \min_{\sigma} \left\{ \frac{1}{n} \sum_{i=1}^{n} \left(c_i^{mkt} - c_{BSM}(S_t, r, X_i, \tilde{T}_i, q; \sigma) \right)^2 \right\}$$

where c_i^{mkt} denotes the observed market price of option i. The CD-ROM, which contains answers to the exercises at the end of this chapter, includes an example of this numerical optimization. Notice that we could, of course, also have simply plugged in an estimate of σ from returns on the underlying asset; however, using the observed market prices of options tends to produce much more accurate model prices.

Using prices on a sample of 106 call options traded on the S&P 500 index on August 29, 2002, we estimate the volatility, which minimizes the MSE to be 1.341285% per day. This was the volatility estimate used in the numerical pricing example. Further details of this calculation can be found on the CD-ROM.

6.3.2. Implied Volatility

From Chapter 1, we know that the assumption of daily asset returns following the normal distribution is grossly violated in the data. We therefore should worry that an option pricing theory based on the normal distribution will not offer an appropriate description of reality. To assess the quality of the normality-based model, consider the so-called implied volatility calculated as

$$\sigma_{BSM}^{iv} = c_{BSM}^{-1}\left(S_t, r, X, \tilde{T}, q, c^{mkt}\right)$$

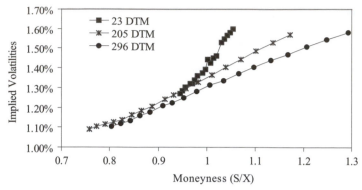

FIGURE 6.2   Implied BSM Daily Volatility from S&P 500 Index Options with 23, 205 and 296 Days to Maturity (DTM). Quoted on August 29, 2002.

where c^{mkt} again denotes the observed market price of the option, and where $c_{BSM}^{-1}(*)$ denotes the inverse of the BSM option pricing formula derived earlier. The implied volatilities can be found contract by contract by using a numerical equation solver.

Returning to the preceding numerical example of the S&P 500 call option traded on August 29, 2002, knowing that the actual market price for the option was 42.60, we can calculate the implied volatility to be

$$\sigma_{BSM}^{iv} = c_{BSM}^{-1}\left(S_t, r, X, \tilde{T}, q, 42.60\right) = 1.528620\%$$

where the $S_t, r, X, \tilde{T}$, and q variables are as in the preceding example. The 1.528620% volatility estimate is such that if we had used it in the BSM formula, then the model price would have equalled the market price exactly, that is,

$$42.60 = c_{BSM}\left(S_t, r, X, \tilde{T}, q, 1.528620\%\right)$$

If the normality assumption imposed on the model were true, then the implied volatility should be roughly constant across strike prices and maturities. However, actual option data displays systematic patterns in implied volatility, thus violating the normality based option pricing theory. Figure 6.2 shows the implied volatility of various S&P 500 index call options on August 29, 2002. The picture shows clear evidence of the so-called *smirk*. Furthermore, the smirk is most evident at shorter horizons. As we will see shortly, this smirk can arise from skewness in the underlying distribution, which is ignored in the BSM model relying on normality. Options on foreign exchange tend to show a more symmetric pattern of implied volatility, which is referred to as the *smile*. The smile can arise from kurtosis in the underlying distribution, which is again ignored in the BSM model.

Smirk and smile patterns in implied volatility constitute evidence of misspecification in the BSM model. Consider for example pricing options with the BSM formula using a daily volatility of approximately 1.3% for all options.

In Figure 6.2, the implied volatility is approximately 1.3% for at-the-money options where $S/X \approx 1$. Therefore, the BSM price would be roughly correct for these options. However, for options that are in the money—that is $S/X > 1$—the BSM implied volatility is higher than 1.3%, which says that the BSM model needs a higher than 1.3% volatility to fit the market data. This is because option prices are increasing in the underlying volatility. Using the BSM formula with a volatility of 1.3% would result in a BSM price that is too low. The BSM is thus said to underprice in-the-money call options. From the put-call formula, we can conclude that the BSM model also underprices out-of-the-money put options.

In the preceding example, the BSM formula calculated the price of a 23-day in-the-money call option to be 39.68 when using a volatility of approximately 1.3% per day. However, the actual market price was 42.60 resulting in an implied volatility of almost 1.53% per day as we also saw earlier. The BSM model underpriced the in-the-money call option in this particular example—a finding that is true more generally.

6.4. ALLOWING FOR SKEWNESS AND KURTOSIS

We now introduce a relatively simple model that is capable of making up for some of the obvious mispricing in the BSM model. We again have one-period returns defined as

$$R_{t+1} = \ln(S_{t+1}) - \ln(S_t)$$

and $\tilde{T}$-period returns as

$$R_{t+1:t+\tilde{T}} = \ln(S_{t+\tilde{T}}) - \ln(S_t).$$

The mean and variance of the daily returns are again defined as $E(R_{t+1}) = \mu$ and $E(R_{t+1} - \mu)^2 = \sigma^2$. In addition, we now define the skewness of the 1-day return as

$$\zeta_{11} = \frac{E(R_{t+1} - \mu)^3}{\sigma^3}$$

Skewness is informative about the degree of asymmetry of the distribution. A negative skewness arises from large negative returns being observed more frequently than large positive returns. Negative skewness is a stylized fact of equity index returns, as we saw in Chapter 1. Kurtosis of the 1-day return is defined as

$$\zeta_{21} = \frac{E(R_{t+1} - \mu)^4}{\sigma^4} - 3$$

which is sometimes referred to as excess kurtosis due to the subtraction by 3. Kurtosis tells us about the degree of tail fatness in the distribution of returns. If large (positive or negative) returns are more likely to occur in the data than in the normal distribution, then the kurtosis is positive. Asset returns typically have positive kurtosis.

Assuming that returns are independent over time, the skewness at horizon $\tilde{T}$ can be written as a simple function of the daily skewness,

$$\zeta_{1\tilde{T}} = \zeta_{11}/\sqrt{\tilde{T}}$$

and correspondingly for kurtosis

$$\zeta_{2\tilde{T}} = \zeta_{21}/\tilde{T}$$

Notice that both skewness and kurtosis will converge to zero as the return horizon, $\tilde{T}$, and thus the maturity of the option increases. This corresponds well with the implied volatility in Figure 6.2, which displayed a more pronounced smirk pattern for short-term as opposed to long term options.

We now define the standardized return at the $\tilde{T}$-day horizon as

$$w_{\tilde{T}} = \frac{R_{t+1:t+\tilde{T}} - \tilde{T}\mu}{\sqrt{\tilde{T}}\sigma}$$

so that

$$R_{t+1:t+\tilde{T}} = \mu\tilde{T} + \sigma\sqrt{\tilde{T}}w_{\tilde{T}}$$

and assume that the standardized returns follow the distribution given by the Gram-Charlier expansion, which is written as

$$f\left(w_{\tilde{T}}\right) = \phi\left(w_{\tilde{T}}\right) - \zeta_{1\tilde{T}}\frac{1}{3!}D^3\phi\left(w_{\tilde{T}}\right) + \zeta_{2\tilde{T}}\frac{1}{4!}D^4\phi\left(w_{\tilde{T}}\right)$$

where $\phi\left(w_{\tilde{T}}\right)$ is the standard normal density, and D^j is its jth derivative. We have

$$D^1\phi(z) = -z\phi(z)$$

$$D^2\phi(z) = \left(z^2 - 1\right)\phi(z)$$

$$D^3\phi(z) = -\left(z^3 - 3z\right)\phi(z)$$

$$D^4\phi(z) = \left(z^4 - 6z^2 + 3\right)\phi(z)$$

The Gram-Charlier density function $f\left(w_{\tilde{T}}\right)$ is an expansion around the normal density function, $\phi\left(w_{\tilde{T}}\right)$, allowing for a nonzero skewness, $\zeta_{1\tilde{T}}$, and kurtosis $\zeta_{2\tilde{T}}$. The Gram-Charlier expansion can approximate a wide range of densities with nonzero higher moments, and it collapses to the standard normal density when skewness and kurtosis are both zero. We notice the similarities with the Cornish-Fisher expansion for value at risk in Chapter 4, which is a similar expansion but for the inverse cumulative density function instead of the density function itself.

To price European options, we can again write the generic risk-neutral call pricing formula as

$$c = e^{-r\tilde{T}} E_t^* \left[Max\{S_{t+\tilde{T}} - X, 0\} \right]$$

Thus, we must solve

$$c = e^{-r\tilde{T}} \int_{\ln X/S_t}^{\infty} \left(S_t \exp(x^*) - X \right) f(x^*)\, dx^*$$

Earlier we relied on x^* following the normal distribution with mean r and variance σ^2 per day. But we now instead define the standardized risk-neutral return at horizon $\tilde{T}$ as

$$w_{\tilde{T}}^* = \frac{(x^* - r\tilde{T})}{\sqrt{\tilde{T}}\sigma}$$

and assume it follows the Gram-Charlier (GC) distribution.

In this case, the call option price can be derived as being approximately equal to

$$c_{GC} \approx S_t \Phi(d) - Xe^{-r\tilde{T}} \Phi\left(d - \sqrt{\tilde{T}}\sigma \right) + S_t \phi(d) \sqrt{\tilde{T}}\sigma \left[\frac{\zeta_{1\tilde{T}}}{3!} \left(2\sqrt{\tilde{T}}\sigma - d \right) \right.$$

$$\left. - \frac{\zeta_{2\tilde{T}}}{4!} \left(1 - d^2 + 3d\sqrt{\tilde{T}}\sigma - 3\tilde{T}\sigma^2 \right) \right]$$

$$= S_t \Phi(d) - Xe^{-r\tilde{T}} \Phi\left(d - \sqrt{\tilde{T}}\sigma \right) + S_t \phi(d) \sigma \left[\frac{\zeta_{11}}{3!} \left(2\sqrt{\tilde{T}}\sigma - d \right) \right.$$

$$\left. - \frac{\zeta_{21}/\sqrt{\tilde{T}}}{4!} \left(1 - d^2 + 3d\sqrt{\tilde{T}}\sigma - 3\tilde{T}\sigma^2 \right) \right]$$

where we have substituted in for skewness using $\zeta_{1\tilde{T}} = \zeta_{11}/\sqrt{\tilde{T}}$ and for kurtosis using $\zeta_{2\tilde{T}} = \zeta_{21}/\tilde{T}$. We will refer to this as the GC option pricing model. The approximation comes from setting the terms involving σ^3 and σ^4 to zero, which also enables us to use the definition of d from the BSM model. Using this approximation, the GC model is just the simple BSM model plus additional terms, which vanish if there is neither skewness ($\zeta_{11} = 0$) nor kurtosis ($\zeta_{21} = 0$) in the data. The GC formula can be extended to allow for a cash flow q in the same manner as the BSM formula shown earlier.

Recall the previous European call option example where

$$S_t = 917.80$$

$$X = 890$$

$$\tilde{T} = 23$$

$$r = 0.004521\%$$

$$q = 0.004360\%$$

Pricing the option using the GC formula, we will use the estimates

$$\sigma = 1.413912\%$$

$$\zeta_{11} = -10.610613$$

$$\zeta_{21} = 0$$

where the kurtosis has been set to zero because skewness is the main source of non-normality in equity index options. Using these estimates, we find

$$d = \frac{\ln\left(S_t/X\right) + \tilde{T}\left(r - q + \sigma^2/2\right)}{\sigma\sqrt{\tilde{T}}} = 0.488047, \quad \text{and} \quad d - \sigma\sqrt{\tilde{T}} = 0.420238$$

which gives

$$\Phi(d) = 0.687242, \quad \text{and} \quad \Phi\left(d - \sigma\sqrt{\tilde{T}}\right) = 0.662844$$

and a GC option price of

$$c_{GC} = 43.66$$

Notice that the GC model price is somewhat higher than the market price of 42.60 but still much closer than the BSM price of 39.68.

6.4.1. Model Implementation

This GC model has three unknown parameters: σ, ζ_{11}, and ζ_{21}. They can be estimated as before using a numerical optimizer minimizing the mean squared error

$$MSE_{GC} = \min_{\sigma, \zeta_{11}, \zeta_{21}} \left\{ \frac{1}{n} \sum_{i=1}^{n} \left(c_i^{mkt} - c_{GC}(S_t, r, X_i, \tilde{T}_i; \sigma, \zeta_{11}, \zeta_{21}) \right)^2 \right\}$$

We can calculate the implied BSM volatilities from the GC model prices by

$$\sigma_{GC}^{iv} = c_{BSM}^{-1}\left(S_t, r, X, \tilde{T}, c_{GC}\right)$$

where $c_{BSM}^{-1}(*)$ is the inverse of the BSM model with respect to volatility. But we can also rely on the following approximate formula for daily implied BSM volatility:

$$\sigma_{GC}^{iv} = c_{BSM}^{-1}\left(S_t, r, X, \tilde{T}, c_{GC}\right) \approx \sigma\sqrt{\tilde{T}}\left[1 - \frac{\zeta_{11}/\sqrt{\tilde{T}}}{3!}d - \frac{\zeta_{21}/\tilde{T}}{4!}\left(1 - d^2\right)\right]$$

Notice this is just volatility times an additional term, which equals one if there is no skewness or kurtosis. Figure 6.3 plots two implied volatility curves for options with 10 days to maturity. One has a skewness of -3 and a kurtosis of 7 and shows the smirk, and the other has no skewness but a kurtosis of 8 and shows a smile.

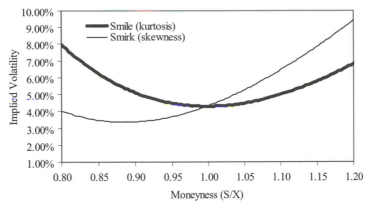

FIGURE 6.3 Implied BSM Volatility from Gram-Charlier Model Prices. The Asymmetric Smirk (from skewness) and the Symmetric Smile (from Kurtosis).

The main advantages of the GC option pricing framework are that it allows for deviations from normality, it provides closed form solutions for option prices, and, most important, it is able to capture the systematic patterns in implied volatility found in observed option data. For example, allowing for negative skewness implies that the GC option price will be higher than the BSM price for in-the-money calls, thus removing the tendency for BSM to underprice in-the-money calls, which we saw evidence of in Figure 6.2.

6.5. GARCH OPTION PRICING MODELS

While the GC model is capable of capturing implied volatility smiles and smirks at a given point in time, it assumes that volatility is constant over time and is thus inconsistent with the empirical observations we made earlier. Put differently, the GC model is able to capture the cross strike price structure but not the cross maturity structure in observed options prices. In Chapters 1 and 2 we saw that variance varies over time in a predictable fashion: High-variance days tend to be followed by high variance days and vice versa, which we modeled using GARCH and other types of models. When returns are independent, the standard deviation of returns at the $\tilde{T}$-day horizon is simply $\sqrt{\tilde{T}}$ times the daily volatility, whereas the GARCH model implies that the term structure of variance depends on the variance today and does not follow the simple square root rule.

We now consider option pricing allowing for the underlying asset returns to follow a GARCH process. The GARCH option pricing model assumes that the expected return on the underlying asset is equal to the risk-free rate, r, plus a premium for volatility risk, λ, as well as a normalization term. The observed daily return is then equal to the expected return plus a noise term. The noise term is conditionally normally distributed with mean zero and variance following a

GARCH(1,1) process with leverage as in Chapter 2. By letting the past return feed into variance in a magnitude depending on the sign of the return, the leverage effect creates an asymmetry in the distribution of returns. This asymmetry is important for capturing the skewness implied in observed option prices.

Specifically we can write the return process as

$$R_{t+1} \equiv \ln(S_{t+1}) - \ln(S_t) = r + \lambda \sigma_{t+1} - \frac{1}{2}\sigma_{t+1}^2 + \sigma_{t+1} z_{t+1}$$

with $z_{t+1} \sim N(0, 1)$, and $\sigma_{t+1}^2 = \omega + \alpha (\sigma_t z_t - \theta \sigma_t)^2 + \beta \sigma_t^2$

Notice that the expected value and variance of tomorrow's return conditional on all the information available at time t are

$$E_t[R_{t+1}] = r + \lambda \sigma_{t+1} - \frac{1}{2}\sigma_{t+1}^2$$

$$V_t[R_{t+1}] = \sigma_{t+1}^2$$

For a generic normally distributed variable $x \sim N(\mu, \sigma^2)$, we have that $E[\exp(x)] = \exp(\mu + \sigma^2/2)$ and thus we have that the conditional mean of one plus the rate of return for the preceding process is

$$E_t[S_{t+1}/S_t] = E_t\left[\exp\left(r + \lambda \sigma_{t+1} - \frac{1}{2}\sigma_{t+1}^2 + \sigma_{t+1} z_{t+1}\right)\right]$$

$$= \exp\left(r + \lambda \sigma_{t+1} - \frac{1}{2}\sigma_{t+1}^2\right) E_t \left[\exp\left(\sigma_{t+1} z_{t+1}\right)\right]$$

$$= \exp\left(r + \lambda \sigma_{t+1} - \frac{1}{2}\sigma_{t+1}^2\right) \exp\left(\frac{1}{2}\sigma_{t+1}^2\right)$$

$$= \exp\left(r + \lambda \sigma_{t+1}\right)$$

where we have used $\sigma_{t+1} z_{t+1} \sim N(0, \sigma_{t+1}^2)$. This expected return equation highlights the role of λ as the price of volatility risk.

We can again solve for the option price using the risk-neutral expectation as in

$$c = \exp(-r\tilde{T}) E_t^*\left[Max\left\{S_{t+\tilde{T}} - X, 0\right\}\right]$$

Under risk neutrality, we must have that

$$E_t^*[S_{t+1}/S_t] = \exp(r)$$

$$V_t^*[R_{t+1}] = \sigma_{t+1}^2$$

so that the expected rate of return on the risky asset equals the risk-free rate and the conditional variance under risk-neutrality is the same as under the original process. Consider the following process:

$$R_{t+1} \equiv \ln(S_{t+1}) - \ln(S_t) = r - \frac{1}{2}\sigma_{t+1}^2 + \sigma_{t+1} z_{t+1}^*$$

with $z_{t+1}^* \sim N(0, 1)$, and $\sigma_{t+1}^2 = \omega + \alpha \left(\sigma_t z_t^* - \lambda \sigma_t - \theta \sigma_t\right)^2 + \beta \sigma_t^2$

In this case, we can check that the conditional mean equals

$$E_t^* [S_{t+1}/S_t] = E_t^* \left[\exp \left(r - \frac{1}{2}\sigma_{t+1}^2 + \sigma_{t+1} z_{t+1}^* \right) \right]$$

$$= \exp \left(r - \frac{1}{2}\sigma_{t+1}^2 \right) E_t^* \left[\exp \left(\sigma_{t+1} z_{t+1}^* \right) \right]$$

$$= \exp \left(r - \frac{1}{2}\sigma_{t+1}^2 \right) \exp \left(\frac{1}{2}\sigma_{t+1}^2 \right)$$

$$= \exp(r)$$

which satisfies the first condition. Furthermore, the conditional variance under the risk neutral process equals

$$V_t^*[R_{t+1}] = E_t^* \left[\omega + \alpha \left(\sigma_t z_t^* - \lambda \sigma_t - \theta \sigma_t \right)^2 + \beta \sigma_t^2 \right]$$

$$= E_t \left[\omega + \alpha \left(R_t - r + \frac{1}{2}\sigma_{t+1}^2 - \lambda \sigma_t - \theta \sigma_t \right)^2 + \beta \sigma_t^2 \right]$$

$$= E_t \left[\omega + \alpha \left(\sigma_t z_t - \theta \sigma_t \right)^2 + \beta \sigma_t^2 \right]$$

$$= \sigma_{t+1}^2$$

where the last equality comes from tomorrow's variance being known at the end of today in the GARCH model. The conclusion is that the conditions for a risk-neutral process are met.

An advantage of the GARCH option pricing approach introduced here is its flexibility: The previous analysis could easily be redone for any of the GARCH variance models introduced in Chapter 2. More important, it is able to fit observed option prices quite well.

6.5.1. Model Implementation

While we have found a way to price the European option under risk neutrality, unfortunately, we do not have a closed-form solution available. Instead, we have to use simulation to calculate the price

$$c = \exp \left(-r\tilde{T} \right) E_t^* \left[Max \{ S_{t+\tilde{T}} - X, 0 \} \right]$$

The simulation can be done as follows: First notice that we can get rid of a parameter by writing

$$\sigma_{t+1}^2 = \omega + \alpha \left(\sigma_t z_t^* - \lambda \sigma_t - \theta \sigma_t \right)^2 + \beta \sigma_t^2$$

$$= \omega + \alpha \left(\sigma_t z_t^* - \lambda^* \sigma_t \right)^2 + \beta \sigma_t^2, \quad \text{with } \lambda^* \equiv \lambda + \theta.$$

Now, for a given conditional variance σ_{t+1}^2, and parameters, $\omega, \alpha, \beta, \lambda^*$, we can use Monte Carlo simulation as in Chapter 5, to create future hypothetical paths of the asset returns. Parameter estimation will be discussed subsequently. Graphically, we can illustrate the simulation of hypothetical daily returns from day $t+1$ to the maturity on day $t + \tilde{T}$ as

$$
\sigma_{t+1}^2 \nearrow \atop \searrow
\begin{array}{cccc}
\check{z}_{1,1}^* \to \check{R}_{1,t+1}^* \to \check{\sigma}_{1,t+2}^2 & \check{z}_{1,2}^* \to \check{R}_{1,t+2}^* \to \check{\sigma}_{1,t+3}^2 & \cdots & \check{z}_{1,\tilde{T}}^* \to \check{R}_{1,t+\tilde{T}}^* \\
\check{z}_{2,1}^* \to \check{R}_{2,t+1}^* \to \check{\sigma}_{2,t+2}^2 & \check{z}_{2,2}^* \to \check{R}_{2,t+2}^* \to \check{\sigma}_{2,t+3}^2 & \cdots & \check{z}_{2,\tilde{T}}^* \to \check{R}_{2,t+\tilde{T}}^* \\
\cdots & \cdots & \cdots & \cdots \\
\cdots & \cdots & \cdots & \cdots \\
\check{z}_{MC,1}^* \to \check{R}_{MC,t+1}^* \to \check{\sigma}_{MC,t+2}^2 & \check{z}_{MC,2}^* \to \check{R}_{MC,t+2}^* \to \check{\sigma}_{MC,t+3}^2 & \cdots & \check{z}_{MC,\tilde{T}}^* \to \check{R}_{MC,t+\tilde{T}}^*
\end{array}
$$

where the $\check{z}_{i,j}^*$s are obtained from a $N(0,1)$ random number generator and where MC is the number of simulated return paths. We need to calculate the expectation term $E_t^*[*]$ in the option pricing formula using the risk-neutral process, thus we calculate the simulated risk-neutral return in period $t+j$ for simulation path i as

$$
\check{R}_{i,t+j}^* = r - \frac{1}{2}\check{\sigma}_{i,t+j}^2 + \check{\sigma}_{i,t+j}\check{z}_{i,j}^*
$$

and the variance is updated by

$$
\check{\sigma}_{i,t+j+1}^2 = \omega + \alpha\left(\check{\sigma}_{i,t+j}\check{z}_{i,j}^* - \lambda^*\check{\sigma}_{i,t+j}\right)^2 + \beta\check{\sigma}_{i,t+j}^2
$$

As in Chapter 5, the simulation paths in the first period all start out from the same σ_{t+1}^2, therefore we have

$$
\check{R}_{i,t+1}^* = r - \frac{1}{2}\sigma_{t+1}^2 + \sigma_{t+1}\check{z}_{i,1}^*
$$

$$
\sigma_{i,t+2}^2 = \omega + \alpha\left(\sigma_{t+1}\check{z}_{i,1}^* - \lambda^*\sigma_{t+1}\right)^2 + \beta\sigma_{t+1}^2
$$

for all i.

Once we have simulated say 5000 paths ($MC = 5000$) each day until the maturity date, $\tilde{T}$, we can calculate the hypothetical risk-neutral asset prices at maturity as

$$
\check{S}_{i,t+\tilde{T}}^* = S_t \exp\left(\sum_{j=1}^{\tilde{T}} \check{R}_{i,t+j}^*\right), \quad i = 1, 2, \ldots, MC
$$

and the option price is calculated taking the average over the future hypothetical payoffs and discounting them to the present as in

$$
c_{GH} = \exp(-r\tilde{T}) E_t^*\left[Max\left\{S_{t+\tilde{T}} - X, 0\right\}\right]
$$

$$
\approx \exp(-r\tilde{T})\frac{1}{MC}\sum_{i=1}^{MC} Max\left\{\check{S}_{i,t+\tilde{T}}^* - X, 0\right\}
$$

where GH denotes GARCH.

Thus, we are using simulation to calculate the average future payoff, which is then used as an estimate of the expected value, $E_t^*[*]$. As the number of Monte Carlo replications gets infinitely large, the average will converge to the expectation. In practice, around 5000 replications suffice to get a reasonably precise estimate. The CD-ROM accompanying this book contains a spreadsheet with a Monte Carlo simulation calculating GARCH option prices.

In theory, we could, of course, estimate all the parameters in the GARCH model using the maximum likelihood method from Chapter 2 on the underlying asset returns. But to obtain a better fit of the option prices, we can instead minimize the option pricing errors directly. Treating the initial variance, σ_{t+1}^2, as a parameter to be estimated, we can estimate the GARCH option pricing model on a daily sample of options by numerically minimizing the mean squared error

$$MSE_{GH} = \min_{\sigma_{t+1}^2, \omega, \alpha, \beta, \lambda^*} \left\{ \frac{1}{n} \sum_{i=1}^{n} \left(c_i^{mkt} - c_{GH}(S_t, r, X_i, \tilde{T}_i; \sigma_{t+1}^2, \omega, \alpha, \beta, \lambda^*) \right)^2 \right\}$$

Notice that for every new parameter vector the numerical optimizer tries, the GARCH options must all be repriced using the MC simulation technique, thus the estimation can be quite time consuming.

6.5.2. A Closed-Form GARCH Option Pricing Model

A significant drawback of the GARCH option pricing framework outlined here is clearly that it does not provide us with a closed-form solution for the option price, which must instead be calculated through simulation. While the simulation technique is straightforward, it does take computing time and introduces an additional source of error arising from the approximation of the simulated average to the expected value.

Fortunately, if we are willing to accept a particular type of GARCH process, then a closed-form pricing formula exists. We will refer to this as the closed-form GARCH or *CFG* model. Assume that returns are generated by the process

$$R_{t+1} \equiv \ln(S_{t+1}) - \ln(S_t) = r + \lambda\sigma_{t+1}^2 + \sigma_{t+1}z_{t+1}$$

with $z_{t+1} \sim N(0, 1)$, and $\sigma_{t+1}^2 = \omega + \alpha(z_t - \theta\sigma_t)^2 + \beta\sigma_t^2$

Notice that the risk premium is now multiplied on the conditional variance not standard deviation, and that z_t enters in the variance innovation term without being scaled by σ_t. Variance persistence in this model can be derived as $\alpha\theta^2 + \beta$ and the unconditional variance as $(\omega + \alpha)/(1 - \alpha\theta^2 - \beta)$.

The risk neutral version of this process is

$$R_{t+1} \equiv \ln(S_{t+1}) - \ln(S_t) = r - \frac{1}{2}\sigma_{t+1}^2 + \sigma_{t+1}z_{t+1}^*$$

with $z_{t+1}^* \sim N(0, 1)$, and $\sigma_{t+1}^2 = \omega + \alpha\left(z_t^* - \theta^*\sigma_t\right)^2 + \beta\sigma_t^2$

To verify that the risky assets earn the risk-free rate under the risk neutral measure, we check again that

$$E_t^*[S_{t+1}/S_t] = E_t^*\left[\exp\left(r - \frac{1}{2}\sigma_{t+1}^2 + \sigma_{t+1}z_{t+1}^*\right)\right]$$

$$= \exp\left(r - \frac{1}{2}\sigma_{t+1}^2\right)E_t^*\left[\exp\left(\sigma_{t+1}z_{t+1}^*\right)\right]$$

$$= \exp\left(r - \frac{1}{2}\sigma_{t+1}^2\right)\exp\left(\frac{1}{2}\sigma_{t+1}^2\right)$$

$$= \exp(r)$$

and the variance can be verified as before as well.

Under this special GARCH process for returns, the European option price can be calculated as

$$c_{CFG} = e^{-r\tilde{T}}E_t^*\left[Max\left(S_{t+\tilde{T}} - X, 0\right)\right] = S_t P_1 - Xe^{-r\tilde{T}}P_2$$

where the formulas for P_1 and P_2 are given in the appendix. Notice that the structure of the option pricing formula is identical to that of the BSM model. As in the BSM model, P_2 is the risk-neutral probability of exercise, and P_1 is the delta of the option.

6.6. IMPLIED VOLATILITY FUNCTION (IVF) MODELS

The option pricing methods surveyed so far in this chapter can be derived from well-defined assumptions about the underlying dynamics of the economy. The next approach to European option pricing we consider is instead completely static and ad hoc but it turns out to offer reasonably good fit to observed option prices, and we therefore give a brief discussion of it here. The idea behind the approach is that the implied volatility smile changes only slowly over time. If we can therefore estimate a functional form on the smile today, then that functional form may work reasonably in pricing options in the near future as well.

The implied volatility smiles and smirks mentioned earlier suggest that option prices may be well captured by the following four-step approach:

1. Calculate the implied BSM volatilities for all the observed option prices on a given day as

$$\sigma_i^{iv} = c_{BSM}^{-1}\left(S_t, r, X_i, \tilde{T}_i, c_i^{mkt}\right) \quad \text{for } i = 1, 2, \ldots, n$$

2. Regress the implied volatilities on a second-order polynomial in moneyness and maturity. That is, use ordinary least squares (OLS) to estimate the a parameters in the regression

$$\sigma_i^{iv} = a_0 + a_1(S_t/X_i) + a_2(S_t/X_i)^2 + a_3\left(\tilde{T}_i/365\right) + a_4\left(\tilde{T}_i/365\right)^2$$
$$+ a_5(S_t/X_i)\left(\tilde{T}_i/365\right) + e_i$$

where e_i is an error term and where we have rescaled maturity to be in years rather than days. The rescaling is done to make the different a coefficients have roughly the same order of magnitude.

3. Compute the fitted values of implied volatility from the regression,

$$\hat{\sigma}^{iv}(S_t/X_i, \tilde{T}_i; \hat{a}) = \hat{a}_0 + \hat{a}_1 (S_t/X_i) + \hat{a}_2 (S_t/X_i)^2 + \hat{a}_3 \left(\tilde{T}_i/365\right)$$

$$+ \hat{a}_4 \left(\tilde{T}_i/365\right)^2 + \hat{a}_5 (S_t/X_i) \left(\tilde{T}_i/365\right)$$

4. Calculate model option prices using the fitted volatilities and the BSM option pricing formula, as in

$$c_{IVF} = c(S_t, r, X_i, \tilde{T}_i; Max(\hat{\sigma}^{iv}(S/X_i, \tilde{T}_i/365; \hat{a}), 0.0001))$$

where the $Max(*)$ function ensures that the volatility used in the option pricing formula is positive.

Notice that this option pricing approach requires only a sequence of simple calculations and it is thus easily implemented.

While this four-step linear estimation approach is standard, one can typically obtain much better model option prices if the following modified estimation approach is taken. We can use a numerical optimization technique to solve for $a = \{a_0, a_1, a_2, a_3, a_4, a_5\}$ by minimizing the mean squared error

MSE_{MIVF}

$$= \min_a \left\{ \frac{1}{n} \sum_{i=1}^{n} \left(c_i^{mkt} - c(S_t, r, X_i, \tilde{T}_i; Max(\sigma^{iv}(S/X_i, \tilde{T}_i/365; a), 0.01)) \right)^2 \right\}$$

The downside of this method is clearly that a numerical solution technique rather than simple OLS is needed to find the parameters. We refer to this approach as the modified implied volatility function (MIVF) technique. Both the IVF and the MIVF techniques are implemented on the CD-ROM, which contains answers to the exercises at the end of the chapter.

6.7. SUMMARY

This chapter has surveyed some key models for pricing European options. First we introduced the famous Black-Scholes-Merton (BSM) model. The key assumption underlying the BSM model is that the underlying asset return dynamics are captured by the normal distribution with constant volatility. While the BSM model provides crucial insight into the pricing of derivative securities, the underlying assumptions are clearly violated by observed asset returns. We therefore next considered a generalization of the BSM model, which was derived from the

Gram-Charlier (GC) expansion around the normal distribution. The GC distribution allows for skewness, and kurtosis and it therefore offers a more accurate description of observed returns than does the normal distribution. However, the GC model still assumes that volatility is constant over time, which we argued in earlier chapters was unrealistic. Next, we thus presented two types of GARCH option pricing models. The first type allowed for a wide range of variance specifications, but the option price had to be calculated using Monte Carlo simulation or another numerical technique as no closed-form formula existed. The second type relied on a particular GARCH specification but in return provided a closed form solution for the option price. Finally, we introduced the ad hoc implied volatility function (IVF) approach, which in essence consists of a second-order polynomial approximation to the implied volatility smile.

6.8. FURTHER RESOURCES

This chapter has focused on option pricing in discrete time in order to remain consistent with the previous chapters. There are many excellent textbooks on options. A popular example is Hull (2002). The classic papers on the BSM model are Black and Scholes (1973) and Merton (1973). The discrete time derivations in this chapter were introduced in Rubenstein (1976) and Brennan (1979). Merton (1976) introduced a continuous time diffusion model with jumps allowing for kurtosis in the distribution of returns. See Andersen and Andreasen (2000) for some recent extensions to Merton's (1976) model. The GC model is derived in Backus *et al.* (1997). The general GARCH option pricing framework is introduced in Duan (1995). Duan and Simonato (1998) discussed Monte Carlo simulation techniques for the GARCH model and Duan *et al.* (1999) contains an analytical approximation to the GARCH model price. Ritchken and Trevor (1999) suggest a trinomial tree method for calculating the GARCH option price. Duan (1999) discusses extensions to the GARCH option pricing model allowing for conditionally non-normal returns. The closed-form GARCH option pricing model is derived in Heston and Nandi (2000). Christoffersen and Jacobs (2002) compares the empirical performance of various GARCH variance specifications for option pricing and found that the simple variance specification including a leverage effect as applied in this chapter works very well compared with the BSM model. Hsieh and Ritchken (2000) compare the GARCH (GH) and the closed-form GARCH (CFG) models and find that the GH model perform the best in terms of out-of-sample option valuation. Hull and White (1987) and Heston (1993) derive continuous time option pricing models with time-varying volatility. Bakshi *et al.* (1997) contains an empirical comparison of Heston's model with more general models and finds that allowing for time-varying volatility is key in fitting observed option prices. Lewis (2000) discusses the implementation of option valuation models with time-varying volatility. The IVF model is described in Dumas *et al.* (1998) and the modified IVF model (MIVF) is examined in Christoffersen and Jacobs (2001) who finds that the MIVF model performs very well empirically compared with the simple BSM model. Berkowitz (2002) provides a theoretical justification for the MIVF approach.

6.9. APPENDIX: THE *CFG* OPTION PRICING FORMULA

The probabilities P_1 and P_2 in the closed-form GARCH (*CFG*) formula are derived by first solving for the conditional moment generating function. The conditional, time-t, moment generating function of the log asset prices as time $t+\tilde{T}$ is

$$f_{t,t+\tilde{T}}(\varphi) = E_t[\exp(\varphi \ln(S_{t+\tilde{T}}))] = E_t\left[S_{t+\tilde{T}}^{\varphi}\right]$$

In the *CFG* model, this function takes a log-linear form (omitting the time subscripts on $f(\varphi)$)

$$f(\varphi) = S_t^{\varphi} * \exp\left(A\left(t; t+\tilde{T}, \varphi\right) + B\left(t; t+\tilde{T}, \varphi\right)\sigma_{t+1}^2\right)$$

where

$$A\left(t; t+\tilde{T}, \varphi\right) = A\left(t+1; t+\tilde{T}, \varphi\right) + \varphi r + B\left(t+1; t+\tilde{T}, \varphi\right)\omega$$
$$- \frac{1}{2}\ln\left(1 - 2\alpha B\left(t+1; t+\tilde{T}, \varphi\right)\right)$$

and

$$B\left(t; t+\tilde{T}, \varphi\right) = \varphi(\lambda+\theta) - \frac{1}{2}\theta^2 + \beta B\left(t+1; t+\tilde{T}, \varphi\right)$$
$$+ \frac{\frac{1}{2}(\varphi-\theta)^2}{1 - 2\alpha B\left(t+1; t+\tilde{T}, \varphi\right)}$$

These functions can be solved by recursing backward one period at a time from the maturity date using the terminal conditions,

$$A\left(t+\tilde{T}; t+\tilde{T}, \varphi\right) = 0, \quad \text{and} \quad B\left(t+\tilde{T}; t+\tilde{T}, \varphi\right) = 0$$

A fundamental result in probability theory establishes the following relationship between the characteristic function, $f(i\varphi)$, and the probability density function $p(x)$:

$$\int_A^{\infty} p(x)\,dx = \frac{1}{2} + \frac{1}{\pi}\int_0^{\infty} \text{Re}\left[\frac{\exp(-i\varphi A)f(i\varphi)}{i\varphi}\right]d\varphi$$

where the Re $(*)$ functions take the real value of the argument.

Using these results, we can calculate the conditional expected payoff as

$$E_t\left[Max\left(S_{t+\tilde{T}}-X,0\right)\right]=E_t\left[Max\left(\exp\left(\ln\left(S_{t+\tilde{T}}\right)\right)-X,0\right)\right]$$

$$=\int_{\ln(X)}^{\infty}\exp(x)p(x)\,dx-X\int_{\ln(X)}^{\infty}p(x)\,dx$$

$$=f(1)\left(\frac{1}{2}+\frac{1}{\pi}\int_0^{\infty}Re\left[\frac{X^{-i\varphi}f(i\varphi+1)}{i\varphi f(1)}\right]d\varphi\right)$$

$$-X\left(\frac{1}{2}+\frac{1}{\pi}\int_0^{\infty}Re\left[\frac{X^{-i\varphi}f(i\varphi)}{i\varphi}\right]d\varphi\right)$$

To price the call option, we use the risk-neutral distribution to get

$$c_{CFG}=e^{-r\tilde{T}}E_t^*\left[Max\left(S_{t+\tilde{T}}-X,0\right)\right]$$

$$=S_t\left(\frac{1}{2}+\frac{1}{\pi}\int_0^{\infty}Re\left[\frac{X^{-i\varphi}f^*(i\varphi+1)}{i\varphi f^*(1)}\right]d\varphi\right)$$

$$-Xe^{-r\tilde{T}}\left(\frac{1}{2}+\frac{1}{\pi}\int_0^{\infty}Re\left[\frac{X^{i\varphi}f^*(i\varphi)}{i\varphi}\right]d\varphi\right)$$

$$\equiv S_t P_1-Xe^{-r\tilde{T}}P_2$$

Where we have used the fact that $f^*(1)=E_t^*\left[S_{t+\tilde{T}}\right]=e^{r\tilde{T}}S_t$. Note that under the risk-neutral distribution, λ is set to $-\frac{1}{2}$, and θ is replaced by θ^*. Finally, we note that the previous integrals must be solved numerically.

6.10. EMPIRICAL EXERCISES ON CD-ROM

Open the Chapter6Data.xls file from the CD-ROM. The file contains European call options on the S&P 500 from August 29, 2002.

1. Calculate the BSM price for each option using a standard deviation of 0.015 per day. Using Solver, find the volatility that minimizes the mean squared pricing error using 0.015 as a starting value. Keep the BSM prices that correspond to this optimal volatility and use these prices below.

2. Scatter plot the BSM pricing errors (actual price less model price) against moneyness defined as (S/X) for the different maturities.

3. Calculate the implied BSM volatility (standard deviation) for each of the options. You can use Excel's Solver to do this. Scatter plot the implied volatilities against moneyness.

4. Fit the Gram-Charlier option price to the data. Estimate a model with skewness only. Use nonlinear least squares (NLS) again.

5. Regress implied volatility on a constant, moneyness, the time-to-maturity divided by 365, each variable squared, and their cross product. Calculate the fitted BSM volatility from the regression for each option. Calculate the ad hoc IVF price for each option using the fitted values for volatility.

6. Redo the IVF estimation using NLS to minimize the mean squared pricing error (MSE). Call this MIVF. Use the IVF regression coefficients as starting values.

7. Calculate the square root of the mean squared pricing error from the IVF and MIVF models and compare them to the square root of the MSE from the standard BSM model and the Gram-Charlier model. Scatter plot the pricing errors from the MIVF model against moneyness and compare them to the plots from question 2.

8. Using GARCH parameters $\omega = 0.00001524, \alpha = 0.1883, \beta = 0.7162, \theta = 0$, and a $\lambda = 0.007452$, simulate the GARCH option price with a strike price of 100 and 20 days to maturity. Assume $r = 0.02/365$ and assume that today's stock price is 100. Assume today's variance is 0.00016. Compare the GARCH price with the BSM price using a daily variance of 0.00016 as well.

   The answers to these exercises can be found in the Chapter6Results.xls file. Previews of the answers follow.

Black-Scholes-Merton Price for Each Option

DTM	Strike	Call	Index	Daily Div	Daily Interest Rate	d	d-σ√T	Φ(d)	Φ(d-σ√T)	BSM Prices	Squared Pricing Errors	Daily Volatility	Mean Squared Errors
23	870	57.60	917.80	0.004360%	0.004521%	0.864	0.800	0.806	0.788	54.30	10.87	1.34%	27.39
23	875	53.70	917.80	0.004360%	0.004521%	0.775	0.711	0.781	0.761	50.43	10.68		
23	880	49.90	917.80	0.004360%	0.004521%	0.687	0.622	0.754	0.733	46.70	10.24		
23	885	46.20	917.80	0.004360%	0.004521%	0.598	0.534	0.725	0.703	43.11	9.54		
23	890	42.60	917.80	0.004360%	0.004521%	0.511	0.447	0.695	0.672	39.68	8.55		
23	900	35.30	917.80	0.004360%	0.004521%	0.337	0.273	0.632	0.608	33.28	4.08		
23	905	32.20	917.80	0.004360%	0.004521%	0.251	0.187	0.599	0.574	30.33	3.50		
23	910	29.00	917.80	0.004360%	0.004521%	0.165	0.101	0.566	0.540	27.55	2.12		
23	915	26.70	917.80	0.004360%	0.004521%	0.080	0.016	0.532	0.506	24.93	3.13		
23	920	23.40	917.80	0.004360%	0.004521%	-0.004	-0.069	0.498	0.473	22.49	0.83		
23	925	20.80	917.80	0.004360%	0.004521%	-0.089	-0.153	0.465	0.439	20.21	0.35		
23	935	16.50	917.80	0.004360%	0.004521%	-0.256	-0.320	0.399	0.374	16.15	0.12		
23	940	14.30	917.80	0.004360%	0.004521%	-0.339	-0.403	0.367	0.343	14.36	0.00		
23	945	12.40	917.80	0.004360%	0.004521%	-0.421	-0.486	0.337	0.314	12.72	0.10		
23	950	10.90	917.80	0.004360%	0.004521%	-0.503	-0.568	0.307	0.285	11.22	0.10		
23	960	8.10	917.80	0.004360%	0.004521%	-0.666	-0.730	0.253	0.233	8.64	0.29		
23	965	6.80	917.80	0.004360%	0.004521%	-0.747	-0.811	0.228	0.209	7.54	0.55		
23	970	5.70	917.80	0.004360%	0.004521%	-0.827	-0.892	0.204	0.186	6.55	0.73		
51	775	148.90	917.80	0.004513%	0.004521%	1.813	1.718	0.965	0.957	143.73	26.75		
51	800	126.70	917.80	0.004513%	0.004521%	1.482	1.386	0.931	0.917	120.31	40.78		
51	825	105.50	917.80	0.004513%	0.004521%	1.161	1.065	0.877	0.857	98.15	54.05		
51	850	85.30	917.80	0.004513%	0.004521%	0.849	0.753	0.802	0.774	77.77	56.77		
51	875	66.70	917.80	0.004513%	0.004521%	0.546	0.451	0.708	0.674	59.67	49.40		
51	885	59.80	917.80	0.004513%	0.004521%	0.428	0.332	0.666	0.630	53.17	44.02		
51	900	49.40	917.80	0.004513%	0.004521%	0.252	0.157	0.600	0.562	44.24	26.61		
51	925	35.10	917.80	0.004513%	0.004521%	-0.034	-0.129	0.487	0.449	31.64	11.96		
51	950	24.00	917.80	0.004513%	0.004521%	-0.312	-0.408	0.377	0.342	21.81	4.80		

QUESTION 1

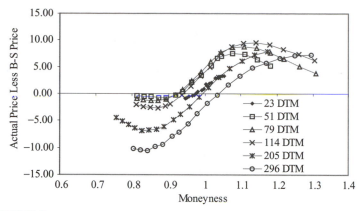

QUESTION 2

DTM	Strike	Call	Index	Daily Div	Daily Interest Rate	Implied BSM Volatilities Implied Volatilities	d	d-σ√T	Φ(d)	Φ(d-σ√T)	BSM Prices	Moneyness	Pricing Errors
23	870	57.60	917.80	0.004360%	0.004521%	1.60%	0.74	0.66	0.77	0.75	57.60	1.05	0.00
23	875	53.70	917.80	0.004360%	0.004521%	1.58%	0.67	0.59	0.75	0.72	53.70	1.05	0.00
23	880	49.90	917.80	0.004360%	0.004521%	1.57%	0.60	0.52	0.73	0.70	49.90	1.04	0.00
23	885	46.20	917.80	0.004360%	0.004521%	1.55%	0.53	0.45	0.70	0.68	46.20	1.04	0.00
23	890	42.60	917.80	0.004360%	0.004521%	1.53%	0.46	0.38	0.68	0.65	42.60	1.03	0.00
23	900	35.30	917.80	0.004360%	0.004521%	1.46%	0.31	0.24	0.62	0.60	35.30	1.02	0.00
23	905	32.20	917.80	0.004360%	0.004521%	1.45%	0.24	0.17	0.59	0.57	32.20	1.01	0.00
23	910	29.00	917.80	0.004360%	0.004521%	1.43%	0.16	0.09	0.56	0.54	29.00	1.01	0.00
23	915	26.70	917.80	0.004360%	0.004521%	1.44%	0.08	0.01	0.53	0.50	26.70	1.00	0.00
23	920	23.40	917.80	0.004360%	0.004521%	1.39%	0.00	-0.07	0.50	0.47	23.40	1.00	0.00
23	925	20.80	917.80	0.004360%	0.004521%	1.38%	-0.08	-0.15	0.47	0.44	20.80	0.99	0.00
23	935	16.50	917.80	0.004360%	0.004521%	1.36%	-0.25	-0.32	0.40	0.38	16.50	0.98	0.00
23	940	14.30	917.80	0.004360%	0.004521%	1.34%	-0.34	-0.40	0.37	0.34	14.30	0.98	0.00
23	945	12.40	917.80	0.004360%	0.004521%	1.32%	-0.43	-0.49	0.33	0.31	12.40	0.97	0.00
23	950	10.90	917.80	0.004360%	0.004521%	1.32%	-0.51	-0.58	0.30	0.28	10.90	0.97	0.00
23	960	8.10	917.80	0.004360%	0.004521%	1.30%	-0.69	-0.75	0.25	0.23	8.10	0.96	0.00
23	965	6.80	917.80	0.004360%	0.004521%	1.28%	-0.78	-0.84	0.22	0.20	6.80	0.95	0.00
23	970	5.70	917.80	0.004360%	0.004521%	1.27%	-0.88	-0.94	0.19	0.17	5.70	0.95	0.00
51	775	148.90	917.80	0.004513%	0.004521%	1.95%	1.28	1.14	0.90	0.87	148.90	1.18	0.00
51	800	126.70	917.80	0.004513%	0.004521%	1.88%	1.09	0.95	0.86	0.83	126.70	1.14	0.00
51	825	105.50	917.80	0.004513%	0.004521%	1.81%	0.89	0.76	0.81	0.78	105.50	1.11	0.00
51	850	85.30	917.80	0.004513%	0.004521%	1.73%	0.68	0.56	0.75	0.71	85.30	1.08	0.00
51	875	66.70	917.80	0.004513%	0.004521%	1.65%	0.46	0.35	0.68	0.64	66.70	1.05	0.00
51	885	59.80	917.80	0.004513%	0.004521%	1.62%	0.37	0.26	0.65	0.60	59.80	1.03	0.00
51	900	49.40	917.80	0.004513%	0.004521%	1.54%	0.23	0.12	0.59	0.55	49.40	1.02	0.00
51	925	35.10	917.80	0.004513%	0.004521%	1.47%	-0.02	-0.13	0.49	0.45	35.10	0.99	0.00
51	950	24.00	917.80	0.004513%	0.004521%	1.43%	-0.29	-0.39	0.39	0.35	24.00	0.96	0.00

QUESTION 3

The Gram-Charlier Option Price Model

DTM	Strike	Call	Index	Daily Div	Daily Interest Rate	d	d-σ√T	Φ(d)	Φ(d-σ√T)	Gram-Charlier Prices	Squared Pricing Errors	Parameters Estimation	
											10.69	Volatility	0.0141
23	870	57.60	917.80	0.004360%	0.004521%	0.82	0.76	0.79	0.78	59.68	4.31	Skewness	-10.6106
23	875	53.70	917.80	0.004360%	0.004521%	0.74	0.67	0.77	0.75	55.59	3.57	Kurtosis	0.0000
23	880	49.90	917.80	0.004360%	0.004521%	0.65	0.59	0.74	0.72	51.55	2.72		
23	885	46.20	917.80	0.004360%	0.004521%	0.57	0.50	0.72	0.69	47.57	1.87		
23	890	42.60	917.80	0.004360%	0.004521%	0.49	0.42	0.69	0.66	43.66	1.13		
23	900	35.30	917.80	0.004360%	0.004521%	0.32	0.26	0.63	0.60	36.11	0.66		
23	905	32.20	917.80	0.004360%	0.004521%	0.24	0.17	0.60	0.57	32.51	0.09		
23	910	29.00	917.80	0.004360%	0.004521%	0.16	0.09	0.56	0.54	29.03	0.00		
23	915	26.70	917.80	0.004360%	0.004521%	0.08	0.01	0.53	0.50	25.69	1.02		
23	920	23.40	917.80	0.004360%	0.004521%	0.00	-0.07	0.50	0.47	22.51	0.79		
23	925	20.80	917.80	0.004360%	0.004521%	-0.08	-0.15	0.47	0.44	19.51	1.67		
23	935	16.50	917.80	0.004360%	0.004521%	-0.24	-0.31	0.41	0.38	14.05	5.99		
23	940	14.30	917.80	0.004360%	0.004521%	-0.32	-0.39	0.38	0.35	11.62	7.18		
23	945	12.40	917.80	0.004360%	0.004521%	-0.40	-0.46	0.35	0.32	9.39	9.05		
23	950	10.90	917.80	0.004360%	0.004521%	-0.47	-0.54	0.32	0.29	7.37	12.47		
23	960	8.10	917.80	0.004360%	0.004521%	-0.63	-0.70	0.26	0.24	3.94	17.32		
23	965	6.80	917.80	0.004360%	0.004521%	-0.71	-0.77	0.24	0.22	2.52	18.30		
23	970	5.70	917.80	0.004360%	0.004521%	-0.78	-0.85	0.22	0.20	1.30	19.39		
51	775	148.90	917.80	0.004513%	0.004521%	1.73	1.62	0.96	0.95	147.27	2.67		
51	800	126.70	917.80	0.004513%	0.004521%	1.41	1.31	0.92	0.90	125.06	2.68		
51	825	105.50	917.80	0.004513%	0.004521%	1.11	1.01	0.87	0.84	103.62	3.52		
51	850	85.30	917.80	0.004513%	0.004521%	0.81	0.71	0.79	0.76	83.11	4.79		
51	875	66.70	917.80	0.004513%	0.004521%	0.52	0.42	0.70	0.66	63.87	7.98		
51	885	59.80	917.80	0.004513%	0.004521%	0.41	0.31	0.66	0.62	56.66	9.89		
51	900	49.40	917.80	0.004513%	0.004521%	0.24	0.14	0.60	0.56	46.46	8.67		
51	925	35.10	917.80	0.004513%	0.004521%	-0.03	-0.13	0.49	0.45	31.45	13.35		

QUESTION 4

	K	L	M	N	O	P	Q	R	S	T
	Implied Volatilities	Call	Daily Interest Rate	Fitted Volatilities	d	d-σ√T	Φ(d)	Φ(d-σ√T)	Ad-hoc Prices	Errors Squared
3										**1.20**
4	1.60%	57.60	0.004521%	1.59%	0.74	0.66	0.77	0.75	57.45	0.02
5	1.58%	53.70	0.004521%	1.58%	0.67	0.59	0.75	0.72	53.60	0.01
6	1.57%	49.90	0.004521%	1.56%	0.60	0.52	0.73	0.70	49.86	0.00
7	1.55%	46.20	0.004521%	1.55%	0.53	0.45	0.70	0.67	46.24	0.00
8	1.53%	42.60	0.004521%	1.54%	0.45	0.38	0.68	0.65	42.74	0.02
9	1.46%	35.30	0.004521%	1.51%	0.31	0.23	0.62	0.59	36.15	0.72
10	1.45%	32.20	0.004521%	1.50%	0.23	0.16	0.59	0.56	33.06	0.74
11	1.43%	29.00	0.004521%	1.49%	0.16	0.08	0.56	0.53	30.12	1.25
12	1.44%	26.70	0.004521%	1.48%	0.08	0.01	0.53	0.50	27.33	0.39
13	1.39%	23.40	0.004521%	1.47%	0.00	-0.07	0.50	0.47	24.69	1.67
14	1.38%	20.80	0.004521%	1.46%	-0.08	-0.15	0.47	0.44	22.21	1.99
15	1.36%	16.50	0.004521%	1.43%	-0.24	-0.30	0.41	0.38	17.72	1.49
16	1.34%	14.30	0.004521%	1.42%	-0.32	-0.38	0.38	0.35	15.71	2.00
17	1.32%	12.40	0.004521%	1.41%	-0.40	-0.46	0.35	0.32	13.86	2.13
18	1.32%	10.90	0.004521%	1.40%	-0.48	-0.55	0.32	0.29	12.16	1.59
19	1.30%	8.10	0.004521%	1.38%	-0.65	-0.71	0.26	0.24	9.20	1.22
20	1.28%	6.80	0.004521%	1.37%	-0.73	-0.80	0.23	0.21	7.93	1.29
21	1.27%	5.70	0.004521%	1.36%	-0.81	-0.88	0.21	0.19	6.80	1.21
22	1.95%	148.90	0.004521%	1.85%	1.35	1.21	0.91	0.89	147.74	1.35
23	1.88%	126.70	0.004521%	1.77%	1.15	1.02	0.87	0.85	125.14	2.43
24	1.81%	105.50	0.004521%	1.70%	0.94	0.82	0.83	0.79	103.56	3.78
25	1.73%	85.30	0.004521%	1.63%	0.72	0.60	0.76	0.73	83.33	3.88
26	1.65%	66.70	0.004521%	1.57%	0.48	0.37	0.69	0.64	64.85	3.44
27	1.62%	59.80	0.004521%	1.54%	0.39	0.28	0.65	0.61	58.03	3.14
28	1.54%	49.40	0.004521%	1.51%	0.24	0.13	0.59	0.55	48.49	0.82
29	1.47%	35.10	0.004521%	1.45%	-0.02	-0.13	0.49	0.45	34.60	0.25

Regression Coefficients (columns V / W)

S/X*(DTM/365)	-0.0152
(DTM/365)^2	-0.0041
DTM/365	0.0161
(S/X)^2	0.0048
S/X	0.0122
Intercept (Constant)	-0.0024
Mean Squared Errors (MSE)	

(Mean Squared Errors (MSE) points to the value 1.20 in column T)

QUESTION 5

QUESTION 6

Modified Implied Volatility Function (MIVF) Technique

DTM	Call	Strike	Index	Daily Div	Index less dividends	Daily Interest Rate	MIVF Volatilities	MIVF Prices	Errors Squared	Coefficients	
									0.810731	Intercept (Constant)	-0.0063
23	57.60	870	917.80	0.004360%	916.88	0.004521%	1.62%	57.93	0.111349	S/X	0.0198
23	53.70	875	917.80	0.004360%	916.88	0.004521%	1.61%	54.10	0.160167	(S/X)^2	0.0017
23	49.90	880	917.80	0.004360%	916.88	0.004521%	1.60%	50.38	0.226461	DTM/365	0.0143
23	46.20	885	917.80	0.004360%	916.88	0.004521%	1.58%	46.77	0.321629	(DTM/365)^2	-0.0007
23	42.60	890	917.80	0.004360%	916.88	0.004521%	1.57%	43.28	0.462643	S/X*(DTM/365)	-0.0165
23	35.30	900	917.80	0.004360%	916.88	0.004521%	1.55%	36.70	1.946722		
23	32.20	905	917.80	0.004360%	916.88	0.004521%	1.53%	33.61	1.982586		
23	29.00	910	917.80	0.004360%	916.88	0.004521%	1.52%	30.66	2.768989		
23	26.70	915	917.80	0.004360%	916.88	0.004521%	1.51%	27.87	1.362400		
23	23.40	920	917.80	0.004360%	916.88	0.004521%	1.50%	25.22	3.314872		
23	20.80	925	917.80	0.004360%	916.88	0.004521%	1.49%	22.73	3.712412		
23	16.50	935	917.80	0.004360%	916.88	0.004521%	1.46%	18.20	2.899079		
23	14.30	940	917.80	0.004360%	916.88	0.004521%	1.45%	16.17	3.506744		
23	12.40	945	917.80	0.004360%	916.88	0.004521%	1.44%	14.30	3.593888		
23	10.90	950	917.80	0.004360%	916.88	0.004521%	1.43%	12.57	2.787843		
23	8.10	960	917.80	0.004360%	916.88	0.004521%	1.41%	9.56	2.119031		
23	6.80	965	917.80	0.004360%	916.88	0.004521%	1.39%	8.26	2.126788		
23	5.70	970	917.80	0.004360%	916.88	0.004521%	1.38%	7.09	1.940781		
51	148.90	775	917.80	0.004513%	915.69	0.004521%	1.87%	147.96	0.877798		
51	126.70	800	917.80	0.004513%	915.69	0.004521%	1.79%	125.42	1.628424		
51	105.50	825	917.80	0.004513%	915.69	0.004521%	1.72%	103.89	2.584341		
51	86.30	850	917.80	0.004513%	915.69	0.004521%	1.65%	83.70	2.556954		
51	66.70	875	917.80	0.004513%	915.69	0.004521%	1.58%	65.22	2.179401		
51	59.80	885	917.80	0.004513%	915.69	0.004521%	1.56%	58.40	1.963139		
51	49.40	900	917.80	0.004513%	915.69	0.004521%	1.52%	48.84	0.312923		
51	35.10	925	917.80	0.004513%	915.69	0.004521%	1.47%	34.88	0.047717		

	Errors Comparison for BSM, GC, IVF and MIVF Models							Pricing Errors from the MIVF model vs. Moneyness			
		Squared Pricing Errors			Square Root of Mean Squared Errors				MIVF Prices	Moneyness	Pricing Errors
BSM	G-C	IVF	MIVF	BSM	G-C	IVF	MIVF			
27.3944	10.6910	1.2006	0.8107	5.2340	3.2697	1.0957	0.9004			
10.8703	4.3145	0.0222	0.1113					57.93	1.053885	-0.333691
10.6763	3.5655	0.0099	0.1602					54.10	1.047863	-0.400208
10.2429	2.7187	0.0015	0.2265					50.38	1.041909	-0.475879
9.5387	1.8748	0.0016	0.3216					46.77	1.036023	-0.567123
8.5548	1.1264	0.0206	0.4626					43.28	1.030202	-0.680179
4.0831	0.6637	0.7187	1.9467					36.70	1.018756	-1.395250
3.5037	0.0932	0.7394	1.9826					33.61	1.013127	-1.408043
2.1166	0.0006	1.2513	2.7690					30.66	1.007560	-1.664028
3.1278	0.1204	0.3943	1.3624					27.87	1.002055	-1.167219
0.8339	0.7874	1.6667	3.3149					25.22	0.996609	-1.820679
0.3482	1.6730	1.9881	3.7124					22.73	0.991222	-1.926762
0.1232	5.9933	1.4911	2.8991					18.20	0.980620	-1.702668
0.0032	7.1842	1.9961	3.5067					16.17	0.975404	-1.872630
0.1002	9.0525	2.1319	3.5939					14.30	0.970243	-1.895755
0.1035	12.4688	1.5879	2.7878					12.57	0.965137	-1.669684
0.2927	17.3199	1.2157	2.1190					9.56	0.955083	-1.455689
0.5474	18.3012	1.2874	2.1268					8.26	0.950135	-1.458351
0.7296	19.3950	1.2078	1.9408					7.09	0.945237	-1.393119
26.7525	2.6717	1.3475	0.8778					147.96	1.181535	0.936909
40.7811	2.6842	2.4321	1.6284					125.42	1.144613	1.276097
54.0515	3.5160	3.7785	2.5843					103.89	1.109927	1.607588
56.7730	4.7918	3.8835	2.5570					83.70	1.077282	1.599048
49.3974	7.9819	3.4395	2.1794					65.22	1.046503	1.476280
44.0168	9.8902	3.1405	1.9631					58.40	1.034678	1.401121
26.6102	8.6687	0.8247	0.3129					48.84	1.017433	0.559395
11.9573	13.3471	0.2514	0.0477					34.88	0.989935	0.218442
4.7969	22.0474	0.4018	0.1955					23.56	0.963884	0.442160

QUESTION 7

REFERENCES

Andersen, L., and J. Andreasen. (2000). "Jump-Diffusion Processes: Volatility Smile Fitting and Numerical Methods for Option Pricing," *Review of Derivatives Research*, 4, 231–262.

Backus, D., S. Foresi, K. Li, and L. Wu. (1997). Accounting for Biases in Black-Scholes, Manuscript, The Stern School at New York University.

Bakshi, G., C. Cao, and Z. Chen. (1997). "Empirical Performance of Alternative Option Pricing Models," *Journal of Finance*, 52, 2003–2050.

Berkowitz, J. (2002). "Frequent Recalibration of Option Pricing Models," Manuscript, University of Houston.

Black, F., and M. Scholes. (1973). "The Pricing of Options and Corporate Liabilities," *Journal of Political Economy*, 81, 637–659.

Brennan, M. (1979). "The Pricing of Contingent Claims in Discrete Time Models," *Journal of Finance*, 34, 53–68.

Christoffersen, P., and K. Jacobs. (2001). "The Importance of the Loss Function in Option Valuation," Manuscript, McGill University and CIRANO.

Christoffersen, P., and K. Jacobs. (2002). "Which Volatility Model for Option Valuation?" Manuscript, McGill University and CIRANO.

Duan, J. (1995). "The GARCH Option Pricing Model," *Mathematical Finance*, 5, 13–32.

Duan, J. (1999). "Conditionally Fat-Tailed Distributions and the Volatility Smile in Options," Manuscript, Hong Kong University of Science and Technology.

Duan, J., G. Gauthier, and J.-G. Simonato. (1999). "An Analytical Approximation for the GARCH Option Pricing Model," *Journal of Computational Finance*, 2, 75–116.

Duan, J., and J.-G. Simonato. (1998). "Empirical Martingale Simulation for Asset Prices," *Management Science*, 44, 1218–1233.

Dumas, B., J. Fleming, and R. Whaley. (1998). "Implied Volatility Functions: Empirical Tests," *Journal of Finance*, 53, 2059–2106.

Heston, S. (1993). "A Closed-Form Solution for Options with Stochastic Volatility, with Applications to Bond and Currency Options," *Review of Financial Studies*, 6, 327–343.

Heston, S., and S. Nandi. (2000). "A Closed-Form GARCH Option Pricing Model," *Review of Financial Studies*, 13, 585–626.

Hsieh, K., and P. Ritchken. (2000). "An Empirical Comparison of GARCH Option Pricing Models," Manuscript, Case Western Reserve University.

Hull, J. (2002). *Options, Futures and Other Derivatives*, 5th ed. Englewood Cliffs, NJ: Prentice-Hall.

Hull, J., and A. White. (1987). "The Pricing of Options on Assets with Stochastic Volatilities," *Journal of Finance*, 42, 281–300.

Lewis, A. (2000). *Option Valuation under Stochastic Volatility.* Newport Beach, CA: Finance Press.

Merton, R. (1973). "Theory of Rational Option Pricing," *Bell Journal of Economics and Management Science*, 4, 141–183.

Merton, R. (1976). "Option Pricing when Underlying Stock Returns are Discontinuous," *Journal of Financial Economics*, 3, 125–144.

Ritchken, P., and R. Trevor. (1999). "Pricing Options under Generalized GARCH and Stochastic Volatility Processes," *Journal of Finance*, 54, 377–402.

Rubenstein, M. (1976). "The Valuation of Uncertain Income Streams and the Pricing of Options," *Bell Journal of Economics and Management Science*, 7, 407–425.

7

MODELING OPTION RISK

7.1. CHAPTER OVERVIEW

In the previous chapter, we gave a brief overview of various models for pricing options. In this chapter, we turn our attention to the key task of incorporating derivative securities into the portfolio risk model, which we developed in previous chapters. Just as the nonlinear payoff function was the key feature from the perspective of option pricing in the previous chapter, it is also driving the risk management discussion in this chapter. The nonlinear payoff creates asymmetry in the portfolio return distribution, even if the return on the underlying asset follows a symmetric distribution. Getting a handle on this asymmetry is a key theme of this chapter.

The chapter is structured as follows:

1. We define the delta of an option, which provides a linear approximation to the nonlinear option price. We then present delta formulas from the various models introduced in the previous chapter.

2. We establish the delta-based approach to portfolio risk management. The idea behind this approach is to linearize the option return and thereby make it fit into the risk models discussed earlier in the book. The downside of this approach is that it ignores the key asymmetry in option payoffs.
3. We define the gamma of an option, which gives a second-order approximation of the option price as a function of the underlying asset price.
4. We use the gamma of an option to construct a quadratic model of the portfolio return distribution. We discuss two implementations of the quadratic model: one relies on the Cornish-Fisher approximation from Chapter 4, and the other relies on the Monte Carlo simulation technique from Chapter 5.
5. We measure the risk of options using the full valuation method, which relies on an accurate but computationally intensive version of the Monte Carlo simulation technique from Chapter 5.
6. Finally, we illustrate all the suggested methods in a simple example. We then discuss a major pitfall in the use of the linear and quadratic approximations in another numerical example. This pitfall, in turn, motivates the use of the full valuation model.

7.2. THE OPTION DELTA

The delta of an option is defined as the partial derivative of the option price with respect to the underlying asset price, S_t. For puts and calls, we define

$$\delta^c \equiv \frac{\partial c}{\partial S_t}$$

$$\delta^p \equiv \frac{\partial p}{\partial S_t}$$

Notice that the deltas are not observed in the market but instead are based on the assumed option pricing model.

Figure 7.1 illustrates the familiar tangent interpretation of a partial derivative. The option price for a generic underlying asset price, S, is approximated by

$$c(S) \approx c(S_t) + \delta(S - S_t)$$

where S_t is the current price of the underlying asset. In Figure 7.1, S_t equals 100.

The delta of an option (in this case, a call option) can be viewed as providing a linear approximation to the nonlinear option price, where the approximation is reasonably good for asset prices close to the current price but it gets gradually worse for prices that deviate significantly from the current price, as Figure 7.1 illustrates. To a risk manager, the poor approximation of delta to the true option price for large underlying price changes is clearly unsettling. Risk management is all about large price changes, and we will therefore consider more accurate approximations here.

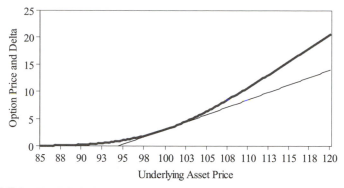

FIGURE 7.1 The Call Option Price (bold) and the Delta Approximation to the Option Plotted against the Price of the Underlying Asset. The Strike Price is 100 and Delta is calculated with an Asset Price of 100.

7.2.1. The Black-Scholes-Merton Model

Recall, from the previous chapter, the Black-Scholes-Merton (BSM) formula for a European call option price

$$c_{BSM} = S_t \Phi(d) - \exp\left(-r\tilde{T}\right)X\Phi\left(d - \sigma\sqrt{\tilde{T}}\,\right)$$

where $\Phi(*)$ is the cumulative density of a standard normal variable, and

$$d = \frac{\ln\left(S_t/X\right) + \tilde{T}\left(r + \sigma^2/2\right)}{\sigma\sqrt{\tilde{T}}}$$

Using basic calculus, we can take the partial derivative of the option price with respect to the underlying asset price, S_t, as follows:

$$\frac{\partial c_{BSM}}{\partial S_t} \equiv \delta_{BSM}^c = \Phi(d)$$

We refer to this as the delta of the option, and it has the interpretation that for small changes in S_t the call option price will change by $\Phi(d)$. Notice that as $\Phi(*)$ is the normal cumulative density function, we have

$$0 \le \delta_{BSM}^c \le 1$$

so that the call option price in the BSM model will change in the same direction as the underlying asset price, but the change will be less than one-for-one.

For a European put option, we have the put call parity stating that

$$S_t + p = c + X\exp(-r\tilde{T}), \text{ or}$$

$$p = c + X\exp(-r\tilde{T}) - S_t$$

so that we can easily derive

$$\frac{\partial p_{BSM}}{\partial S_t} \equiv \delta^p_{BSM} = \frac{\partial c_{BSM}}{\partial S_t} - 1 = \Phi(d) - 1$$

Notice that we have

$$-1 \le \delta^p_{BSM} \le 0$$

so that the BSM put option price moves in the opposite direction of the underlying asset, and again the option price will change by less (in absolute terms) than the underlying asset price.

In the case where a dividend or interest is paid on the underlying asset at a rate of q per day, the deltas will be

$$\delta^c_{BSM} = \exp(-q\tilde{T})\Phi(d),$$

$$\delta^p_{BSM} = \exp(-q\tilde{T})(\Phi(d) - 1)$$

where

$$d = \frac{\ln(S_t/X) + \tilde{T}(r - q + \sigma^2/2)}{\sigma\sqrt{\tilde{T}}}$$

The deltas of the European call and put options from the BSM model are shown in Figure 7.2 for $X = 100$ and for S_t varying from 50 to 150. Notice that delta changes most dramatically when the option is close to at the money—that is, when $S_t \approx X$. This in turn means that a risk management model that relies on a fixed initial delta is likely to be misleading if the portfolio contains a significant amount of at-the-money options.

Figure 7.3 shows the delta of three call options with different strike prices ($X = 80$, 100, and 120, respectively) for maturity, $\tilde{T}$, ranging from 1 to 365 calendar days. The asset price S_t is held fixed at 100 throughout the graph. Notice when the maturity gets shorter (we move from right to left in the graph), the

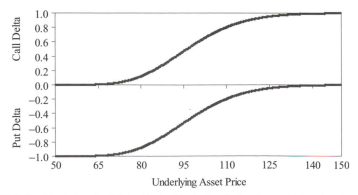

FIGURE 7.2   The Delta of a Call Option (top) and a Put Option (bottom) Plotted against the Price of the Underlying Asset. The Strike Price is 100.

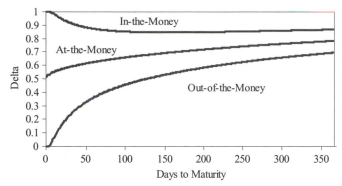

FIGURE 7.3 The Delta of Three call Options with Different Strike Prices Plotted against the Number of Days to Maturity.

deltas diverge: the delta from the in-the-money call option increases to 1, the delta from the out-of-the-money option decreases to 0, and the delta from the at-the-money option converges to 0.5. An in-the-money call option with short maturity is almost certain to pay off $S_t - X$, which is why its price moves in tandem with the asset price S_t and its delta is close to 1. An out-of-the money option with short maturity is almost certain to pay 0, which is why its price is virtually constant and its delta is close to 0.

7.2.2. The Gram-Charlier Model

As the delta is a partial derivative of an option pricing model with respect to the underlying asset price, it is fundamentally model dependent. The preceding deltas were derived from the BSM model, but different option pricing models imply different formulas for the deltas. We saw in the previous chapter that the BSM model sometimes misprices traded options quite severely. We therefore want to consider using more accurate option pricing models for calculating the options delta.

In the case of the Gram-Charlier option pricing model, we have

$$c_{GC} \approx S_t \Phi(d) - Xe^{-r\tilde{T}} \Phi\left(d - \sqrt{\tilde{T}}\sigma\right) + S_t\phi(d)\sigma\left[\frac{\zeta_{11}}{3!}\left(2\sqrt{\tilde{T}}\sigma - d\right)\right.$$

$$\left. - \frac{\zeta_{21}/\sqrt{\tilde{T}}}{4!}\left(1 - d^2 + 3d\sqrt{\tilde{T}}\sigma - 3\tilde{T}\sigma^2\right)\right]$$

and the partial derivative with respect to the asset price in this case is

$$\delta_{GC} = \frac{\partial c_{GC}}{\partial S_t} = \Phi(d) - \frac{\zeta_{11}/\sqrt{\tilde{T}}}{3!}\phi(d)\left(1 - d^2 + 3\sigma\sqrt{\tilde{T}} - 2\sigma^2\tilde{T}\right)$$

$$+ \frac{\zeta_{21}/\tilde{T}}{4!}\phi(d)\left[3d\left(1 + 2\sigma^2\tilde{T}\right) + 4d^2\sigma\sqrt{\tilde{T}} - d^3 - 4\sigma\sqrt{\tilde{T}} + 3\sigma^3\tilde{T}^{3/2}\right]$$

which collapses to the BSM delta of $\Phi(d)$ when skewness, ζ_{11}, and excess kurtosis, ζ_{21}, are both zero. Again, we can easily calculate the put option delta from

$$\delta_{GC}^p \equiv \frac{\partial p_{GC}}{\partial S_t} = \frac{\partial c_{GC}}{\partial S_t} - 1$$

7.2.3. The GARCH Option Pricing Models

Calculating deltas from the general GARCH option pricing model, we are immediately faced with the issue that the option price is not available in closed form but must be simulated. We have in general

$$c_{GH} = \exp\left(-r\tilde{T}\right)E_t^*\left[Max\{S_{t+\tilde{T}} - X, 0\}\right]$$

which we compute by simulation as

$$c_{GH} \approx \exp\left(-r\tilde{T}\right)\frac{1}{MC}\sum_{i=1}^{MC} Max\left\{\check{S}_{i,t+\tilde{T}}^* - X, 0\right\}$$

where $\check{S}_{i,t+\tilde{T}}^*$ is the hypothetical GARCH asset price on option maturity date $t + \tilde{T}$ for Monte Carlo simulation path i, where the simulation is done under the risk neutral distribution.

The partial derivative of the GARCH option price with respect to the underlying asset price can be shown to be

$$\delta_{GH}^c = \exp\left(-r\tilde{T}\right)E_t^*\left[\frac{S_{t+\tilde{T}}}{S_t}\mathbf{1}\left(S_{t+\tilde{T}} \geq X\right)\right]$$

where the function $\mathbf{1}(*)$ takes the value 1 if the argument is true and zero otherwise.

The GARCH delta must also be found by simulation as

$$\delta_{GH}^c \approx \exp\left(-r\tilde{T}\right)\frac{1}{MC}\sum_{i=1}^{MC}\frac{\check{S}_{i,t+\tilde{T}}^*}{S_t}\mathbf{1}\left(\check{S}_{i,t+\tilde{T}}^* \geq X\right)$$

where $\check{S}_{i,t+\tilde{T}}^*$ is again the simulated future risk-neutral asset price. The delta of the European put option can still be derived from the call-put parity formula.

In the special case of the closed-form GARCH process, we have the European call option pricing formula

$$c_{CFG} = S_t P_1 - Xe^{-r\tilde{T}}P_2$$

and the delta of the call option is

$$\delta_{CFG}^c = P_1$$

The formula for P_1 is given in the appendix to the previous chapter.

7.3. PORTFOLIO RISK USING DELTA

Equipped with a formula for delta from our option pricing formula of choice, we are now ready to adapt our portfolio distribution model from earlier chapters to include portfolios of options.

Consider a portfolio consisting of just a call option on a stock. The change in the dollar value (or the dollar return) of the option portfolio, $DV_{PF,t+1}$, is then just the change in the value of the option

$$DV_{PF,t+1} \equiv c_{t+1} - c_t$$

Using the delta of the option, we have that for small changes in the underlying asset price

$$\delta \approx \frac{c_{t+1} - c_t}{S_{t+1} - S_t}$$

Defining geometric returns on the underlying stock as

$$R_{t+1} = \frac{S_{t+1} - S_t}{S_t} \approx \ln\left(S_{t+1}/S_t\right)$$

and combining the three above equations, we get the change in the option portfolio value to be

$$DV_{PF,t+1} \approx \delta\left(S_{t+1} - S_t\right) \approx \delta S_t R_{t+1}$$

The upshot of this formula is that we can write the change in the dollar value of the option as a known value δS_t times the future return of the underlying asset, R_{t+1}, if we rely on the delta approximation to the option pricing formula.

Notice that a portfolio consisting of an option on a stock corresponds to a stock portfolio with δS_t shares. Similarly, we can think of holdings in the underlying asset as having a delta of 1 per share of the underlying asset. Trivially, the derivative of a stock price with respect to the stock price is 1. Thus, holding one share corresponds to having $\delta = 1$, and holding 100 shares corresponds to having a $\delta = 100$.

Similarly, a short position of 10 identical calls corresponds to setting $\delta = -10\delta^c$, where δ^c is the delta of each call option. The delta of a short position in call options is negative, and the delta of a short position in put options is positive as the delta of a put option itself is negative.

The variance of the portfolio in the delta-based model is

$$\sigma_{DV,t+1}^2 \approx \delta^2 S_t^2 \sigma_{t+1}^2$$

where σ_{t+1}^2 is the conditional variance of the return on the underlying stock.

Assuming conditional normality, the dollar value at risk (VaR) in this case is

$$\$VaR_{t+1}^p = -\sigma_{DV,t+1} * \Phi_p^{-1} \approx -abs(\delta)S_t\sigma_{t+1} * \Phi_p^{-1}$$

where the absolute value, $abs(*)$, comes from having taken the square root of the portfolio change variance, $\sigma_{DV,t+1}^2$. Notice that since $DV_{PF,t+1}$ is measured in dollars, we are calculating dollar VaRs directly and not percentage VaRs as in previous chapters. The percentage VaR can be calculated immediately from the dollar VaR by dividing it by the current value of the portfolio.

In case we are holding a portfolio of several options on the *same* underlying asset, we can simply add up the deltas. The delta of a portfolio of options on the same underlying asset is just the weighted sum of the individual deltas as in

$$\delta = \sum_j m_j \delta_j$$

where the weight, m_j, equals the number of the particular option contract j. A short position in a particular type of options corresponds to a negative m_j.

In the general case where the portfolio consists of options on n underlying assets, we have

$$DV_{PF,t+1} \approx \sum_{i=1}^{n} \delta_i S_{i,t} R_{i,t+1}$$

In this delta-based model, the variance of the dollar change in the portfolio value is again

$$\sigma_{DV,t+1}^2 \approx \sum_{i=1}^{n}\sum_{j=1}^{n} abs(\delta_i)abs(\delta_j) S_{i,t} S_{j,t} \sigma_{ij,t+1}$$

Under conditional normality, the dollar VaR of the portfolio is again just

$$\$VaR_{t+1}^p = -\sigma_{DV,t+1} * \Phi_p^{-1}$$

Thus, in this case we can use the risk management framework established in Chapters 2 and 3 without modification. The linearization of the option prices through the use of delta, together with the assumption of normality, makes the calculation of the VaR and other risk measures very easy.

Notice that if we allow for the standard deviations, $\sigma_{i,t+1}$, to be time varying as in GARCH, then the option deltas should ideally be calculated from the GARCH model also. We recall that for horizons beyond 1 day, the GARCH returns are no longer normal, in which case the return distribution must be simulated. We will discuss simulation-based approaches to option risk management later.

When volatility is assumed to be constant and returns are assumed to be normally distributed, we can calculate the dollar VaR at horizon K by

$$\$VaR^p_{t+1:t+K} = -\sigma_{DV}\sqrt{K} * \Phi^{-1}_p$$

where σ_{DV} is the daily portfolio volatility and where K is the risk management horizon measured in trading days.

7.4. THE OPTION GAMMA

The linearization of the option using the delta approach outlined here often does not offer a sufficiently accurate description of the risk from the option. When the underlying asset price makes large moves in a short time, the option price will change by more than the delta approximation would suggest. Figure 7.1 illustrates this point. If the underlying price today is $100 and it moves to $115, then the nonlinear option price increase is substantially larger than the linear increase in the delta approximation. Risk managers, of course, care deeply about large moves in asset prices and this shortcoming of the delta approximation is therefore a serious issue. A possible solution to this problem is to apply a quadratic rather than just a linear approximation to the option price. The quadratic approximation attempts to accommodate part of the error made by the linear delta approximation.

The Greek letter gamma, γ, is used to denote the rate of change of δ with respect to the price of the underlying asset—that is,

$$\gamma \equiv \frac{\partial \delta}{\partial S_t} = \frac{\partial^2 c}{\partial S_t^2}$$

Figure 7.4 shows a call option price as a function of the underlying asset price. The gamma approximation is shown along with the model option price. The model option price is approximated by the second-order Taylor expansion

$$c(S) \approx c(S_t) + \delta (S - S_t) + \frac{1}{2}\gamma (S - S_t)^2$$

For a European call or put on an underlying asset paying a cash flow at the rate q, and relying on the BSM model, the gamma can be derived as

$$\gamma^c = \gamma^p = \frac{\phi(d)e^{-q\tilde{T}}}{S_t \sigma \sqrt{\tilde{T}}}, \text{ where}$$

$$d = \frac{\ln(S_t/X) + \tilde{T}(r - q + \sigma^2/2)}{\sigma\sqrt{\tilde{T}}}$$

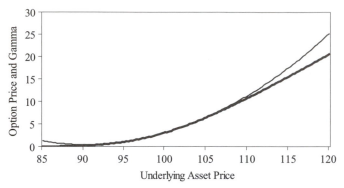

FIGURE 7.4   The Call Option Price (bold) and the Gamma Approximation Plotted against the Price of the Underlying Asset. The Strike Price is 100 and Delta is calculated with an Asset Price of 100.

and where $\phi(*)$ as before is the probability density function for a standard normal variable,

$$\phi(d) \equiv \frac{1}{\sqrt{2\pi}} \exp\left(-d^2/2\right)$$

Figure 7.5 shows the gamma for an option using the same parameters as in Figure 7.2 where we plotted the deltas. When the option is close to at the money, the gamma is relatively large and when the option is deep out of the money or deep in the money, the gamma is relatively small. This is because the nonlinearity of the option price is highest when the option is close to at the money. Deep in-the-money call option prices move virtually one-for-one with the price of the underlying asset because the options will almost surely be exercised.

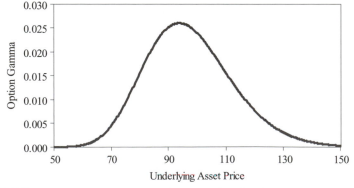

FIGURE 7.5   The Gamma of an Option with a Strike Price of 100 Plotted against the Price of the Underlying Asset.

Deep out-of-the money options will almost surely not be exercised, and they are therefore virtually worthless regardless of changes in the underlying asset price.

All this, in turn, implies that for European options, ignoring gamma is most crucial for at-the-money options. For these options, the linear delta-based model can be highly misleading.

7.5. PORTFOLIO RISK USING GAMMA

In the previous delta-based model, when considering a portfolio consisting of options on one underlying asset, we have

$$DV_{PF,t+1} \approx \delta S_t R_{t+1}$$

where δ denotes the weighted sum of the deltas on all the individual options in the portfolio.

When incorporating the second derivative, gamma, we instead rely on the quadratic approximation

$$DV_{PF,t+1} \approx \delta S_t R_{t+1} + \frac{1}{2} \gamma S_t^2 R_{t+1}^2$$

where the portfolio δ and γ are calculated as

$$\delta = \sum_j m_j \delta_j$$

$$\gamma = \sum_j m_j \gamma_j$$

where again m_j denotes the number of option contract j in the portfolio.

7.5.1. The Cornish-Fisher Approximation

If we assume that the underlying asset return, R_{t+1}, is normally distributed with mean zero and constant variance, σ^2, and rely on the preceding quadratic approximation, then the first three moments of the distribution of changes in the value of a portfolio of options can be written as

$$\mu_{DV} \approx \frac{1}{2} \gamma S_t^2 \sigma^2$$

$$\sigma_{DV}^2 \approx \delta^2 S_t^2 \sigma^2 + \frac{1}{2} \gamma^2 S_t^4 \sigma^4$$

$$\zeta_{1,DV} \approx \frac{\frac{9}{2} \delta^2 \gamma S_t^4 \sigma^4 + \frac{15}{8} \gamma^3 S_t^6 \sigma^6 - 3 \left(\delta^2 S_t^2 \sigma^2 + \frac{3}{4} \gamma^2 S_t^4 \sigma^4 \right) \mu_{DV} + 2 \mu_{DV}^3}{\sigma_{DV}^3}$$

For example, we can derive the expected value as

$$\mu_{DV} \equiv E\left[DV_{PF,t+1}\right] \approx E\left[\delta S_t R_{t+1}\right] + E\left[\frac{1}{2}\gamma S_t^2 R_{t+1}^2\right]$$

$$= \delta S_t * 0 + \frac{1}{2}\gamma S_t^2 \sigma^2 = \frac{1}{2}\gamma S_t^2 \sigma^2$$

The K-day horizon moments can be calculated by scaling σ by $\sqrt{K}$ everywhere.

Notice that because the change in the portfolio value now depends on the squares of the individual returns, the portfolio return is no longer normally distributed, even if the underlying asset returns are normally distributed. In particular, we notice that even if the underlying return has mean zero, the portfolio mean is no longer zero. More important, the variance formula changes and the portfolio skewness are no longer zero, even if the underlying asset has no skewness. The asymmetry of the options payoff itself creates asymmetry in the portfolio distribution. The linear-normal model presented earlier fails to capture this skewness, but the quadratic model considered here captures the skewness at least approximately. In this way, the quadratic model can offer a distinct improvement over the linear model.

The approximate value at risk of the portfolio can be calculated using the Cornish-Fisher approach discussed in Chapter 4. The Cornish-Fisher VaR allowing for skewness is

$$\$VaR_{t+1}^P = -\mu_{DV} - \left(\Phi_p^{-1} + \frac{1}{6}\left(\left(\Phi_p^{-1}\right)^2 - 1\right)\zeta_{1,DV}\right)\sigma_{DV}$$

Unfortunately, the analytical formulas for the moments of options portfolios with many underlying assets are quite cumbersome, and they rely on the unrealistic assumption of normality and constant variance. We will therefore now consider a much more general but simulation-based technique that builds on the Monte Carlo method introduced in Chapter 5. Later, we will illustrate the Cornish-Fisher quadratic VaR in a numerical example.

7.5.2. The Simulation-Based Gamma Approximation

Consider again the simple case where the portfolio consists of options on only one underlying asset and we are interested in the K-day $\$VaR$. We have

$$DV_{PF,t+K} \approx \delta S_t R_{t+1:t+K} + \frac{1}{2}\gamma S_t^2 R_{t+1:t+K}^2$$

Using the assumed model for the physical distribution of the underlying asset return, we can simulate MC pseudo K-day returns on the underlying asset

$$\left\{\widehat{R}_h^K\right\}_{h=1}^{MC}$$

and calculate the hypothetical changes in the portfolio value as

$$\widehat{DV}_{PF,h}^{K} \approx \delta S_t \widehat{R}_h^K + \frac{1}{2} \gamma S_t^2 \left(\widehat{R}_h^K\right)^2$$

from which we can calculate the value at risk as

$$\$VaR_{t+1:t+K}^{p} = -Percentile \left\{ \left\{\widehat{DV}_{PF,h}^{K}\right\}_{h=1}^{MC}, 100p \right\}$$

In the general case of options on n underlying assets, we have

$$DV_{PF,t+K} \approx \sum_{i=1}^{n} \delta_i S_{i,t} R_{i,t+1:t+K} + \sum_{i=1}^{n} \frac{1}{2} \gamma_i S_{i,t}^2 R_{i,t+1:t+K}^2$$

where δ_i and γ_i are the aggregate delta and gamma of the portfolio with respect to the ith return.

If we in addition allow for derivatives that depend on several underlying assets, then we write

$$DV_{PF,t+K} \approx \sum_{i=1}^{n} \delta_i S_{i,t} R_{i,t+1:t+K} + \sum_{i=1}^{n}\sum_{j=1}^{n} \frac{1}{2} \gamma_{ij} S_{i,t} S_{j,t} R_{i,t+1:t+K} R_{j,t+1:t+K}$$

which includes the so-called cross-gammas, γ_{ij}. For a call option, for example, we have

$$\gamma_{ij}^c \equiv \frac{\partial^2 c}{\partial S_i \partial S_j}, \quad \text{for } i \neq j$$

Cross-gammas are relevant for options with multiple sources of uncertainty. An option written on the U.S. dollar value of the Tokyo stock index is an example of such an option.

We now simulate a vector of underlying returns from the multivariate distribution

$$\left\{\hat{R}_{i,h}^K\right\}_{h=1}^{MC}, \quad \text{for } i = 1, 2, \ldots, n$$

and we calculate $\widehat{DV}$s by summing over the different assets using

$$\widehat{DV}_{PF,h}^{K} \approx \sum_{i=1}^{n} \delta_i S_{i,t} \hat{R}_{i,h}^K + \sum_{i=1}^{n}\sum_{j=1}^{n} \frac{1}{2} \gamma_{ij} S_{i,t} S_{j,t} \hat{R}_{i,h}^K \hat{R}_{j,h}^K$$

The great benefit of this approach is that we are aggregating all the options on one particular asset into a delta and a gamma for that asset. Thus, if the portfolio consists of a thousand different types of option contract but only written on 100 different underlying assets, then the dimension of the approximated portfolio distribution is only 100.

As these formulas suggest, we could, in principle, simulate the distribution of the future asset returns at any horizon and calculate the portfolio value at risk for that horizon. However, a key problem with the delta and the delta-gamma approaches is that if we calculate the VaR for a horizon longer than 1 day, the delta and gamma numbers may not be reliable approximations to the risk of the option position. We therefore next consider an approach that is computationally intensive but does not suffer from the problems arising from approximating the options by delta and gamma.

7.6. PORTFOLIO RISK USING FULL VALUATION

Linear and quadratic approximations to the nonlinearity arising from options can in some cases give a highly misleading picture of the risk from options. Particularly, if the portfolio contains options with different strike prices, then problems are likely to arise. We will give an explicit example of this type of problem.

In such complex portfolios, we may be forced to calculate the risk measure using what we will call full valuation. Full valuation consists of simulating future hypothetical underlying asset prices and using the option pricing model to calculate the corresponding future hypothetical option prices. For each hypothetical future asset price, every option written on that asset must be priced. While full valuation is precise, it is unfortunately also computationally intensive. Full valuation can be done with any of the option pricing models discussed in Chapter 6.

7.6.1. The Single Underlying Asset Case

Consider first the simple case where our position consists of a short position in one call option. The dollar change at horizon K can be written

$$DV_{PF,t+K} = -1 * \left(c(S_{t+K}, r, X, \tilde{T} - \tau, q; \sigma) - c^{mkt} \right)$$

where c^{mkt} is the current market price.

The τ is the risk horizon measured in calendar days because the option maturity, $\tilde{T}$, is measured in calendar days. The risk management horizon in trading days is denoted by K. For example, if we have a 2 week VaR horizon, then K is 10 and τ is 14.

We can think of full valuation as pretending that we have arrived on the risk management horizon date and want to price all the options in the portfolio. As we do not know the price of the underlying asset K days into the future, we value the options for a range of hypothetical future prices of the underlying. Assuming a particular physical distribution of the return on the underlying asset, and applying the Monte Carlo methods discussed in Chapter 5, we can simulate future hypothetical returns on the underlying asset

$$\left\{ \hat{R}_h^K \right\}_{h=1}^{MC}$$

and calculate future hypothetical asset prices

$$\left\{ \hat{S}_h^K = S_t \exp\left(\hat{R}_h^K\right) \right\}_{h=1}^{MC}$$

We can now calculate the hypothetical changes in the portfolio value as

$$\widehat{DV}_{PF,h}^K = -1 * \left(c(\hat{S}_h^K, r, X, \tilde{T} - \tau, q; \sigma) - c^{mkt} \right),$$

$$\text{for } h = 1, 2, \ldots, MC$$

The VaR can now be calculated as in Chapter 5 using

$$\$VaR_{t+1:t+K}^p = -Percentile\left\{ \left\{ \widehat{DV}_{PF,h}^K \right\}_{h=1}^{MC}, 100p \right\}$$

Thus, we sort the portfolio value changes in $\left\{ \widehat{DV}_{PF,h}^K \right\}_{h=1}^{MC}$ in ascending order and choose the $\$VaR_{t+1:t+K}^p$ to be the number such that only $100p\%$ of the observations are smaller than the $\$VaR_{t+1:t+K}^p$.

7.6.2. The General Case

More generally, consider again the portfolio of linear assets such as stocks. We have

$$DV_{PF,t+K} = \sum_{i=1}^n \tilde{w}_i \left(S_{i,t+K} - S_{i,t} \right)$$

where $\tilde{w}_i$ is the dollar value of the holding in share i.

If we add, for example, call options to the portfolio, we would have

$$DV_{PF,t+K} = \sum_{i=1}^n \tilde{w}_i \left(S_{i,t+K} - S_{i,t} \right) + \sum_{i=1}^n \sum_j m_{i,j} \left(c(S_{i,t+K}, r, X_{i,j}, \tilde{T}_{i,j} - \tau, \right.$$

$$\left. q_{i,j}; \sigma_i) - c_{i,j}^{mkt} \right)$$

where $m_{i,j}$ is the number of options of type j on the underlying asset i.

The value at risk from full valuation can be calculated from simulation again. Using the model for the returns distribution, we can simulate future returns and thus future asset prices

$$\left\{ \hat{S}_{i,h}^K \right\}_{h=1}^{MC}, \quad \text{for } i = 1, 2, \ldots, n$$

and calculate the hypothetical changes in the portfolio value as

$$\widehat{DV}_{PF,h}^K = \sum_{i=1}^n \tilde{w}_i \left(\hat{S}_{i,h} - S_{i,t} \right) + \sum_{i=1}^n \sum_j m_{i,j} \left(c(\hat{S}_{i,h}^K, r, X_{i,j}, \tilde{T}_{i,j} - \tau, q_{i,j}; \sigma_i) \right.$$

$$\left. -c_{i,j}^{mkt} \right)$$

From these simulated value changes, we can calculate the dollar value at risk as

$$\$VaR_{t+1:t+K}^{p} = -Percentile\left\{\left\{\widehat{DV}_{PF,h}^{K}\right\}_{h=1}^{MC}, 100p\right\}$$

The full valuation approach has the benefit of being conceptually very simple; furthermore it does not rely on approximations to the option price. It does, however, require much more computational effort as all the future hypothetical prices of every option contract have to be calculated for every simulated future underlying asset price. Considerations of computational speed therefore sometimes dictate the choice between the more precise but slow full valuation method and the approximation methods, which are faster to implement.

7.7. A SIMPLE EXAMPLE

To illustrate the three approaches to option risk management, consider the following example. On August 29, 2002, we want to compute the 10-day $\$VaR$ of a portfolio consisting of a short position in one S&P 500 call option. The option has 51 calendar days to maturity, and it has a strike price of 925. The price of the option is $35.10, and the underlying index is 917.8. The expected flow of dividends per day is 0.004513%, and the risk-free interest rate is 0.0045205% per day. For simplicity, we assume a constant standard deviation of 1.5% per calendar day (for option pricing and delta calculation) or equivalently $0.015 * \sqrt{365/252} = 0.0181$ per trading day (for calculating VaR in trading days). We will use the BSM model for calculating δ, γ as well as the full valuation option prices. We thus have

$$S_t = 917.80$$

$$X = 925$$

$$\tilde{T} = 51$$

$$r = 0.0045205\%$$

$$q = 0.004513\%$$

$$\sigma = 1.5\% \text{ per calendar day}$$

from which we can calculate the delta and gamma of the option as

$$d = \frac{\ln\left(S_t/X\right) + \tilde{T}\left(r - q + \sigma^2/2\right)}{\sigma\sqrt{\tilde{T}}} = -0.0194$$

$$\delta = \exp\left(-q\tilde{T}\right)\Phi(d) = 0.491149$$

$$\gamma = \frac{\phi\left(d\right)e^{-q\tilde{T}}}{S_t\sigma\sqrt{\tilde{T}}} = 0.004048$$

for the portfolio, which is short one option; we thus have

$$m * \delta = -1 * 0.491149$$

$$m * \gamma = -1 * 0.004048$$

where the -1 comes from the position being short.

In the delta-based model, the dollar VaR is

$$\$VaR^{0.01}_{t+1:t+10} = -abs(\delta) * S_t * \sigma * \sqrt{10} * \Phi^{-1}_{0.01}$$

$$\approx -abs(-1 * 0.491149) * 917.8 * 0.0181 * \sqrt{10} * (-2.33)$$

$$\approx \$59.73$$

where we now use volatility in trading days.

Using the quadratic model and relying on the Cornish-Fisher approximation to the portfolio dollar return distribution, we calculate the first three moments for the K-day change in portfolio values, when the underlying return follows the $N(0, K\sigma^2)$ distribution. Setting $K = 10$, we get

$$\mu_{DV} \approx \frac{1}{2} S_t^2 \gamma K\sigma^2 = -5.5558,$$

$$\sigma^2_{DV} \approx S_t^2 \delta^2 K\sigma^2 + \frac{1}{2} S_t^4 \gamma^2 K^2\sigma^4 = 723.9459$$

$$\zeta_{1,DV} \approx \frac{\frac{9}{2} S_t^4 \delta^2 \gamma K^2\sigma^4 + \frac{15}{8} S_t^6 \gamma^3 K^3\sigma^6 - 3\left(S_t^2 \delta^2 K\sigma^2 + \frac{3}{4} S_t^4 \gamma^2 K^2\sigma^4\right)\mu_{DV} + 2\mu^3_{DV}}{\sigma^3_{DV}}$$

$$= -1.2037$$

where we use volatility denoted in trading days as K is denoted in trading days. The dollar VaR is then

$$\$VaR^{.01}_{t+1:t+10} = -\mu_{DV} - \left(\Phi^{-1}_p + \frac{1}{6}\left(\left(\Phi^{-1}_p\right)^2 - 1\right)\zeta_{1,DV}\right)\sigma_{DV} = \$91.96$$

which is **much** higher than the VaR from the linear model. The negative skewness coming from the option γ and captured by $\zeta_{1,DV}$ increases the quadratic VaR in comparison with the linear VaR, which implicitly assumes a skewness of 0.

Using instead the simulated quadratic model, we generate 5000 10-trading day returns, $\hat{R}_h, h = 1, 2, \ldots, 5000$ with a standard deviation of $0.0181 * \sqrt{10}$. Using the δ and γ calculated earlier, we find

$$\$VaR^{0.01}_{t+1:t+10} = -Percentile\left\{\left\{\delta S_t \hat{R}_h + \frac{1}{2}\gamma S_t^2 * \hat{R}_h^2\right\}^{MC}_{h=1}, 1\right\}$$

$$= -Percentile\left\{\left\{(-1 * 0.491149) * 917.8 * \hat{R}_h\right.\right.$$

$$+\frac{1}{2}\left.(-1*0.004048)*917.8^2*\hat{R}_h^2\right\}_{h=1}^{MC},1\Bigg\}$$

$$\approx \$95.52$$

Notice again that due to the relatively high γ of this option, the quadratic VaR is more than 50% higher than the linear VaR.

Finally, we can use the full valuation approach to find the most accurate VaR. Using the simulated asset returns $\hat{R}_h$ to calculate hypothetical future stock prices, $\hat{S}_h$, we calculate the simulated option portfolio value changes as

$$\widehat{DV}_{PF,h} = -1*\left(c(\hat{S}_h, r, X, \tilde{T}-14, q; \sigma)-35.10\right), \text{ for } h=1,2,\dots,5000$$

where 14 is the number of calendar days in the 10-trading-day risk horizon. We then calculate the full valuation VaR as

$$\$VaR_{t+1:t+10}^{0.01} = -Percentile\left\{\left\{\widehat{DV}_{PF,h}\right\}_{h=1}^{MC},1\right\}$$

$$\approx \$97.31$$

In this example, the full valuation VaR is slightly higher than the quadratic VaR. The quadratic VaR thus provides a pretty good approximation in this simple portfolio of one option.

To gain further insight into the difference among the three VaRs, we plot the entire distribution of the hypothetical future 10-day portfolio dollar returns under the three models. Figure 7.6 shows a normal distribution with mean zero and variance $\delta^2 S_t^2 10\sigma^2 = 659.17$. Figure 7.7 shows the histogram from the quadratic model using the 5000 simulated portfolio returns. Finally, Figure 7.8 shows the histogram of the 5000 simulated full valuation dollar returns. Notice the stark differences between the delta-based method and the other two. The linear model assumes a normal distribution where there is no skewness. The quadratic model

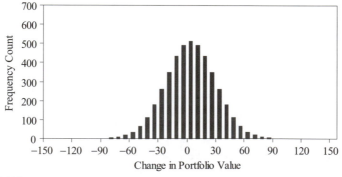

FIGURE 7.6   Histogram of Portfolio Value Changes from Simple Option Portfolio Using the Delta-Based Model.

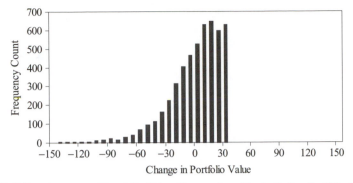

FIGURE 7.7 Histogram of Portfolio Value Changes from Simple Option Portfolio Using the Gamma-Based Model.

allows for skewness arising from the gamma of the option. The portfolio dollar return distribution has a negative skewness of around -1.25. Finally, the full valuation distribution is slightly more skewed at -1.43. The difference in skewness arises from the asymmetry of the distribution now being simulated directly from the option returns rather than being approximated by the gamma of the option.

Further details on all the calculations in this section can be found on the CD-ROM.

7.8. PITFALL IN THE DELTA AND GAMMA APPROACHES

While the previous example suggests that the quadratic approximation yields a sufficiently precise approximation to the true option portfolio distribution,

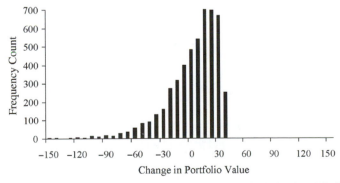

FIGURE 7.8 Histogram of Portfolio Value Changes from Simple Option Portfolio Using Full Valuation.

we now show a different example, which illustrates that even the gamma approximation can sometimes be highly misleading.

To illustrate the potential problem with the approximations, consider an options portfolio that consists of three types of options, all on the same asset, and that has a price of $S_t = 100$, all with $\tilde{T} = 28$ calendar days to maturity. The risk-free rate is $0.02/365$, and the volatility is 0.015 per calendar day. We take a short position in 1 put with a strike of 95, a short position in 1.5 calls with a strike of 95, and a long position in 2.5 calls with a strike of 105. Using the BSM model to calculate the delta and gamma of the individual options, we get

Type of Option:	Put	Call	Call
Strike, X_j:	95	95	105
Option Price:	1.1698	6.3155	1.3806
Delta, δ_j:	−0.2403	0.7597	0.2892
Gamma, γ_j:	0.03919	0.03919	0.04307
Position, m_j:	−1	−1.5	2.5

We are now interested in assessing the accuracy of the delta and gamma approximation for the portfolio over a 5 trading day or equivalently 7 calendar day horizon. Rather than computing VaRs, we will take a closer look at the complete payoff profile of the portfolio for different future values of the underlying asset price, S_{t+5}. We refer to the value of the portfolio today as VPF_t and to the hypothetical future value as $VPF_{t+5}(S_{t+5})$.

We first calculate the value of the portfolio today as

$$VPF_t = -1 * 1.1698 - 1.5 * 6.3155 + 2.5 * 1.3806$$

$$= -7.1916$$

The delta of the portfolio is similarly

$$\delta = -1 * (-0.2403) - 1.5 * 0.7597 + 2.5 * 0.2892$$

$$= -0.1761$$

Now, the delta approximation to the portfolio value in 5 trading days is easily calculated as

$$VPF_{t+5}(S_{t+5}) \approx VPF_t + \delta(S_{t+5} - S_t)$$

$$= -7.1916 - 0.1761(S_{t+5} - 100)$$

The gamma of the portfolio is

$$\gamma = -1 * 0.03919 - 1.5 * 0.03919 + 2.5 * 0.04307$$

$$= 0.0096898$$

and the gamma approximation to the portfolio value in 5 trading days is

$$VPF_{t+5}(S_{t+5}) = VPF_t + \delta(S_{t+5} - S_t) + \frac{1}{2}\gamma(S_{t+5} - S_t)^2$$

$$= -7.1916 - 0.1761 * (S_{t+5} - 100) + 0.004845 * (S_{t+5} - 100)^2$$

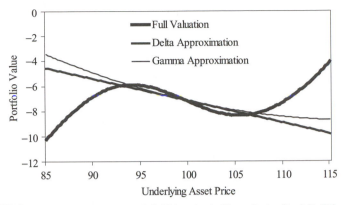

FIGURE 7.9   The Five Day Future Portfolio Values for the Three-Option Portfolio Using the Delta, Gamma and Full Valuation Methods Plotted against the Future Price of the Underlying Asset.

Finally, relying on full valuation, we must calculate the future hypothetical portfolio values as

$$VPF_{t+5}(S_{t+5}) = -1*p_{BSM}(S_{t+5}, r=0.02/365, X=95, \tilde{T}=28-7; \sigma=0.015)$$

$$-1.5*c_{BSM}(S_{t+5}, r=0.02/365, X=95, \tilde{T}=28-7; \sigma=0.015)$$

$$+2.5*c_{BSM}(S_{t+5}, r=0.02/365, X=105, \tilde{T}=28-7; \sigma=0.015)$$

where we subtract 7 calendar days from the time to maturity corresponding to the risk management horizon of 5 trading days.

Letting the hypothetical future underlying stock price vary from 85 to 115, the three-option portfolio values are shown in Figure 7.9. Notice how the exact portfolio value is akin to a third-order polynomial. The nonlinearity is arising from the fact that we have two strike prices. Both approximations are fairly poor when the stock price makes a large move, and the gamma-based model is even worse than the delta-based approximation when the stock price drops. Further details on all the calculations in this section can be found on the CD-ROM.

The important lesson of this three-option example is as follows: The different strike prices and the different exposures to the underlying asset price around the different strikes create higher-order nonlinearities, which are not well captured by the simple linear and quadratic approximations. In realistic option portfolios consisting of thousands of contracts, there may be no alternative to using the full valuation method.

7.9. SUMMARY

This chapter has presented three methods for incorporating options into the risk management model.

First, the delta-based approach consists of a complete linearization of the nonlinearity in the options. This crude approximation essentially allows us to use the methods in the previous chapters without modification. We just have to use the options delta when calculating the portfolio weight of the option.

Second, we considered the quadratic, gamma-based approach, which attempts to capture the nonlinearity of the option while still mapping the option returns into the underlying asset returns. In general, we have to rely on simulation to calculate the portfolio distribution using the gamma approach, but we only simulate the underlying returns and not the option prices.

The third approach is referred to as full valuation. It avoids approximating the option price, but it involves much more computational work. We simulate returns on the underlying asset and then use an option pricing model to value each option in the portfolio for each of the future hypothetical underlying asset prices.

In a simple example of a portfolio consisting of just one short call option, we showed how a relatively large gamma would cause the delta-based VaR to differ substantially from the gamma and full valuation VaRs.

In another example involving a portfolio of three options with different strike prices and with large variations in the delta across the strike prices, we saw how the gamma and delta approaches were both quite misleading with respect to the future payoff profile of the options portfolio.

The main lesson from the chapter is that for nontrivial options portfolios and for risk management horizons beyond just a few days, the full valuation approach may be the only reliable choice.

7.10. FURTHER RESOURCES

The delta, gamma, and other risk measures are introduced and discussed in detail in Hull (2002). Backus *et al.* (1997) gives the formula for delta in the Gram-Charlier model. Duan (1995) provides the delta in the GARCH option pricing model. Garcia and Renault (1998) discuss further the calculation of delta in the GARCH option pricing model. Heston and Nandi (2000) provided the formula for delta in the closed-form GARCH option pricing model.

The sample portfolio used to illustrate the pitfalls in the use of the delta and gamma approximations is taken from Britten-Jones and Schaefer (1999), which also contains the analytical VaR formulas for the gamma approach assuming normality.

The important issue of accuracy versus computation speed in the full valuation versus delta and gamma approaches is analyzed in Pritsker (1997).

In this and the previous chapter, we have restricted attention to European options. American options and many types of exotic options can be priced using binomial trees. Deltas and gammas can be calculated from the tree approach as well. Hull (2002) contains a thorough introduction to binomial trees as an approximation to the normal distribution with constant variance. Ritchken and

Trevor (1999) price American options under GARCH using a time-varying tri-nomial tree. Duan and Simonato (2001) price American options under GARCH using instead a Markov chain simulation approach. Longstaff and Schwartz (2001) establish a convenient least squares Monte Carlo method for pricing Ameri-can and certain exotic options. Derman (1999), Derman and Kani (1994), and Rubinstein (1994) suggest binomial trees, which allow for implied volatility smiles as in the implied volatility function (IVF) approach in the previous chapter.

Whether one relies on the delta, gamma, or full valuation approach, an option pricing model is needed to measure the risk of the option position. As all models are inevitably approximations, they introduce an extra source of risk referred to as model risk. Analysis of the various aspects of model risk can be found in Gibson (2000).

7.11. EMPIRICAL EXERCISES ON CD-ROM

Open the Chapter7Data.xls file. The file contains European call options on the S&P 500 from August 29, 2002.

1. Assume a volatility of 0.015 per calendar day for option pricing and a volatility of $0.015 * \sqrt{365/252} = 0.0181$ per trading day for return volatility. Calculate the delta and gamma of a short position of one option. Do this for every option in the sample. Calculate the delta-based portfolio variance for each option and the 10-trading-day (that is, 14-calendar-day) 1% delta-based dollar VaR for each option.

2. Assume a portfolio that consists of a short position of one in each of the option contracts. Calculate the 10-day, 1% dollar VaRs using the delta-based and the gamma-based models. Assume a normal distribution with the variance as in question 1. Use MC = 5000 simulated returns for the 10-trading-day return. Compare the simulated quadratic VaR with the one using the Cornish-Fisher expansion formula.

3. Assume a short position of one option contract with 51 days to maturity and a strike price of 925. Using the preceding 5000 random normal numbers, calculate the changes in the 10-day portfolio value according to the delta-based, the gamma-based, and the full valuation approach. Calculate the 10-day, 1% dollar VaRs using the simulated data from the three approaches. Make histograms of the distributions of the changes in the portfolio value for these three approaches using the simulated data. Calculate the Cornish-Fisher VaR as well.

4. Replicate Figure 7.9.

The answers to these exercises can be found in the Chapter7Results.xls file. Previews of the answers follow.

Calculating Delta, Gamma and 10-day 1% linear VaR of short position of each option

Initial Data		DTM	Strike	Call (Bid)	Index	Daily Div	r	d	Delta	Portfolio Variances	1% 10-day VaR
Daily Volatility (Calendar Day)	1.50%	23	870	57.60	917.8	0.004360%	0.004521%	0.7800	-0.7815	167.67	95.26
Daily Volatility (Trading Day)	1.81%	23	875	53.70	917.8	0.004360%	0.004521%	0.7003	-0.7574	157.47	92.32
Horizon (Trading Days)	10	23	880	49.90	917.8	0.004360%	0.004521%	0.6211	-0.7320	147.10	89.22
Horizon (Calendar	14	23	885	46.20	917.8	0.004360%	0.004521%	0.5424	-0.7055	136.64	85.99
Number of options	-1	23	890	42.60	917.8	0.004360%	0.004521%	0.4640	-0.6780	126.20	82.64
		23	900	35.30	917.8	0.004360%	0.004521%	0.3087	-0.6206	105.73	75.64
		23	905	32.20	917.8	0.004360%	0.004521%	0.2317	-0.5910	95.89	72.04
		23	910	29.00	917.8	0.004360%	0.004521%	0.1551	-0.5611	86.42	68.39
		23	915	26.70	917.8	0.004360%	0.004521%	0.0790	-0.5309	77.38	64.71
		23	920	23.40	917.8	0.004360%	0.004521%	0.0032	-0.5008	68.84	61.04
		23	925	20.80	917.8	0.004360%	0.004521%	-0.0721	-0.4708	60.84	57.38
		23	935	16.50	917.8	0.004360%	0.004521%	-0.2216	-0.4119	46.57	50.20
		23	940	14.30	917.8	0.004360%	0.004521%	-0.2958	-0.3833	40.34	46.72
		23	945	12.40	917.8	0.004360%	0.004521%	-0.3695	-0.3555	34.70	43.33
		23	950	10.90	917.8	0.004360%	0.004521%	-0.4429	-0.3286	29.64	40.05
		23	960	8.10	917.8	0.004360%	0.004521%	-0.5884	-0.2778	21.19	33.87
		23	965	6.80	917.8	0.004360%	0.004521%	-0.6606	-0.2542	17.73	30.98
		23	970	5.70	917.8	0.004360%	0.004521%	-0.7325	-0.2317	14.74	28.24
		51	775	148.90	917.8	0.004513%	0.004521%	1.6323	-0.9465	245.94	115.37
		51	800	126.70	917.8	0.004513%	0.004521%	1.3360	-0.9071	225.90	110.57
		51	825	105.50	917.8	0.004513%	0.004521%	1.0487	-0.8509	198.75	103.71

QUESTION I

QUESTION 2

Calculating 10-day 1% VaR for portfolio consisting of one short position of each option

Initial Data		DTM	Strike	Call (Bid)	Weights (# of contracts)	Index	Daily Div	r	d	Delta	Gamma	Portfolio		Simulated Random Normal Numbers	10-day Rate of Return
Daily Volatility (Calendar Day)	1.50%	23	870	57.60	-1	917.8	0.004360%	0.004521%	0.7800	0.7815	0.0045	Delta	-53.6224	-0.3002	-0.0171
Daily Volatility (Trading Day)	1.81%	23	875	53.70	-1	917.8	0.004360%	0.004521%	0.7003	0.7574	0.0047	Gamma	-0.26629	-1.2777	-0.0729
Horizon (Trading Days)	10	23	880	49.90	-1	917.8	0.004360%	0.004521%	0.6211	0.7320	0.0050			0.2443	0.0139
Horizon (Calendar Days)	14	23	885	46.20	-1	917.8	0.004360%	0.004521%	0.5424	0.7055	0.0052			1.2765	0.0729
		23	890	42.60	-1	917.8	0.004360%	0.004521%	0.4640	0.6780	0.0054			1.1984	0.0684
		23	900	35.30	-1	917.8	0.004360%	0.004521%	0.3087	0.6206	0.0058			1.7331	0.0989
		23	905	32.20	-1	917.8	0.004360%	0.004521%	0.2317	0.5910	0.0059			-2.1836	-0.1247
		23	910	29.00	-1	917.8	0.004360%	0.004521%	0.1551	0.5611	0.0059			-0.2342	-0.0134
		23	915	26.70	-1	917.8	0.004360%	0.004521%	0.0790	0.5309	0.0060			1.0950	0.0625
		23	920	23.40	-1	917.8	0.004360%	0.004521%	0.0032	0.5008	0.0060			-1.0867	-0.0620
		23	925	20.80	-1	917.8	0.004360%	0.004521%	-0.0721	0.4708	0.0060			-0.6902	-0.0394
		23	935	16.50	-1	917.8	0.004360%	0.004521%	-0.2216	0.4119	0.0059			-1.6904	-0.0965
		23	940	14.30	-1	917.8	0.004360%	0.004521%	-0.2968	0.3833	0.0058			-1.8469	-0.1054
		23	945	12.40	-1	917.8	0.004360%	0.004521%	-0.3696	0.3555	0.0056			-0.9776	-0.0558
		23	950	10.90	-1	917.8	0.004360%	0.004521%	-0.4429	0.3286	0.0055			-0.7735	-0.0442
		23	960	8.10	-1	917.8	0.004360%	0.004521%	-0.5884	0.2778	0.0051			-2.1179	-0.1209
		23	965	6.80	-1	917.8	0.004360%	0.004521%	-0.6606	0.2542	0.0049			-0.5679	-0.0324
		23	970	5.70	-1	917.8	0.004360%	0.004521%	-0.7325	0.2317	0.0046			-0.4040	-0.0231
		51	775	148.90	-1	917.8	0.004513%	0.004521%	1.6323	0.9465	0.0011			0.1349	0.0077
		51	800	126.70	-1	917.8	0.004513%	0.004521%	1.3360	0.9071	0.0017			-0.3655	-0.0209
		51	825	105.50	-1	917.8	0.004513%	0.004521%	1.0487	0.8909	0.0023			-0.3270	-0.0187
		51	850	85.30	-1	917.8	0.004513%	0.004521%	0.7700	0.7776	0.0030			-0.3702	-0.0211
		51	875	66.70	-1	917.8	0.004513%	0.004521%	0.4994	0.6897	0.0036			1.3426	0.0766
		51	885	59.80	-1	917.8	0.004513%	0.004521%	0.3933	0.6515	0.0037			-0.0863	-0.0049
		51	900	49.40	-1	917.8	0.004513%	0.004521%	0.2364	0.5921	0.0039			-0.1862	-0.0106
		51	925	36.10	-1	917.8	0.004513%	0.004521%	-0.0194	0.4911	0.0040			-0.5132	-0.0293
		51	950	24.00	-1	917.8	0.004513%	0.004521%	-0.2683	0.3933	0.0039			1.9722	0.1126
		51	975	14.80	-1	917.8	0.004513%	0.004521%	-0.5108	0.3040	0.0036			0.8657	0.0494
		51	995	9.90	-1	917.8	0.004513%	0.004521%	-0.7003	0.2413	0.0032			2.3757	0.1356
		51	1025	5.00	-1	917.8	0.004513%	0.004521%	-0.9776	0.1637	0.0025			-0.6649	-0.0374
		51	1050	2.60	-1	917.8	0.004513%	0.004521%	-1.2026	0.1143	0.0020			1.6615	0.0948
		51	1075	1.40	-1	917.8	0.004513%	0.004521%	-1.4223	0.0773	0.0015			-1.6124	-0.0920
		51	1100	0.60	-1	917.8	0.004513%	0.004521%	-1.6369	0.0507	0.0011			0.5389	0.0308
		51	1125	0.20	-1	917.8	0.004513%	0.004521%	-1.8467	0.0323	0.0007			0.9022	0.0615
		79	700	221.00	-1	917.8	0.004795%	0.004521%	2.0969	0.9783	0.0004			1.9189	0.1095
		79	725	197.90	-1	917.8	0.004795%	0.004521%	1.8337	0.9630	0.0006			-0.0845	-0.0048
		79	750	175.30	-1	917.8	0.004795%	0.004521%	1.5795	0.9393	0.0009			-0.5238	-0.0299
		79	775	153.30	-1	917.8	0.004795%	0.004521%	1.3335	0.9054	0.0013			0.6751	0.0386
		79	800	132.00	-1	917.8	0.004795%	0.004521%	1.0954	0.8601	0.0018			-0.3813	-0.0218
		79	825	111.60	-1	917.8	0.004795%	0.004521%	0.8646	0.8033	0.0022			0.7576	0.0432
		79	850	92.50	-1	917.8	0.004795%	0.004521%	0.6407	0.7363	0.0026			-1.4442	-0.0824
		79	875	74.70	-1	917.8	0.004795%	0.004521%	0.4232	0.6614	0.0030			-0.8472	-0.0484
		79	900	58.30	-1	917.8	0.004795%	0.004521%	0.2119	0.5817	0.0032			-1.5216	-0.0869
		79	925	44.10	-1	917.8	0.004795%	0.004521%	0.0064	0.5007	0.0032			-0.3629	-0.0207

Calculating 10-day 1% VaR for full valuation, linear and quadratic models for portfolio consistng of one short option

Initial Data		DTM	Strike	Call (Bid)	Index	Daily Dividends	r	d	Delta	Gamma	First three moments			Full Valuation	Linear
											Mean	Variance	Skewness		10-da
Daily Volatility (Calendar Day)	1.50%	51	925	35.10	917.8	0.004513%	0.004521%	-0.0194	-0.4911	-0.0040	-5.5558	723.9459	-1.2037	97.31	59.73
Daily Volatility (Trading Day)	1.81%														
Horizon (Trading Days)	10														
Horizon (Calendar Days)	14														
Number of options	-1														

QUESTION 3

Replicating Figure 7.9

Initial Data		DTM	Current Stock Price	r	d Calls @ 95	d Calls @ 105	d Puts	Today's Value of the Portfolio	Future Value of the Portfolio	Delta Approximation	Gamma Approximation
Daily Volatility (Calendar Day)	1.50%	28	100.00	0.005479%	0.7053	-0.5557	0.7053	-7.19			
# of Calls	-1.5	21	85.00	0.005479%	-1.5670	-3.0230	-1.5670		-10.24	-4.55	-3.46
Strike	95	21	85.25	0.005479%	-1.5243	-2.9803	-1.5243		-10.03	-4.59	-3.54
# of Calls	2.5	21	85.50	0.005479%	-1.4817	-2.9377	-1.4817		-9.82	-4.64	-3.62
Strike	105	21	85.75	0.005479%	-1.4392	-2.8952	-1.4392		-9.61	-4.68	-3.70
Puts	-1	21	86.00	0.005479%	-1.3968	-2.8528	-1.3968		-9.41	-4.73	-3.78
Strike	95	21	86.25	0.005479%	-1.3546	-2.8106	-1.3546		-9.21	-4.77	-3.85
Initial δ	-0.1761	21	86.50	0.005479%	-1.3125	-2.7685	-1.3125		-9.02	-4.81	-3.93
Initial γ	0.0097	21	86.75	0.005479%	-1.2705	-2.7265	-1.2705		-8.83	-4.86	-4.01
		21	87.00	0.005479%	-1.2286	-2.6846	-1.2286		-8.64	-4.90	-4.08
		21	87.25	0.005479%	-1.1869	-2.6429	-1.1869		-8.46	-4.95	-4.16
		21	87.50	0.005479%	-1.1453	-2.6013	-1.1453		-8.28	-4.99	-4.23
		21	87.75	0.005479%	-1.1038	-2.5598	-1.1038		-8.11	-5.03	-4.31
		21	88.00	0.005479%	-1.0624	-2.5184	-1.0624		-7.95	-5.08	-4.38
		21	88.25	0.005479%	-1.0211	-2.4771	-1.0211		-7.79	-5.12	-4.45
		21	88.50	0.005479%	-0.9800	-2.4360	-0.9800		-7.63	-5.17	-4.53
		21	88.75	0.005479%	-0.9389	-2.3949	-0.9389		-7.48	-5.21	-4.60
		21	89.00	0.005479%	-0.8980	-2.3540	-0.8980		-7.34	-5.25	-4.67
		21	89.25	0.005479%	-0.8572	-2.3132	-0.8572		-7.20	-5.30	-4.74
		21	89.50	0.005479%	-0.8165	-2.2725	-0.8165		-7.07	-5.34	-4.81
		21	89.75	0.005479%	-0.7759	-2.2319	-0.7759		-6.94	-5.39	-4.88
		21	90.00	0.005479%	-0.7355	-2.1915	-0.7355		-6.83	-5.43	-4.95
		21	90.25	0.005479%	-0.6951	-2.1511	-0.6951		-6.72	-5.47	-5.01
		21	90.50	0.005479%	-0.6549	-2.1109	-0.6549		-6.61	-5.52	-5.08
		21	90.75	0.005479%	-0.6147	-2.0707	-0.6147		-6.51	-5.56	-5.15

QUESTION 4

REFERENCES

Backus, D., S. Foresi, K. Li, and L. Wu. (1997). "Accounting for Biases in Black-Scholes," Manuscript, The Stern School at NYU.

Britten-Jones, M., and S. Schaefer. (1999). "Non-Linear Value at Risk," *European Finance Review*, 2, 161–187.

Derman, E. (1999, April). "Regimes of Volatility," *Risk*, 55–59.

Derman, E., and I. Kani. (1994). "The Volatility Smile and Its Implied Tree," *Quantitative Strategies Research Note*, Goldman Sachs.

Duan, J. (1995). "The GARCH Option Pricing Model," *Mathematical Finance*, 5, 13–32.

Duan, J., and J. Simonato. (2001). "American Option Pricing under GARCH by a Markov Chain Approximation," *Journal of Economic Dynamics and Control*, 25, 1689–1718.

Garcia, R., and E. Renault. (1998). "A Note on Hedging in ARCH and Stochastic Volatility Option Pricing Models," *Mathematical Finance*, 8, 153–161.

Gibson, R. (2000). *Model Risk: Concepts, Calibration and Pricing*. London: Risk Books.

Heston, S., and S. Nandi. (2000). "A Closed-Form GARCH Option Pricing Model," *Review of Financial Studies*, 13, 585–626.

Hull, J. (2002). *Options, Futures and Other Derivatives*, 5th ed. Englewood Cliffs, NJ: Prentice-Hall.

Longstaff, F., and E. Schwartz. (2001). "Valuing American Options by Simulation: A Simple Least Squares Approach," *Review of Financial Studies*, 14, 113–147.

Pritsker, M. (1997). "Evaluating Value at Risk Methodologies: Accuracy versus Computational Time," *Journal of Financial Services Research*, 12, 201–241.

Ritchken, P., and R. Trevor. (1999). "Pricing Options under Generalized GARCH and Stochastic Volatility Processes," *Journal of Finance*, 54, 377–402.

Rubinstein, M. (1994). "Implied Binomial Trees," *Journal of Finance*, 49, 771–818.

8

BACKTESTING AND STRESS TESTING

8.1. CHAPTER OVERVIEW

The first seven chapters covered various methods for constructing risk management models. Along the way we also considered several ways of diagnostic checking. For example, in Chapter 1 we looked at the autocorrelations of returns to see if the assumption of a constant mean was valid. In Chapter 2 we looked at the autocorrelation function of returns squared divided by the time varying variance to assess if we had modeled the variance dynamics properly. We also ran variance regressions to assess the forecasting performance of the suggested GARCH models. In Chapter 4 we studied the so-called QQ plots to see if the distribution we assumed for standardized returns captured the extreme observations in the sample. In Chapter 5 we looked at the reaction of various risk models to an extreme event such as the 1987 stock market crash. Finally, in Chapter 6 we illustrated option pricing model misspecification in terms of implied volatility smiles and smirks.

The objective in this chapter is to consider the ex ante risk measure forecasts from the model and compare it with the ex post realized portfolio return. The risk measure forecast could take the form of a value at risk (VaR), an expected shortfall (ES), the shape of the entire return distribution, or perhaps the shape of the left tail of the distribution only. We want to be able to backtest any of these risk measures of interest. The backtest procedures developed in this chapter can be seen as a final diagnostic check on the aggregate risk model, thus complementing the various specific diagnostics covered in previous chapters. The discussion on backtesting is followed up by a section on stress testing at the end of the chapter. The material in the chapter will be covered as follows:

1. We take a brief look at the performance of some real-life VaRs from six large (and anonymous) commercial banks. The clustering of VaR violations in these real-life VaRs provides sobering food for thought.
2. We establish procedures for backtesting VaRs. We start by introducing a simple unconditional test for the average probability of a VaR violation. We then test the independence of the VaR violations. Finally, we combine the unconditional test and the independence test in a test of correct conditional VaR coverage.
3. We consider using explanatory variables to backtest the VaR. This is done in a regression-based framework.
4. We establish backtesting procedures for the expected shortfall measure. As discussed in Chapter 4, expected shortfall often contains more information than the VaR measure, which, however, is more commonly used.
5. We broaden the focus to include the entire shape of the distribution of returns. The distributional forecasts can be backtested as well, and we suggest ways to do so. Risk managers typically care most about having a good forecast of the left tail of the distribution, and we therefore modify the distribution test to focus on backtesting the left tail of the distribution only.
6. We define stress testing and give a critical survey of the way it is often implemented. Based on this critique we suggest a coherent framework for stress testing.

Before we get into the technical details of backtesting VaRs and other risk measures, it is instructive to take a look at the performance of some real-life VaRs. Figure 8.1 shows the exceedences (measured in return standard deviations) of the VaR in six large (and anonymous) U.S. commercial banks during the January 1998 to March 2001 period. Whenever the realized portfolio return is worse than the VaR, the difference between the two is shown. Whenever the returns is better, zero is shown. The difference is divided by the standard deviation of the portfolio across the period. The return is daily, and the VaR is reported for a 1% coverage rate. To be exact, we plot the time series of

$$Min\left\{R_{PF,t+1} - \left(-VaR_{t+1}^{.01}\right), 0\right\}/\sigma_{PF,t+1}$$

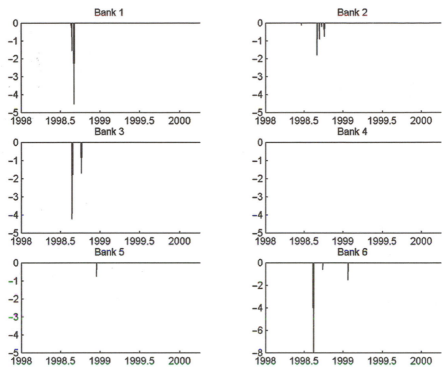

FIGURE 8.1   Value-at-Risk Exceedences From six Major Commercial Banks Reprinted from Berkowitz and O'Brien (2002).

Bank 4 has no violations at all, and in general the banks have fewer violations than expected. Thus, the banks on average report a VaR that is higher than it should be. This could either be due to the banks deliberately wanting to be cautious or the VaR systems being biased. Another culprit is that the returns reported by the banks contain nontrading-related profits, which increase the average return without substantially increasing portfolio risk.

More important, notice the clustering of VaR violations. The violations for each of Banks 1, 2, 3, and 5 fall within a very short time span and often on adjacent days. This clustering of VaR violations is a serious sign of risk model misspecification. These banks are most likely relying on a technique such as historical simulation (HS), which is very slow at updating the VaR when market volatility increases. This issue was discussed in the context of the 1987 stock market crash in Chapter 5.

Notice also how the VaR violations tend to be clustered across banks. Many violations appear to be related to the Russia default and long-term capital management bailout in the fall of 1998. The clustering of violations across banks is important from a regulator perspective as it raises the possibility of a country-wide banking crisis.

Motivated by this sobering evidence of misspecification in existing commercial bank VaRs, we now introduce a set of statistical techniques for backtesting risk management models.

8.2. BACKTESTING VaRs

Recall that a VaR_{t+1}^p measure promises that the actual return will only be worse than the VaR_{t+1}^p forecast $p*100\%$ of the time. If we observe a time series of past ex ante VaR forecasts and past ex post returns, we can define the "hit sequence" of VaR violations as

$$
I_{t+1} = \begin{cases} 1, & if\ R_{PF,t+1} < -VaR_{t+1}^p \\ 0, & if\ R_{PF,t+1} > -VaR_{t+1}^p \end{cases}
$$

The hit sequence returns a 1 on day $t + 1$ if the loss on that day was larger than the VaR number predicted in advance for that day. If the VaR was not violated, then the hit sequence returns a 0. When backtesting the risk model, we construct a sequence $\{I_{t+1}\}_{t=1}^{T}$ across T days indicating when the past violations occurred.

8.2.1. The Null Hypothesis

If we are using the perfect VaR model, then given all the information available to us at the time the VaR forecast is made, we should not be able to predict whether the VaR will be violated. Our forecast of a VaR violation should be simply $100*p\%$ every day. If we could predict the VaR violations, then that information could be used to construct a better risk model. In other words, the hit sequence of violations should be completely unpredictable and therefore distributed independently over time as a Bernoulli variable. We write

$$
H_0 : I_{t+1} \sim i.i.d.\ \text{Bernoulli}(p)
$$

If p is one half, then the $i.i.d.$ Bernoulli distribution describes the distribution of getting a "head" when tossing a fair coin. The Bernoulli distribution function is written

$$
f(I_{t+1}; p) = (1 - p)^{1-I_{t+1}} p^{I_{t+1}}
$$

When backtesting risk models, p will not be one-half but instead on the order of 0.01 or 0.05 depending on the coverage rate of the VaR. The hit sequence from a correctly specified risk model should thus look like a sequence of random tosses of a coin, which comes up heads 1% or 5% of the time depending on the VaR coverage rate.

8.2.2. Unconditional Coverage Testing

We first want to test if the fraction of violations obtained for a particular risk model, call it π, is significantly different from the promised fraction, p. We call this the unconditional coverage hypothesis. To test it, we write the likelihood of an $i.i.d.$ Bernoulli(π) hit sequence

$$L(\pi) = \prod_{t=1}^{T}(1 - \pi)^{1-I_{t+1}}\pi^{I_{t+1}} = (1 - \pi)^{T_0}\pi^{T_1}$$

where T_0 and T_1 are the number of 0s and 1s in the sample. We can easily estimate π from $\hat{\pi} = T_1/T$—that is, the observed fraction of violations in the sequence. Plugging the maximum likelihood (ML) estimates back into the likelihood function gives the optimized likelihood as

$$L(\hat{\pi}) = (1 - T_1/T)^{T_0}(T_1/T)^{T_1}$$

Under the unconditional coverage null hypothesis that $\pi = p$, where p is the known VaR coverage rate, we have the likelihood

$$L(p) = \prod_{t=1}^{T}(1 - p)^{1-I_{t+1}}p^{I_{t+1}} = (1 - p)^{T_0}p^{T_1}$$

We can check the unconditional coverage hypothesis using a likelihood ratio test

$$LR_{uc} = -2\ln\left[L(p)/L(\hat{\pi})\right]$$

Asymptotically, that is, as the number of observations, T, goes to infinity, the test will be distributed as a χ^2 with one degree of freedom. Substituting in the likelihood functions, we write

$$LR_{uc} = -2\ln\left[(1 - p)^{T_0}p^{T_1}\Big/\left\{(1 - T_1/T)^{T_0}(T_1/T)^{T_1}\right\}\right] \sim \chi_1^2$$

Choosing a significance level of say 10% for the test, we will have a critical value of 2.7055 from the χ_1^2 distribution. If the LR_{uc} test value is larger than 2.7055, then we reject the VaR model at the 10% level. Alternatively, we can calculate the P-value associated with our test statistic. The P-value is defined as the probability of getting a sample that conforms even less to the null hypothesis than the sample we actually got—given that the null hypothesis is true. In this case, the P-value is calculated as

$$\text{P-value} \equiv 1 - F_{\chi_1^2}(LR_{uc})$$

where $F_{\chi_1^2}(*)$ denotes the cumulative density function of a χ^2 variable with one degree of freedom. If the P-value is below the desired significance level, then we reject the null hypothesis. If we, for example, obtain a test value of 3.5, then the associated P-value is

$$\text{P-value} = 1 - F_{\chi_1^2}(3.5) = 1 - 0.9386 = 0.0614$$

If we have a significance level of 10%, then we would reject the null hypothesis, but if our significance level is only 5%, then we would not reject the null that the risk model is correct on average.

The choice of significance level comes down to an assessment of the costs of making two types of mistakes: We could reject a correct model (Type I error) or we could fail to reject (that is, accept) an incorrect model (Type II error). Increasing the significance level implies larger Type I errors but smaller Type II errors and vice versa. In academic work, a significant level of 1%, 5%, or 10% is typically used. In risk management, the Type II errors may be very costly so that a significance level of 10% may be appropriate.

Often we do not have a large number of observations available for backtesting, and we certainly will typically not have a large number of violations, T_1, which are the informative observations. It is therefore often better to rely on Monte Carlo simulated P-values rather than those from the χ^2 distribution. The simulated P-values for a particular test value can be calculated by first generating 999 samples of random $i.i.d.$ Bernoulli(p) variables, where the sample size equals the actual sample at hand. Given these artificial samples, we can calculate 999 simulated test statistics, call them $\left\{\widetilde{LR}_{uc}(i)\right\}_{i=1}^{999}$. The simulated P-value is then calculated as the share of simulated LR_{uc} values, which are larger than the actually obtained LR_{uc} test value. We can write

$$\text{P-value} = \frac{1}{1000}\left\{1 + \sum_{i=1}^{999} \mathbf{1}\left(\widetilde{LR}_{uc}(i) > LR_{uc}\right)\right\}$$

where $\mathbf{1}(*)$ takes on the value of one if the argument is true and zero otherwise.

To calculate the tests in the first place, we need samples where VaR violations actually occurred—that is, we need some ones in the hit sequence. If we, for example, discard simulated samples with zero or one violations before proceeding with the test calculation, then we are in effect conditioning the test on having observed at least two violations.

8.2.3. Independence Testing

Imagine all of the VaR violations or "hits" in a sample happening around the same time, which was the case in Figure 8.1. Would you then be happy with a VaR with correct average (or unconditional) coverage? The answer is clearly no. For example, if the 5% VaR gave exactly 5% violations but all of these violations came during a 3-week period, then the risk of bankruptcy would be much higher than if the violations came scattered randomly through time. We therefore would very much like to reject VaR models which imply violations that are clustered in time. Such clustering can easily happen in a VaR constructed from the historical simulation method in Chapter 5, if the underlying portfolio return has a clustered variance, which is common in asset returns and which we studied in Chapter 2.

If the VaR violations are clustered, then the risk manager can essentially predict that if today is a violation, then tomorrow is more than $p*100\%$ likely to be a violation as well. This is clearly not satisfactory. In such a situation, the risk manager should increase the VaR in order to lower the conditional probability of a violation to the promised p.

Our task is to establish a test that will be able to reject a VaR with clustered violations. To this end, assume the hit sequence is dependent over time and that it can be described as a so-called first-order Markov sequence with transition probability matrix

$$\Pi_1 = \begin{bmatrix} 1 - \pi_{01} & \pi_{01} \\ 1 - \pi_{11} & \pi_{11} \end{bmatrix}$$

These transition probabilities simply mean that conditional on today being a nonviolation (that is, $I_t = 0$), then the probability of tomorrow being a violation (that is, $I_{t+1} = 1$) is π_{01}. The probability of tomorrow being a violation given today is also a violation is

$$\pi_{11} = \Pr(I_t = 1 \text{ and } I_{t+1} = 1)$$

The first-order Markov property refers to the assumption that only today's outcome matters for tomorrow's outcome—that the exact sequence of past hits does not matter, only the value of I_t matters. As only two outcomes are possible (zero and one), the two probabilities π_{01} and π_{11} describe the entire process. The probability of a nonviolation following a nonviolation is $1 - \pi_{01}$, and the probability of a nonviolation following a violation is $1 - \pi_{11}$.

If we observe a sample of T observations, then we can write the likelihood function of the first-order Markov process as

$$L(\Pi_1) = (1 - \pi_{01})^{T_{00}} \pi_{01}^{T_{01}} (1 - \pi_{11})^{T_{10}} \pi_{11}^{T_{11}}$$

where T_{ij}, $i, j = 0, 1$ is the number of observations with a j following an i. Taking first derivatives with respect to π_{01} and π_{11} and setting these derivatives to zero, one can solve for the maximum likelihood estimates

$$\hat{\pi}_{01} = \frac{T_{01}}{T_{00} + T_{01}}$$

$$\hat{\pi}_{11} = \frac{T_{11}}{T_{10} + T_{11}}$$

Using then the fact that the probabilities have to sum to one, we have

$$\hat{\pi}_{00} = 1 - \hat{\pi}_{01}$$

$$\hat{\pi}_{10} = 1 - \hat{\pi}_{11}$$

which gives the matrix of estimated transition probabilities

$$\hat{\Pi}_1 \equiv \begin{bmatrix} \hat{\pi}_{00} & \hat{\pi}_{01} \\ \hat{\pi}_{10} & \hat{\pi}_{11} \end{bmatrix} = \begin{bmatrix} 1 - \hat{\pi}_{01} & \hat{\pi}_{01} \\ 1 - \hat{\pi}_{11} & \hat{\pi}_{11} \end{bmatrix} = \begin{bmatrix} \frac{T_{00}}{T_{00}+T_{01}} & \frac{T_{01}}{T_{00}+T_{01}} \\ \frac{T_{10}}{T_{10}+T_{11}} & \frac{T_{11}}{T_{10}+T_{11}} \end{bmatrix}$$

Allowing for dependence in the hit sequence corresponds to allowing π_{01} to be different from π_{11}. We are typically worried about positive dependence, which amounts to the probability of a violation following a violation (π_{11}) being larger than the probability of a violation following a nonviolation (π_{01}). If, on the other hand, the hits are independent over time, then the probability of a violation tomorrow does not depend on today being a violation or not, and we write $\pi_{01} = \pi_{11} = \pi$. Under independence, the transition matrix is thus

$$\hat{\Pi} = \begin{bmatrix} 1 - \hat{\pi} & \hat{\pi} \\ 1 - \hat{\pi} & \hat{\pi} \end{bmatrix}$$

We can test the independence hypothesis that $\pi_{01} = \pi_{11}$ using a likelihood ratio test

$$LR_{ind} = -2 \ln \left[L\left(\hat{\pi}\right) / L(\hat{\Pi}_1) \right] \sim \chi_1^2$$

where $L\left(\hat{\pi}\right)$ is the likelihood under the alternative hypothesis from the LR_{uc} test.

In large samples, the distribution of the LR_{ind} test statistic is also χ^2 with one degree of freedom. But we can calculate the P-value using simulation as we did before. We again generate 999 artificial samples of $i.i.d.$ Bernoulli variables, calculate 999 artificial test statistics, and find the share of simulated test values that are larger than the actual test value.

As a practical matter, when implementing the LR_{ind} tests one may incur samples where $T_{11} = 0$. In this case, we simply calculate the likelihood function as

$$L(\hat{\Pi}_1) = \left(1 - \hat{\pi}_{01}\right)^{T_{00}} \hat{\pi}_{01}^{T_{01}}$$

8.2.4. Conditional Coverage Testing

Ultimately, we care about simultaneously testing if the VaR violations are independent and the average number of violations is correct. We can test jointly for independence and correct coverage using the conditional coverage test

$$LR_{cc} = -2 \ln \left[L(p)/L(\hat{\Pi}_1) \right] \sim \chi_2^2$$

which corresponds to testing that $\pi_{01} = \pi_{11} = p$.

Notice that the LR_{cc} test takes the likelihood from the null hypothesis in the LR_{uc} test and combines it with the likelihood from the alternative hypothesis in the LR_{ind} test. Therefore,

$$LR_{cc} = -2 \ln \left[L(p)/L(\hat{\Pi}_1) \right]$$

$$= -2 \ln \left[\{ L(p)/L(\hat{\pi}) \} \{ L(\hat{\pi})/L(\hat{\Pi}_1) \} \right]$$
$$= -2 \ln \left[L(p)/L(\hat{\pi}) \right] - 2 \ln \left[L(\hat{\pi})/L(\hat{\Pi}_1) \right]$$
$$= LR_{uc} + LR_{ind}$$

so that the joint test of conditional coverage can be calculated by simply summing the two individual tests for unconditional coverage and independence. As before, the P-value can be calculated from simulation.

8.3. INCREASING THE INFORMATION SET

The preceding tests are quick and easy to implement. But as they only use information on past VaR violations, they might not have much power to detect misspecified risk models. To increase the testing power, we consider using the information in past market variables, such as interest rate spreads or volatility measures. The basic idea is to test the model using information that may explain when violations occur. The advantage of increasing the information set is not only to increase power but also to help us understand the areas in which the risk model is misspecified. This understanding is key in improving the risk models further.

If we define the vector of variables available to the risk manager at time t as X_t, then the null hypothesis of a correct risk model can be written as

$$H_0 : \Pr \left(I_{t+1} = 1 | X_t \right) = p \Leftrightarrow E \left[I_{t+1} | X_t \right] = p$$

The first hypothesis says that the conditional probability of getting a VaR violation on day $t+1$ should be independent of any variable observed at time t, and it should simply be equal to the promised VaR coverage rate, p. This hypothesis is equivalent to the conditional expectation of a VaR violation being equal to p. The reason for the equivalence is that I_{t+1} can only take on one of two values: 0 and 1. Thus, we can write the conditional expectation as

$$E \left[I_{t+1} | X_t \right] = 1 * \Pr \left(I_{t+1} = 1 | X_t \right) + 0 * \Pr \left(I_{t+1} = 0 | X_t \right) = \Pr \left(I_{t+1} = 1 | X_t \right)$$

Thinking of the null hypothesis in terms of a conditional expectation immediately leads us to consider a regression-based approach, because regressions are essentially conditional mean functions.

8.3.1. A Regression Approach

Consider regressing the hit sequence on the vector of known variables, X_t. In a simple linear regression, we would have

$$I_{t+1} = b_0 + b_1' X_t + e_{t+1}$$

where the error term e_{t+1} is assumed to be independent of the regressor, X_t.

The hypothesis that $E\left[I_{t+1}|X_t\right] = p$ is then equivalent to

$$E\left[b_0 + b_1' X_t + e_{t+1}|X_t\right] = p$$

As X_t is known, taking expectations yields

$$b_0 + b_1' X_t = p$$

which can only be true if $b_0 = p$ and $b_1 = 0$. In this linear regression framework, the null hypothesis of a correct risk model would therefore correspond to the hypothesis

$$H_0 : b_0 = p, b_1 = 0$$

which can be tested using a standard F-test. The P-value from the test can be calculated using simulated samples as described earlier.

There is, of course, no particular reason why the explanatory variables should enter the conditional expectation in a linear fashion. But nonlinear functional forms could be tested as well.

8.4. BACKTESTING EXPECTED SHORTFALL

In Chapter 4 we argued that the value at risk had certain drawbacks as a risk measure, and we defined expected shortfall (ES),

$$ES_{t+1}^p = -E_t\left[R_{PF,t+1}|R_{PF,t+1} < -VaR_{t+1}^p\right]$$

as a viable alternative. We now want to think about how to backtest the ES risk measure.

Consider again a vector of variables, X_t, which are known to the risk manager and which may help explain potential portfolio losses beyond what is explained by the risk model. The *ES* risk measure promises that whenever we violate the VaR, the expected value of the violation will be equal to ES_{t+1}^p. We can therefore test the *ES* measure by checking if the vector X_t has any ability to explain the deviation of the observed shortfall or loss, $-R_{PF,t+1}$, from the expected shortfall on the days where the VaR was violated. Mathematically, we can write

$$-R_{PF,t+1} - ES_{t+1}^p = b_0 + b_1' X_t + e_{t+1}, \text{ for } t+1 \text{ where } R_{PF,t+1} < -VaR_{t+1}^p$$

where $t+1$ now refers only to days where the VaR was violated. The observations where the VaR was not violated are simply removed from the sample. The error term e_{t+1} is again assumed to be independent of the regressor, X_t.

To test the null hypothesis that the risk model from which the *ES* forecasts were made uses all information optimally ($b_1 = 0$), and that it is not biased ($b_0 = 0$), we can jointly test that $b_0 = b_1 = 0$.

Notice that now the magnitude of the violation shows up on the left-hand side of the regression. But notice that we can still only use information in the tail to backtest. The ES measure does not reveal any particular properties about the remainder of the distribution, and therefore we only use the observations where the losses were larger than the VaR.

8.5. BACKTESTING THE ENTIRE DISTRIBUTION

Rather than focusing on particular risk measures from the return distribution such as the value at risk or the expected shortfall, we could instead decide to backtest the entire return distribution from the risk model. This would have the benefit of potentially increasing further the power to reject bad risk models. Notice, however, that we are again changing the object of interest: If only the VaR is reported, for example, from historical simulation, then we cannot test the distribution.

Assuming that the risk model produces a cumulative distribution forecast for returns, call it $F_t(*)$. Then at the end of every day, after having observed the actual portfolio return, we can calculate the risk model's probability of observing a return below the actual. We will denote this so-called transform probability by $\tilde{p}_{t+1}$:

$$\tilde{p}_{t+1} \equiv F_t\left(R_{PF,t+1}\right)$$

If we are using the correct risk model to forecast the return distribution, then we should not be able to forecast the risk model's probability of falling below the actual return. In other words, the time series of observed probabilities $\tilde{p}_{t+1}$ should be distributed independently over time as a Uniform(0, 1) variable. We therefore want to consider tests of the null hypothesis

$$H_0 : \tilde{p}_{t+1} \sim i.i.d. \text{ Uniform } (0, 1)$$

The Uniform(0, 1) distribution function is flat on the interval 0 to 1 and zero everywhere else. As the $\tilde{p}_{t+1}$ variable is a probability, it is must lie in the zero to one interval. A visual diagnostic on the distribution would be to simply construct a histogram and check to see if it looks reasonably flat. If systematic deviations from a flat line appear in the histogram, then we would conclude that the distribution from the risk model is misspecified.

For example, if the true portfolio return data follows a fat tailed Student's $t(d)$ distribution, but the risk manager uses a normal distribution model, then we will see too many $\tilde{p}_{t+1}$s close to zero and one, too many around 0.5, and too few elsewhere. This would just be another way of saying that the observed returns data have more observations in the tails and around zero than the normal distribution allows for. Figure 8.2 shows the histogram of a $\tilde{p}_{t+1}$ sequence, obtained from taking $F_t\left(R_{PF,t+1}\right)$ to be normal distribution with zero mean and variance $d/(d-2)$, when it should have been Student's $t(d)$, with $d=6$. Thus, we use the correct mean and variance to forecast the returns, but the shape of our density forecast is incorrect.

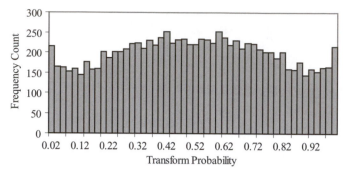

FIGURE 8.2   Histogram of the Transform Probability, $\hat{p}_{t+1}$. The returns follow an *i.i.d.* Student's $t(6)$ distribution, but they are forecasted by an *i.i.d.* $N(0, 2/(d-2))$, with $d = 6$.

The histogram check is, of course, not a proper statistical test, and it does not test the time variation in $\tilde{p}_{t+1}$. If we can predict $\tilde{p}_{t+1}$ using information available on day t, then $\tilde{p}_{t+1}$ is not *i.i.d.*, and the conditional distribution forecast, $F_t(R_{PF,t+1})$, is therefore not correctly specified either. We want to consider proper statistical tests here.

Unfortunately, testing the *i.i.d.* uniform distribution hypothesis is cumbersome due to the restricted support of the uniform distribution. We therefore transform the *i.i.d.* Uniform $\tilde{p}_{t+1}$ to an *i.i.d.* standard normal variable, $\tilde{z}_{t+1}$ using the inverse cumulative distribution function, Φ^{-1}. We write

$$H_0 : \tilde{p}_{t+1} \sim i.i.d.\ Uniform\ (0, 1) \Leftrightarrow$$
$$H_0 : \tilde{z}_{t+1} = \Phi^{-1}\left(\tilde{p}_{t+1}\right) = \Phi^{-1}\left(F_t\left(R_{PF,t+1}\right)\right) \sim i.i.d.\ N\ (0, 1)$$

We are now left with a test of a variable conforming to the standard normal distribution, which can easily be implemented.

We proceed by specifying a model that we can use to test against the null hypothesis. Assume again, for example, that we think a variable X_t may help forecast $\tilde{z}_{t+1}$. Then we can write

$$\tilde{z}_{t+1} = b_0 + b_1' X_t + \sigma z_{t+1}, \text{ with } z_{t+1} \sim i.i.d.\ N(0, 1)$$

The log-likelihood of a sample of T observations of $\tilde{z}_{t+1}$ under the alternative hypothesis is then

$$\ln L\left(b_0, b_1, \sigma^2\right) = -\frac{T}{2}\ln\left(2\pi\right) - \frac{T}{2}\ln\left(\sigma^2\right) - \sum_{t=1}^{T}\left(\frac{\left(\tilde{z}_{t+1} - b_0 - b_1' X_t\right)^2}{2\sigma^2}\right)$$

where we have conditioned on an initial observation.

The parameter estimates $\widehat{b_0}, \widehat{b_1}, \hat{\sigma}^2$ can be obtained from maximum likelihood or, in this simple case, from linear regression. We can then write a likelihood ratio test of correct risk model distribution as

$$LR = -2 \left(\ln L\,(0, 0, 1) - \ln L\left(\widehat{b}_0, \widehat{b}_1, \widehat{\sigma}^2 \right) \right) \sim \chi^2_{nb+2}$$

where the degrees of freedom in the χ^2 distribution will depend on the number of parameters, nb, in the vector b_1. If one does not have much of an idea about how to choose X_t, then lags of $\tilde{z}_{t+1}$ itself would be obvious choices.

8.5.1. Backtesting Only the Left Tail of the Distribution

In risk management, we often only really care about forecasting the left tail of the distribution correctly. Testing the entire distribution as we did earlier, may lead us to reject risk models that capture the left tail of the distribution well, but not the rest of the distribution. Instead, we should construct a test that directly focuses on assessing the risk model's ability to capture the left tail of the distribution, which contains the largest losses.

Consider restricting attention to the tail of the distribution to the left of the VaR^p_{t+1}—that is, to the $100p\%$ largest losses.

If we want to test that the $\tilde{p}_{t+1}$ observations from, for example, the 10% largest losses are themselves uniform, then we can construct a rescaled $\tilde{p}_{t+1}$ variable as

$$\tilde{p}^*_{t+1} = \begin{cases} 10\tilde{p}_{t+1}, & \text{if } \tilde{p}_{t+1} < 0.10 \\ \text{Else not defined} \end{cases}$$

Then we can write the null hypothesis that the risk model provides the correct tail distribution as

$$H_0 : \tilde{p}^*_{t+1} \sim i.i.d.\ \text{Uniform}\,(0, 1)$$

or equivalently

$$H_0 : \tilde{z}^*_{t+1} = \Phi^{-1}\left(\tilde{p}^*_{t+1} \right) \sim i.i.d.\ N\,(0, 1)$$

Figure 8.3 shows the histogram of $\tilde{p}^*_{t+1}$ corresponding to the 10% smallest returns. The data again follows a Student's $t(d)$ distribution, but the density forecast model assumes the normal distribution. We have simply zoomed in on the leftmost 10% of the histogram from Figure 8.2. The systematic deviation from a flat histogram is again obvious.

To do formal statistical testing, we can again construct an alternative hypothesis as in

$$\tilde{z}^*_{t+1} = b_0 + b'_1 X_t + \sigma z_{t+1}, \quad \text{with } z_{t+1} \sim i.i.d.\ N(0, 1)$$

for $t + 1$ such that $R_{PF,t+1} < -VaR^p_{t+1}$. We can then calculate a likelihood ratio test

$$LR = -2 \left(\ln L(0, 0, 1) - \ln L\left(\widehat{b}_0, \widehat{b}_1, \widehat{\sigma}^2 \right) \right) \sim \chi^2_{nb+2}$$

where nb again is the number of elements in the parameter vector b_1.

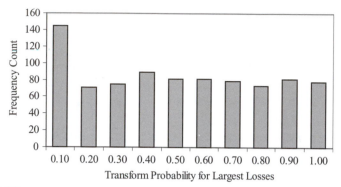

FIGURE 8.3   Histogram of the Transform Probability, $\hat{p}_{t+1}$ from the 10% Largest Losses. The returns follow an $i.i.d.$ Student's $t(6)$ distribution, but they are forecasted by an $i.i.d.N(0, 2/(d-2))$, with $d = 6$.

8.6. STRESS TESTING

Due to the practical constraints from managing large portfolios, risk managers often work with relatively short data samples. This can be a serious issue if the historical data available do not adequately reflect the potential risks going forward. The available data may, for example, lack extreme events such as an equity market crash, which occurs very infrequently.

To make up for the inadequacies of the available data, it can be useful to artificially generate extreme scenarios of the main factors driving the portfolio returns (see the exposure mapping discussion in Chapter 3) and then assess the resulting output from the risk model. This is referred to as stress testing, as we are *stressing* the model by exposing it to data different from the data used when specifying and estimating the model.

At first pass, the idea of stress testing may seem vague and ad hoc. Two key issues appear to be, first, how should one interpret the output of the risk model from the stress scenarios, and second, how should one create the scenarios in the first place? We deal with each of these issues in turn.

8.6.1. Combining Distributions for Coherent Stress Testing

Standard implementation of stress testing amounts to defining a set of scenarios, running them through the risk model using the current portfolio weights, and if a scenario results in an extreme loss, then the portfolio manager may decide to rebalance the portfolio. Notice how this is very different from deciding to rebalance the portfolio based on an undesirably high VaR or expected shortfall (ES). VaR and ES are proper probabilistic statements: What is the loss such that I will lose more only 1% of the time (VaR)? Or what is the expected loss when I exceed my VaR (ES)? Standard stress testing does not tell the probability manager anything about the probability of the scenario happening, and it is therefore not at all clear what the portfolio rebalancing decision should be. The portfolio manager may end up overreacting to an extreme scenario, which occurs with very low probability, and underreact to a less extreme scenario, which occurs much more frequently. Unless a probability of occurring is assigned to each scenario, then the portfolio manager really has no idea how to react.

On the other hand, once scenario probabilities are assigned, then stress testing can be very useful. To be explicit, consider a simple example of one stress scenario, which we define as a probability distribution $f_{stress}(*)$ of the vector of factor returns. We simulate a vector of risk factor returns from the risk model, calling it $f(*)$, and we also simulate from the scenario distribution, $f_{stress}(*)$. If we assign a probability α of a draw from the scenario distribution occurring, then we can combine the two distributions as in

$$f_{comb}(*) = \begin{cases} f(*), & \text{with probability } (1 - \alpha) \\ f_{stress}(*), & \text{with probability } \alpha \end{cases}$$

Data from the combined distribution is generated by drawing a random variable U_i from a Uniform(0,1) distribution. If U_i is smaller than α, then we draw a return from $f_{stress}(*)$; otherwise we draw it from $f(*)$. The combined distribution can easily be generalized to multiple scenarios, each of which has its own preassigned probability of occurring.

Notice that by simulating from the combined distribution, we are effectively creating a new data set that reflects our available historical data as well our view of the deficiencies of it. The deficiencies are rectified by including data from the stress scenarios in the new combined data set.

Once we have simulated data from the combined data set, we can calculate the VaR or ES risk measure on the combined data using the previous risk model. If the risk measure is viewed to be inappropriately high, then the portfolio can be rebalanced. Notice that now the rebalancing is done taking into account both the magnitude of the stress scenarios and their probability of occurring.

Assigning the probability, α, also allows the risk manager to backtest the VaR system using the combined probability distribution $f_{comb}(*)$. Any of these can be used to test the risk model using the data drawn from $f_{comb}(*)$. If the risk model, for example, has too many VaR violations on the combined data, or if the VaR violations come in clusters, then the risk manager should consider respecifying the risk model. Ultimately, the risk manager can use the combined data set to specify and estimate the risk model.

8.6.2. Choosing Scenarios

Having decided to do stress testing, a key challenge to the risk manager is to create relevant scenarios. The scenarios of interest will typically vary with the type of portfolio under management and with the factor returns applied. The exact choice of scenarios will therefore be situation specific, but in general, certain types of scenarios should be considered. The risk manager ought to do the following:

- *Simulate shocks that are more likely to occur than the historical database suggests.* For example, the available database may contain a few high variance days, but if in general the recent historical period was unusually calm, then the high variance days can simply be replicated in the stress scenario.
- *Simulate shocks that have never occurred but could.* Our available sample may not contain any stock market crashes, but one could occur.
- *Simulate shocks reflecting the possibility that current statistical patterns could break down.* Our available data may contain a relatively low persistence in variance, whereas longer samples suggest that variance is highly persistent. Ignoring the potential persistence in variance could lead to a clustering of large losses going forward.
- *Simulate shocks that reflect structural breaks that could occur.* A prime example in this category would be the sudden float of the previously fixed Thai baht currency in the summer of 1997.

Even if we have identified a set of scenario types, pinpointing the specific scenarios is still difficult. But the long and colorful history of financial crises may serve a source of inspiration. Examples could include crises set off by political events or natural disasters. For example, the 1995 Nikkei crisis was set off by the Kobe earthquake, and the 1979 oil crisis was rooted in political upheaval. Other crises such as the 1997 Thai baht float and subsequent depreciation mentioned earlier could be the culmination of pressures such as a continuing real appreciation building over time resulting in a loss of international competitiveness.

The effects of market crises can also be very different. They can result in relatively brief market corrections, as was the case after the October 1987 stock market crash, or they can have longer lasting effects, such as the Great Depression in the 1930s. Figure 8.4 depicts the 10 largest daily declines in the Dow-Jones

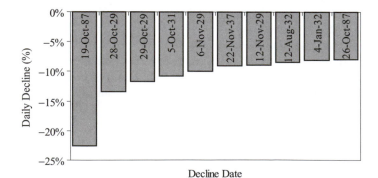

FIGURE 8.4   The Ten-Largest One-day Percentage Declines in the Dow Jones Industrial Average, 1915–2002.

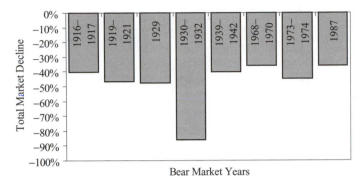

FIGURE 8.5   Example of Bear Markets: Decline of at Least 30% During at Least 50 Days in the Dow Jones Industrial Average, 1915–2002.

Industrial Average during the past 100 years. It clearly shows that the October 19, 1987, decline was very large even on a historical scale.

Figure 8.5 shows 10 episodes of prolonged market downturn—or bear markets—defined as at least a 30% decline over at least 50 days. Figure 8.5 shows that the bear market following the 1987 market crash was relatively modest compared to previous episodes. Stress testing scenarios should include both rapid corrections, such as the 1987 episode, as well as prolonged downturns that prevailed previously.

8.7. SUMMARY

The backtesting of a risk model can be seen as a final step in model building procedure, and it therefore represents the final chapter in this book. The clustering in time of VaR violations as seen in actual commercial bank risk models can pose a serious threat to the financial health of the institution. In this chapter, we have therefore developed backtesting procedures capable of capturing such clustering. Backtesting tools were introduced for various risk measures including VaR, expected shortfall (ES), the entire return density, and the left tail of the density.

The more information is provided in the risk measure, the higher statistical power we will have to reject a misspecified risk model. The popular VaR risk measure does not, unfortunately, convey a lot of information about the portfolio risk. It tells us a return threshold, which we will only exceed with a certain probability, but it does not tell us about the magnitude of violations that we should expect. The lack of information in the VaR makes it harder to backtest. All we can test is that the VaR violations fall randomly in time and in the proportion matching the promised coverage rate. Purely from a backtesting perspective, other risk measures such as ES and the distribution shape are therefore preferred.

Backtesting ought to be supplemented by stress testing, and we have outlined a framework for doing so. Standard stress testing procedures do not specify the probability with which the scenario under analysis will occur. The failure to specify a probability renders the interpretation of stress testing scenarios very difficult. It is not clear how one should react to a large VaR from an extreme scenario unless the likelihood of the scenario occurring is assessed. While it is, of course, difficult to pinpoint the likelihood of extreme events, doing so enables the risk manager to construct a pseudo data set that combines the actual data with the stress scenarios. This combined data set can be used to backtest the model. Stress testing and backtesting is then done in an integrated fashion.

8.8. FURTHER RESOURCES

The VaRs exceedences from the six U.S. commercial banks in Figure 8.1 are taken from Berkowitz and O'Brien (2002). Jorion (2002) argues that the temporal clustering of violations in bank VaRs is due to smoothing constraints imposed on the risk management systems by regulators. The VaR backtests of unconditional coverage, independence, and conditional coverage are derived from Christoffersen (1998). Kupiec (1995) restricts attention to unconditional testing. The regression-based approach is used in Christoffersen and Diebold (2000). Christoffersen and Pelletier (2003) discuss further details in implementing the Monte Carlo simulated P-values, which are originally derived by Dufour (2000). Christoffersen, Hahn, and Inoue (2001) develop tests for comparing different VaR models. Andreou and Ghysels (2002) consider ways of detecting structural breaks in the return process for the purpose of financial risk management. Procedures for backtesting the expected shortfall risk measures can be found in McNeil and Frey (2000). Graphical tools for assessing the quality of density forecasts are suggested in Diebold, Gunther, and Tay (1998) and in Diebold, Hahn and Tay (1999). Crnkovic and Drachman (1996) and Berkowitz (2001) establish formal statistical density evaluation tests, and Berkowitz (2001), in addition, suggests focusing attention to backtesting the left tail of the density.

A useful general discussion of stress testing can be found on www.erisk.com. The coherent framework for stress testing is spelled out in Berkowitz (2000). The May 1998 issue of the *World Economic Outlook*, published by the International Monetary Fund (see www.imf.org), contains a useful discussion of financial crises during the past quarter of a century. Kindleberger (2000) takes an even longer historical view.

8.9. EMPIRICAL EXERCISES ON CD-ROM

Open the Chapter8Data.xls file from the CD-ROM.

1. Compute the daily variance of the returns on the S&P 500 for the period starting January 2, 1992, using the RiskMetrics approach. Use the first 2 years of data to calculate the variance of the return on January 2, 1992.

2. Compute the 1% and 5% 1-day value at risk for each day using RiskMetrics and historical simulation with 500 observations. Again, the first 2 years of data should be used to calculate the value at risk on January 2, 1992.

3. For the 1% and 5% value at risk, calculate the indicator "hit" sequence for both the RiskMetrics and historical simulation models. The hit sequence takes on the value 1 if the return is below the (negative of the) VaR and 0 otherwise.

4. Calculate the LR_{uc}, LR_{ind}, and LR_{cc} tests on the hit sequence from the RiskMetrics and historical simulation models. (*Excel Hint*: Use the CHIINV function.) Can you reject the VaR model using a 10% significance level?

5. Using the RiskMetrics variances calculated in question 1, compute the uniform transform variable. Plot the histogram of the uniform variable. Does it look flat?

6. Transform the uniform variable to a normal variable using the inverse cumulative density function (cdf) of the normal distribution. Plot the histogram of the normal variable. What is the mean, standard deviation, skewness, and kurtosis? Does the variable appear to be normally distributed?

7. Take all the values of the uniform variable that are less than or equal to 0.1. Multiply each number by 10. Plot the histogram of this new uniform variable. Does it look flat? Why should it?

8. Transform the new uniform variable to a normal variable using the inverse cdf of the normal distribution. Plot the histogram of the normal variable. What is the mean, standard deviation, skewness, and kurtosis? Does the variable appear to be normally distributed?

The answers to these exercises can be found in the Chapter8Results.xls file. Previews of the answers follow.

Computing Risk Metrics Daily Variance

	DATA			$\lambda =$	0.94
Date	Close	Return	Variance		
26-Mar-92	407.86	0.08%	0.00002865		
27-Mar-92	403.50	-1.07%	0.00002697		
30-Mar-92	403.00	-0.12%	0.00003228		
31-Mar-92	403.69	0.17%	0.00003044		
01-Apr-92	404.23	0.13%	0.00002879		
02-Apr-92	400.50	-0.93%	0.00002717		
03-Apr-92	401.55	0.26%	0.00003069		
06-Apr-92	405.59	1.00%	0.00002926		
07-Apr-92	398.06	-1.87%	0.00003352		
08-Apr-92	394.50	-0.90%	0.00005258		
09-Apr-92	400.64	1.54%	0.00005427		
10-Apr-92	404.29	0.91%	0.00006532		
13-Apr-92	406.08	0.44%	0.00006634		
14-Apr-92	412.39	1.54%	0.00006353		
15-Apr-92	416.28	0.94%	0.00007398		
16-Apr-92	416.05	-0.06%	0.00007483		
20-Apr-92	410.16	-1.43%	0.00007036		
21-Apr-92	410.26	0.02%	0.00007834		
22-Apr-92	409.81	-0.11%	0.00007364		
23-Apr-92	411.60	0.44%	0.00006929		
24-Apr-92	409.02	-0.63%	0.00006628		
27-Apr-92	408.45	-0.14%	0.00006467		
28-Apr-92	409.11	0.16%	0.00006091		
29-Apr-92	412.02	0.71%	0.00005741		
30-Apr-92	414.95	0.71%	0.00005698		
01-May-92	412.53	-0.58%	0.00005657		
04-May-92	416.91	1.06%	0.00005523		
05-May-92	416.84	-0.02%	0.00005561		

QUESTION I

Computing Risk Metrics & Historical Simulations 1% & 5% VaRs

	A	B	C	D	E	F	G	H
		DATA			Risk Metrics VaR		Historical Simulation VaR	
	Date	Close	Return	RM Variance	1.00%	5.00%	1.00%	5.00%
510	02-Jan-92	417.26	0.04%	0.00009075	2.22%	1.57%	2.49%	1.43%
511	03-Jan-92	419.34	0.50%	0.00008532	2.15%	1.52%	2.49%	1.43%
512	06-Jan-92	417.96	-0.33%	0.00008168	2.10%	1.49%	2.49%	1.43%
513	07-Jan-92	417.40	-0.13%	0.0007743	2.05%	1.45%	2.49%	1.43%
514	08-Jan-92	418.10	0.17%	0.00007288	1.99%	1.40%	2.49%	1.43%
515	09-Jan-92	417.61	-0.12%	0.00006869	1.93%	1.36%	2.49%	1.43%
516	10-Jan-92	415.10	-0.60%	0.00006465	1.87%	1.32%	2.49%	1.43%
517	13-Jan-92	414.34	-0.18%	0.00006295	1.85%	1.31%	2.49%	1.43%
518	14-Jan-92	420.44	1.46%	0.00005938	1.79%	1.27%	2.39%	1.43%
519	15-Jan-92	420.77	0.08%	0.00006863	1.93%	1.36%	2.39%	1.43%
520	16-Jan-92	418.21	-0.61%	0.00006455	1.87%	1.32%	2.39%	1.43%
521	17-Jan-92	418.86	0.16%	0.00006291	1.85%	1.30%	2.39%	1.43%
522	20-Jan-92	416.36	-0.60%	0.00005928	1.79%	1.27%	2.39%	1.43%
523	21-Jan-92	412.64	-0.90%	0.00005787	1.77%	1.25%	2.39%	1.43%
524	22-Jan-92	418.13	1.32%	0.00005923	1.79%	1.27%	2.28%	1.42%
525	23-Jan-92	414.96	-0.76%	0.00006616	1.89%	1.34%	2.28%	1.42%
526	24-Jan-92	415.48	0.13%	0.00006567	1.89%	1.33%	2.28%	1.42%
527	27-Jan-92	414.99	-0.12%	0.00006182	1.83%	1.29%	2.28%	1.42%
528	28-Jan-92	414.96	-0.01%	0.00005819	1.77%	1.25%	2.28%	1.42%
529	29-Jan-92	410.34	-1.12%	0.00005470	1.72%	1.22%	2.28%	1.42%
530	30-Jan-92	411.63	0.31%	0.00005894	1.79%	1.26%	2.28%	1.42%
531	31-Jan-92	408.79	-0.69%	0.00005600	1.74%	1.23%	2.28%	1.42%
532	03-Feb-92	409.53	0.18%	0.00005551	1.73%	1.23%	2.28%	1.42%
533	04-Feb-92	413.85	1.05%	0.00005238	1.68%	1.19%	2.28%	1.42%
534	05-Feb-92	413.84	0.00%	0.00005584	1.74%	1.23%	2.28%	1.42%
535	06-Feb-92	413.82	0.00%	0.00005249	1.69%	1.19%	2.28%	1.42%
536	07-Feb-92	411.09	-0.66%	0.00004934	1.63%	1.16%	2.28%	1.42%

QUESTION 2

Calculating "hit" sequence for 1% & 5% VaRs for both Risk Metrics & Historical Simulation

	DATA				Risk Metrics VaR		Historical Simulation VaR		RM "hit" sequence		HS "hit" sequence	
	Date	Close	Return	RM Variance	1.00%	5.00%	1.00%	5.00%	1.00%	5.00%	1.00%	5.00%
510	02-Jan-92	417.26	0.04%	0.00009075	2.22%	1.57%	2.49%	1.43%	0	0	0	0
511	03-Jan-92	419.34	0.50%	0.00008532	2.15%	1.52%	2.49%	1.43%	0	0	0	0
512	06-Jan-92	417.96	-0.33%	0.00008168	2.10%	1.49%	2.49%	1.43%	0	0	0	0
513	07-Jan-92	417.40	-0.13%	0.00007743	2.05%	1.45%	2.49%	1.43%	0	0	0	0
514	08-Jan-92	418.10	0.17%	0.00007289	1.99%	1.40%	2.49%	1.43%	0	0	0	0
515	09-Jan-92	417.61	-0.12%	0.00006889	1.93%	1.36%	2.49%	1.43%	0	0	0	0
516	10-Jan-92	415.10	-0.60%	0.00006465	1.87%	1.32%	2.49%	1.43%	0	0	0	0
517	13-Jan-92	414.34	-0.18%	0.00006295	1.85%	1.31%	2.49%	1.43%	0	0	0	0
518	14-Jan-92	420.44	1.46%	0.00005938	1.79%	1.27%	2.39%	1.43%	0	0	0	0
519	15-Jan-92	420.77	0.08%	0.00006863	1.93%	1.36%	2.39%	1.43%	0	0	0	0
520	16-Jan-92	418.21	-0.61%	0.00006455	1.87%	1.32%	2.39%	1.43%	0	0	0	0
521	17-Jan-92	418.86	0.16%	0.00006291	1.85%	1.30%	2.39%	1.43%	0	0	0	0
522	20-Jan-92	416.36	-0.60%	0.00005928	1.79%	1.27%	2.39%	1.43%	0	0	0	0
523	21-Jan-92	412.64	-0.90%	0.00005787	1.77%	1.25%	2.39%	1.43%	0	0	0	0
524	22-Jan-92	418.13	1.32%	0.00005923	1.79%	1.27%	2.28%	1.42%	0	0	0	0
525	23-Jan-92	414.96	-0.76%	0.00006616	1.89%	1.34%	2.28%	1.42%	0	0	0	0
526	24-Jan-92	415.48	0.13%	0.00006567	1.89%	1.33%	2.28%	1.42%	0	0	0	0
527	27-Jan-92	414.99	-0.12%	0.00006182	1.83%	1.29%	2.28%	1.42%	0	0	0	0
528	28-Jan-92	414.96	-0.01%	0.00005819	1.77%	1.25%	2.28%	1.42%	0	0	0	0
529	29-Jan-92	410.34	-1.12%	0.00005470	1.72%	1.22%	2.28%	1.42%	0	0	0	0
530	30-Jan-92	411.63	0.31%	0.00005894	1.79%	1.26%	2.28%	1.42%	0	0	0	0
531	31-Jan-92	408.79	-0.69%	0.00005600	1.74%	1.23%	2.28%	1.42%	0	0	0	0
532	03-Feb-92	409.53	0.18%	0.00005551	1.73%	1.23%	2.28%	1.42%	0	0	0	0
533	04-Feb-92	413.85	1.05%	0.00005238	1.68%	1.19%	2.28%	1.42%	0	0	0	0
534	05-Feb-92	413.84	0.00%	0.00005584	1.74%	1.23%	2.28%	1.42%	0	0	0	0
535	06-Feb-92	413.82	0.00%	0.00005249	1.69%	1.19%	2.28%	1.42%	0	0	0	0
536	07-Feb-92	411.09	-0.66%	0.00004934	1.63%	1.16%	2.28%	1.42%	0	0	0	0

QUESTION 3

QUESTION 4

Risk Metrics

	1%	5%
T_0	2468	2391
T_1	53	130
T_{00}	2420	2270
T_{01}	48	121
T_{10}	48	121
T_{11}	5	9
π	0.0210	0.0516
π_{01}	0.0194	0.0506
π_{11}	0.0943	0.0692
LR_{uc}	23.4940	0.1290
LR_{ind}	7.8445	0.7980
LR_{cc}	31.3385	0.9270

Chi-test

Significance	10%	Significance	10%
LR_{uc}	Reject VaR Model	LR_{uc}	Don't Reject VaR Model
LR_{ind}	Reject VaR Model	LR_{ind}	Don't Reject VaR Model
LR_{cc}	Reject VaR Model	LR_{cc}	Don't Reject VaR Model

Historical Simulation

	1%	5%
T_0	2486	2375
T_1	35	146
T_{00}	2453	2237
T_{01}	33	138
T_{10}	33	138
T_{11}	2	8
π	0.0139	0.0579
π_{01}	0.0133	0.0581
π_{11}	0.0571	0.0548
LR_{uc}	3.4260	3.1696
LR_{ind}	2.7670	0.0281
LR_{cc}	6.1930	3.1977

Chi-test

Significance	10%	Significance	10%
LR_{uc}	Reject VaR Model	LR_{uc}	Reject VaR Model
LR_{ind}	Reject VaR Model	LR_{ind}	Don't Reject VaR Model
LR_{cc}	Reject VaR Model	LR_{cc}	Don't Reject VaR Model

Calculating Uniorm Transfrom Variable

Histogram of the Uniform Transform Variable

Date	Close	Return	Variance	Uniform Transform Variable	Bin	Frequency
02-Jan-92	417.26	0.04%	0.00009075	0.5171	0.00	0
03-Jan-92	419.34	0.50%	0.00008532	0.7048	0.05	130
06-Jan-92	417.96	-0.33%	0.00008168	0.3577	0.10	97
07-Jan-92	417.40	-0.13%	0.00007743	0.4394	0.15	98
08-Jan-92	418.10	0.17%	0.00007289	0.5778	0.20	84
09-Jan-92	417.61	-0.12%	0.00006869	0.4437	0.25	100
10-Jan-92	415.10	-0.60%	0.00006465	0.2267	0.30	114
13-Jan-92	414.34	-0.18%	0.00006295	0.4087	0.35	142
14-Jan-92	420.44	1.46%	0.00005938	0.9711	0.40	134
15-Jan-92	420.77	0.08%	0.00006863	0.5377	0.45	164
16-Jan-92	418.21	-0.61%	0.00006455	0.2238	0.50	124
17-Jan-92	418.86	0.16%	0.00006291	0.5776	0.55	154
20-Jan-92	416.36	-0.60%	0.00005928	0.2184	0.60	126
21-Jan-92	412.64	-0.90%	0.00005787	0.1191	0.65	148
22-Jan-92	418.13	1.32%	0.00005923	0.9570	0.70	151
23-Jan-92	414.96	-0.76%	0.00006616	0.1747	0.75	130
24-Jan-92	415.48	0.13%	0.00006567	0.5614	0.80	115
27-Jan-92	414.99	-0.12%	0.00006182	0.4403	0.85	128
28-Jan-92	414.96	-0.01%	0.00005819	0.4962	0.90	125
29-Jan-92	410.34	-1.12%	0.00005470	0.0650	0.95	107
30-Jan-92	411.63	0.31%	0.00005894	0.6687	1.00	151
31-Jan-92	408.79	-0.69%	0.00005600	0.1774		
03-Feb-92	409.53	0.18%	0.00005551	0.5959		
04-Feb-92	413.85	1.05%	0.00005238	0.9265		
05-Feb-92	413.84	0.00%	0.00005584	0.4987		
06-Feb-92	413.82	0.00%	0.00005249	0.4973		
07-Feb-92	411.09	-0.66%	0.00004934	0.1730		

QUESTION 5

QUESTION 6

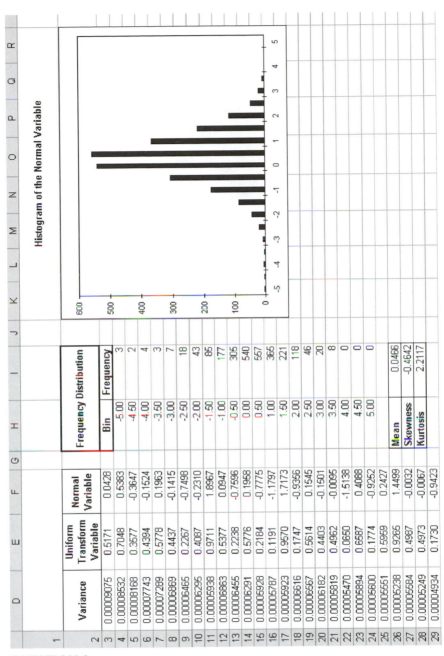

Histogram of the Normal Variable

Variance	Uniform Transform Variable	Normal Variable		Frequency Distribution	
				Bin	**Frequency**
0.00009075	0.5171	0.0428		-5.00	3
0.00008532	0.7048	0.5383		-4.50	2
0.00008168	0.3577	-0.3647		-4.00	4
0.00007743	0.4394	-0.1524		-3.50	3
0.00007289	0.5778	0.1963		-3.00	7
0.00006869	0.4437	-0.1415		-2.50	18
0.00006465	0.2267	-0.7498		-2.00	43
0.00006295	0.4087	-0.2310		-1.50	85
0.00005938	0.9711	1.8967		-1.00	177
0.00006863	0.5377	0.0947		-0.50	305
0.00006455	0.2238	-0.7596		0.00	540
0.00006291	0.5776	0.1958		0.50	557
0.00005928	0.2184	-0.7775		1.00	365
0.00005787	0.1191	-1.1797		1.50	221
0.00005923	0.9570	1.7173		2.00	118
0.00006616	0.1747	-0.9356		2.50	46
0.00006567	0.5614	0.1545		3.00	20
0.00006182	0.4403	-0.1501		3.50	8
0.00005819	0.4962	-0.0095		4.00	0
0.00005470	0.0650	-1.5138		4.50	0
0.00005894	0.6587	0.4088		5.00	0
0.00005600	0.1774	-0.9252			
0.00005551	0.5959	0.2427			
0.00005238	0.9265	1.4499		**Mean**	0.0466
0.00005584	0.4987	-0.0032		**Skewness**	-0.4642
0.00005249	0.4973	-0.0067		**Kurtosis**	2.2117
0.00004934	0.1730	-0.9423			

Uniform Transform Variable less than 0.1	Rank	Sorted	Frequency Distribution	
			Bin	Frequency
	1	0.0000000	0.00	0
	2	0.0000007	0.05	35
	3	0.0000027	0.10	18
	4	0.0000045	0.15	11
	5	0.0000079	0.20	6
	6	0.0000461	0.25	14
	7	0.0000598	0.30	10
	8	0.0001008	0.35	5
	9	0.0002346	0.40	6
	10	0.0009349	0.45	8
	11	0.0013507	0.50	11
	12	0.0021041	0.55	6
	13	0.0031239	0.60	7
	14	0.0036587	0.65	16
	15	0.0045206	0.70	10
	16	0.0060448	0.75	8
	17	0.0074659	0.80	6
	18	0.0110166	0.85	10
0.6604	19	0.0124296	0.90	9
	20	0.0139702	0.95	7
	21	0.0148592	1.00	5
	22	0.0192207		
	23	0.0245537		
	24	0.0247126		
	25	0.0265031		
	26	0.0294776		
	27	0.0304742		
	28	0.0310000		

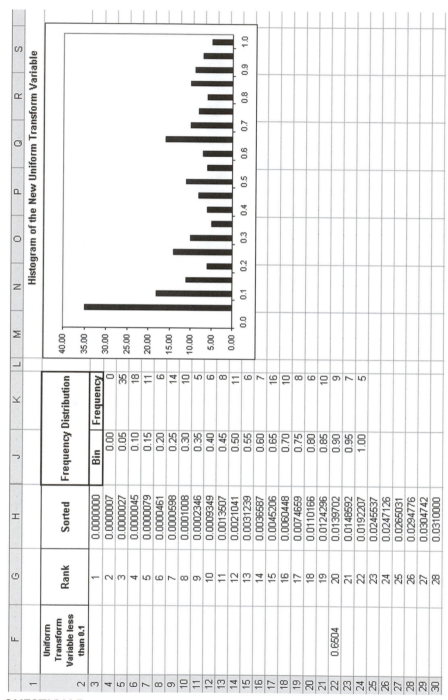

Histogram of the New Uniform Transform Variable

QUESTION 7

QUESTION 8

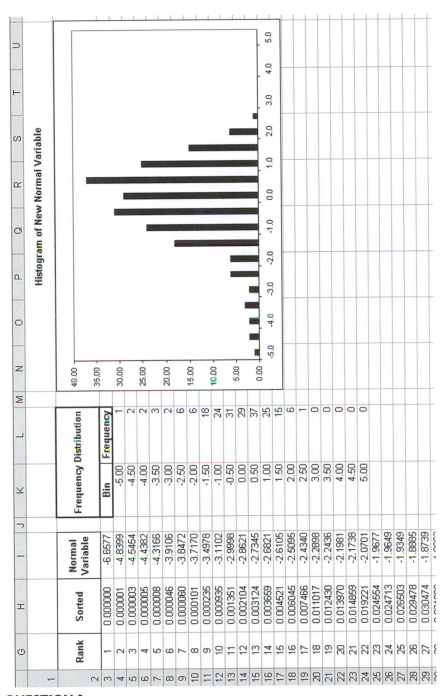

Histogram of New Normal Variable

Rank	Sorted	Normal Variable		Bin	Frequency
			Frequency Distribution		
1	0.000000	-6.6577		-5.00	1
2	0.000001	-4.8399		-4.50	2
3	0.000003	-4.5454		-4.00	2
4	0.000005	-4.4382		-3.50	3
5	0.000008	-4.3166		-3.00	2
6	0.000046	-3.9106		-2.50	6
7	0.000060	-3.8472		-2.00	6
8	0.000101	-3.7170		-1.50	18
9	0.000235	-3.4978		-1.00	24
10	0.000935	-3.1102		-0.50	31
11	0.001351	-2.9998		0.00	29
12	0.002104	-2.8621		0.50	37
13	0.003124	-2.7345		1.00	25
14	0.003659	-2.6821		1.50	15
15	0.004521	-2.6105		2.00	6
16	0.006045	-2.5095		2.50	1
17	0.007466	-2.4340		3.00	0
18	0.011017	-2.2898		3.50	0
19	0.012430	-2.2436		4.00	0
20	0.013970	-2.1981		4.50	0
21	0.014859	-2.1738		5.00	0
22	0.019221	-2.0701			
23	0.024554	-1.9677			
24	0.024713	-1.9649			
25	0.026503	-1.9349			
26	0.029478	-1.8885			
27	0.030474	-1.8739			

REFERENCES

Andreou and Ghysels. (2002). "Quality Control for Value at Risk: Monitoring Disruptions in the Distribution of Risk Exposure," Manuscript, University of North Carolina.

Berkowitz, J. (2000, Winter). "A Coherent Framework for Stress Testing," *Journal of Risk.*

Berkowitz, J. (2001). "Testing Density Forecasts, Applications to Risk Management," *Journal of Business and Economic Statistics*, 19, 465–474.

Berkowitz, J., and J. O'Brien. (2002). "How Accurate Are the Value-at-Risk Models at Commercial Banks?" *Journal of Finance*, 57, 1093–1112.

Christoffersen, P. (1998). "Evaluating Interval Forecasts," *International Economic Review*, 39, 841–862.

Christoffersen, P., and F. Diebold. (2000). "How Relevant Is Volatility Forecasting for Financial Risk Management?" *Review of Economics and Statistics*, 82, 12–22.

Christoffersen, P., J. Hahn, and A. Inoue. (2001). "Testing and Comparing Value-at-Risk Measures," *Journal of Empirical Finance*, 8, 325–342.

Christoffersen, P., and D. Pelletier. (2003). "Backtesting Portfolio Risk Measures: A Duration-Based Approach," Manuscript, McGill University and CIRANO.

Crnkovic, C., and J. Drachman. (1996, September). "Quality Control," *Risk*, 138–143.

Diebold, F. X., T. Gunther, and A. Tay. (1998). "Evaluating Density Forecasts, with Applications to Financial Risk Management," *International Economic Review*, 39, 863–883 .

Diebold, F. X., J. Hahn, and A. Tay. (1999). "Multivariate Density Forecast Evaluation and Calibration in Financial Risk Management: High-Frequency Returns on Foreign Exchange," *Review of Economics and Statistics*, 81, 661–673.

Dufour, J.-M. (2000). "Monte Carlo Tests with Nuisance Parameters: A General Approach to Finite Sample Inference and Non-Standard Asymptotics," Manuscript, Universite de Montreal.

International Monetary Fund. (1998, May). *World Economic Outlook.*

Jorion, P. (2002). "Fallacies about the Effects of Market Risk Management Systems," *Journal of Risk*, 5, 75–96.

Kindleberger, C. (2000). *Manias, Panics and Crashes: A History of Financial Crisis.* New York: John Wiley & Sons.

Kupiec, P. (1995). "Techniques for Verifying the Accuracy of Risk Measurement Models," *Journal of Derivatives*, 3, 73–84.

McNeil, A., and R. Frey. (2000). "Estimation of Tail-Related Risk Measures for Heteroskedastic Financial Time Series: An Extreme Value Approach," *Journal of Empirical Finance*, 7, 271–300.

INDEX